PATTERNS OF THINKING

PATTERNS
OF THINKING

Integrating Learning Skills in Content Teaching

JOHN H. CLARKE

UNIVERSITY OF VERMONT

Foreword by Arthur L. Costa

Allyn and Bacon
Boston   London   Toronto   Sydney   Tokyo   Singapore

Library of Congress Cataloging-in-Publication Data

Clarke, John H.
    Patterns of thinking : integrating learning skills in content
teaching / John H. Clarke.
        p.   cm.
    Includes bibliographical references.
    ISBN 0–205–12361–9
    1. Thought and thinking—Study and teaching—United States.
I. Title.
LB1590.3.C53   90–31470
370.15′2—dc20   CIP

Printed in the United States of America
10 9 8 7 6 5 4 3 2 1   94 93 92 91 90

To Ethan, Jesse, Cindy,
and all the other children

Contents

8   Mapping Concept Networks   163

9   Modeling Causal Relations   197

10   Planning to Solve Problems   231

Foreword

Have YOU EVER HEARD YOURSELF SAY TO YOUR OWN child or a student in your class, "Think about it," or "Think hard"? Have you ever heard yourself or a colleague say, "These students just don't think"? Interestingly, the term *thinking* is a broad, vague, fuzzy term that has diffuse meanings for different people. Furthermore, students often don't have the foggiest idea of what we expect from them when we say, "Now *think!*" Do we want them to generate creative new ideas, focus on a task, make connections with past knowledge, explore consequences, or simply guess what's in our head?

Have you ever asked a student to describe how he or she solved a problem—to discuss the mental steps he or she used in the problem-solving process? Did you receive a blank stare or perhaps a response like, "I don't know. I just did it."

The goal of this book is to have students be able to say instead, "Yes, let me show you how I did it." Furthermore, we'd like them to say, "Let's compare how I solved it with how others did it," or "I know some other ways I could do it; let me show you," or "If I were to find a similar problem elsewhere, here are some ways I would use to solve it."

It has been said that true intelligent behavior is knowing how to behave when you don't know the answer to a problem. It is not how many answers you do know; rather, it is how you behave when you don't know that counts. Helping students know how to behave when they don't know the answers, therefore, is what education is—or should be—about.

Patterns of Thinking offers a wide range of suggestions for ways to represent complex, covert thought processes—those internal mental manipulations that we all engage in but seldom discuss and rarely illustrate. The intent is to make the covert more overt, the implicit more explicit, the hidden more obvious. As a result, students should become more aware of their own thought processes, more able to entertain a range and repertoire of problem-solving strategies, and, with discussion and visual representation, able to apply them more deliberately and productively to a broader range of life problems that they will encounter.

In this book, the processes of thinking, decision making, and conceptualizing are not only described, they are also graphically represented—displayed metacognition—picturing what goes on in our heads when we think. The intent is to help the student understand, monitor, and take charge of her or his own thinking abilities. Both students and teachers can become aware of the steps in the thinking process. They can discuss and illustrate what is happening in their heads when they are in the process of problem solving. They can represent an idea in a form that offers permanence to processes that are fleeting. The benefits of such discussion will prove to have a profound effect on students' mental growth. Students will demonstrate greater empathy for each others' point of view; they will acquire a wider repertoire of problem-solving processes; they will gain a sense of efficacy, empowerment, and command of their own thought processes; and they will better understand their own thought processes because they have explained them graphically to others. They will gain a healthy respect for each other when someone else takes the opportunity to listen to an explanation and to analyze a diagram displaying the intricacies of each other's complex thought processes. Powerful stuff!

Furthermore, teachers will listen more and better appreciate how students are processing their reality; how they approach problems in what may seem to be an awkward, inefficient way. By observing students graphically represent their thinking, teachers can better appreciate, mediate, and enhance the productiveness of student thinking because they have presented a "cognitive map" of their thoughts—including the backroads, side trips, excursions, dead ends, and pathways the mind took on their journey to find meaning.

Too often, we teachers view education as something we do to or for students. We sometimes forget that we are also reciprocals of the teaching-learning act. Teachers, too, will learn from this process when they display their thinking. The strategic act of teaching also requires thoughtful planning before, metacognitive awareness during, and reflective analysis after the act of instruction. Teachers who map their own thought processes of teaching will graphically display their strategies of instruction to themselves, to other teachers, and, most importantly, to their students. Strangely, many teachers keep secret from their students their own thought processes about their intended instructional outcomes, their planning procedures, their instructional strategies, and their methods of self-evaluation. Graphically representing them and sharing them with students will invite students to become partners in the teaching-learning process.

Even without training or formal education, the human mind is capable of myriad complex mental processes. Humans are innately endowed with the capacity to compare and contrast, to classify and categorize, to induce and deduce, to retrieve and transfer, to seriate and reverse, to collect data through sensory pathways, to infer and generalize, to find patterns and predict, and to think spatially, numerically, and temporally. Humans do this because they are human, not because they are educated.

Educated humans, however, are not satisfied with the mere performance of such mental processes. We also have a strong inner desire to perfect those skills. Improvement is in evidence when our cognitive abilities become more broadly applied, more spontaneously generated, more precisely focused, more intricately complex, more metaphorically abstract, and more insightfully divergent. The enlargement of our knowledge base, our continual search into the unknown, our insatiable curiosity, our compulsion to resolve discrepancies, all serve as testimony to this human desire for enhancing, applying, and perfecting our cognitive functioning.

Thus, a distinction between an educated and an uneducated person may not only be in terms of the amount of knowledge acquired, the number of years of schooling, or the number of degrees collected. Rather, a person also may be considered educated because he or she continues to learn how to learn. Lifetimes are spent in the pursuit of knowledge and skills. Our ability to learn from experience, to reflect upon and abstract from our history, and to modify our future actions may well be the definition of an educated human. The capacity for self-modification may be the essential attribute of the autonomous person.

In this universe, there will be the need for a new conception of the educated person as one who is continually self-analyzing, self-evaluating, and self-modifying, continually adapting to change.

Education today must respond to the projected need for this new form of literate citizen for tomorrow's world. This requires the preparation of today's students with the awareness of, the desire for, and the skills of self-modification. I believe this book, in combination with a devoted, skillful teacher and a stimulating curriculum, can contribute greatly to the mediation of students' understanding of problem-solving strategies, the awareness of their own metacognitive functioning, and the application of a range of useful strategies when confronted with problems, the resolution of which are not readily apparent.

Arthur L. Costa, Ed.D.
California State University
Sacramento, CA

Preface

EDUCATION FROM GRADE SCHOOL THOUGH COLLEGE HAS entered yet another crisis period. Calls for reform have pointed out disarray in the curriculum and widespread demoralization among teachers at all levels. Students complain that their studies are not meaningful. *Patterns of Thinking* aims to help teachers develop specific strategies that help students think about subject area content and learn to enjoy managing the work of their minds. A focus on thinking can bring coherence to a curriculum that is badly fragmented. It can provide a common goal to faculty in all subject areas, without undercutting the importance of specific content knowledge. Its purpose is to allow students to derive meaning from their encounter with academic content. *Thinking* is not just another add-on; it is essential to effective learning in all subject areas.

A SHORT LOCAL HISTORY

Thinking Across the Disciplines of the University

I developed a personal interest in thinking skills instruction more than ten years ago while working as an instructional design consultant to the teaching faculty of the University of Vermont. As I worked with university teachers within the narrow frame of the academic disciplines, I began to notice recurring patterns in the way they thought about their subject areas. Sociologists tended to think in similar ways; so did biologists; so did literature teachers. But literature teachers did not think like biologists. When sociologists mentioned "models" for social behavior, biologists looked quite blank; when biologists described "systems" of organisms supporting life, literature teachers appeared to cringe; when literature teachers mentioned evidence supporting a "tone" or "motif" in a piece of writing, teachers of other disciplines turned attention to the coffee urn. Virtually all the college teachers put the "facts" of their own discipline at a subordinate level to governing ideas. Yet, each accused the other disciplines of being "fact dominated." Higher-level thinking skills may have been a common interest of all of us, but we had no common language that would let us talk about that interest. This book proposes a graphic language for talking about basic thinking patterns in all the sub-ject areas.

In 1979, I helped organize a seminar for our faculty that enabled them to explain to each other the assumptions about thinking that char-acterized their disciplines. Called "Teaching Students to Think," the col-loquium brought interested faculty to a lounge at noon to eat sandwiches and to talk about thinking. There, a classics professor described connec-tions between thought and language. A chemist showed how a visualiza-tion of physical phenomenon could be explored more carefully through the scientific method. An historian talked about laborious induction from primary source material—and the limits of inductive thinking. Lit-erature teachers described making intuitive connections across a great expanse of text that made thinking about literature exciting. Writing teachers talked about the experience of writing and revision as an explo-ration of thinking. What was clear in the faculty presentations was that we were all able to talk about thinking within the frame of our subject areas—but none of us had ever been asked to do so. Thinking was the common thread that linked all of our work to one purpose.

With support from the academic vice presidents of the New England Land Grant Colleges, we expanded the seminar to include college teach-ers from all six states in the Northeast region. Meeting in Amherst, Mas-sachusetts, the regional seminars continued for three years, growing to the size of regional conference. The question that brought us together was simple: *What does it mean to "think" within your discipline? How do you help students recognize and practice the skills of thinking appro-priate to your subject area?* For all of us, the focus on thinking skills seemed to bring purpose and coherence to our own teaching. Although thinking was a different kind of activity in different disciplines, the focus on thinking brought us together as a regional faculty with a common mission beyond our institutions and specialized concerns. Talking about thinking became a way for us to talk about teaching—our profession.

Thinking Across the K–12 Curriculum

As faculty interest in writing and thinking across the disciplines contin-ued, a group of teachers from several academic departments at the Uni-versity of Vermont began to recognize the importance of enlarging the discussion to include public school teachers. We saw that we could not succeed in supporting the development of thinking abilities at the college level unless we involved K–12 teachers. Also, several public school teach-ers in Vermont had already developed innovative programs in thinking and learning skills. To test for wider interest among K–12 teachers, we put together a one-day colloquium, presented jointly by public school teachers and university instructors. When several hundred teachers showed up from across the state, we decided we needed three more years and set up an Institute in Thinking and Writing Across the Disciplines. The Institute had two components: a summer course on the university campus and individual courses taught during the school year within specific school districts. This book is a result from the work of teachers in the summer institutes and from school improvement projects carried out by teachers during the regular school year.

The examples of thinking skills curriculum in this book were developed by teachers for their own students and subject areas. Since 1982, the College of Education and Social Services at the University of Vermont has linked up with school districts across the state to offer Masters degree programs for teachers within their schools. In the Off-Campus Masters Program, a group of teachers (K–12) from schools within one district take courses together in their own school (see Clarke & Hood, 1984). A program of courses for any district may be targeted at specific regional goals. Each course in a school district requires teachers to design an individual action project aimed at local school improvement. At any one time, 20 to 30 teachers within one district may be carrying out school improvement projects for the local course in which they are all enrolled. In a school district, the cumulative effect of many projects from many teachers over a three-year period may be quite large indeed. In looking through the examples included here, you may have to imagine the scope and power of the projects from which they came.

The examples in this book have a strong regional flavor. Vermont teachers often embed apple picking, sugar making, logging, and other local events in their classes. Hopefully, the unmistakable regional flavor of those examples will provide a constant reminder to the reader that a general thinking skills approach cannot be imported or exported. It must be developed by individual teachers within particular schools for their own students. There is strong national support for integrating thinking in all the content areas. Research will continue to provide new insights and cautionary notes. Over the last ten years, research in human cognition has been active and very productive. No matter what support is available, however, the process of integrating thinking skills with content instruction must be designed and managed at last by the individual teacher. Watching fine teachers from all the grade levels work together to design instruction for their schools inspired the writing of this book.

ACKNOWLEDGMENTS

What does it mean to "think" within your discipline? How do you help students recognize and practice the skills of thinking appropriate to your subject area? Can you design a learning experience for your students that will show them something about thinking? In response to questions like these, more than 30 teachers, K–12, contributed examples of their materials for this book, designed to promote some aspect of thinking among their students. I will thank them all now but you will meet many of these teachers by name in the chapters that follow. In the process of compiling this book, I have derived the greatest pleasure from being allowed to work with these teachers and to watch some of them practice their profession. I sincerely hope that the brief examples included here will let the reader imagine the talent that all of these people bring to the classroom.

Throughout this period, Ken Hood at the University of Vermont's College of Education and Social Services has provided leadership and unswerving support to me and to the Arts and Sciences faculty who developed the summer institutes, the school-based courses and workshops. I want also to thank the group itself, Toby Fulwiler (English), Lynda McIntyre (Art), Mike Strauss (Chemistry), Herb Leff (Psychology), and Hank Steffens (History) of the Institute on Writing and Thinking Across the Disciplines. It takes considerable courage and conviction to cross the lines of discipline in a university context. I have greatly enjoyed our shadowy association. I would also like to thank Dean Jim Raths for supporting my effort to write the book and helping me think more clearly about evaluation.

I would like to express appreciation to Superintendent Glenn Yankee who helped us bring an early course on Thinking Across the Curriculum to Marshfield, Vermont, our most rural area for a field test. The course then moved to Bristol, Vermont, where Superintendent Jim Lombardo had begun a massive curriculum review and Curriculum Coordinator Judy Carr was organizing support for the teachers in the labors of K–12 curriculum design. I would like to express my appreciation to each of them, as well as my admiration for their approach to school improvement. In its last run before I began writing, the course moved to Missisquoi High School and the region of Swanton, Vermont, on the Canadian border. I would like to thank Superintendent John Robb for his support and Curriculum Coordinator Bill Williams for helping this large group design some truly remarkable curriculum projects.

My task in compiling this book has been to arrange and explain specific examples supplied by teachers and their students to fit a general model for cognition. I have adapted a general frame for thinking developed by Art Costa (1985), who has also provided much encouragement. I have used three books from ASCD as texts for my courses: *Developing Minds: A Resource Book for Teaching Thinking* (Costa, 1985); *Strategic Teaching and Learning: Cognitive Instruction in the Content Areas* (Jones et al., 1987); and Ron Brandt of ASCD Publications allowed an early draft of *Dimensions of Thinking* (1988) to be used as a text in a Burlington Institute, for which I am grateful.

Five talented writers read drafts of chapters or sections and helped me find my way. Art Costa, then President of ASCD, read sample chapters and suggested ways that I could create a "bridge" from academic applications to intelligent behavior in life itself. "When else do students need to think this way?" he asked. (I have tried to guide the reader toward that question.) Toby Fulwiler read an early draft and gave me encouragement. "Tell the story," he said, "Write the way you talk." (I have kept a "story" for each chapter.) Judy Carr put aside her own writing and work with teachers to read and encourage me as well. "Show what teachers have done," she said. I hope the book celebrates fine teaching. Professor Ann Nevin read carefully and offered close notes. "What does this mean?" she asked. Sometimes I couldn't answer. Nancy Cornell, to whom I am married, gave me the benefit of her ten years of experience as a professional writer to guide me along. "Some days," she said, "That's just the way it goes." (With her support, I have tried to keep going.) Joan Carrassi edited and produced the final manuscript. To all of these people I want to express my thanks.

John H. Clarke
South Starksboro, Vermont

PATTERNS OF THINKING

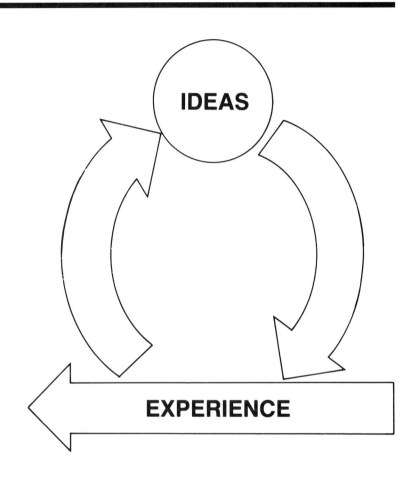

*Teaching
Thinking*

Introduction: Thinking Across the Disciplines

T̲HE PURPOSE OF THIS BOOK IS TO HELP TEACHERS OF CONventional subjects integrate thinking skills in content instruction. The book specifically shows how graphic organizers can be used as a medium for expressing different thinking processes. It provides a general framework for understanding the kind of thinking required in the study of academic subjects. This framework is represented graphically—as a cycle or Thinking Wheel—throughout the book (see Figure I.1). You will notice that the metaphor of the wheel takes on different purposes and meanings as the book progresses. Throughout the book, however, the Thinking Wheel reflects the mind's interaction with physical reality. The human mind can turn impressions from the senses into abstract concepts. It can then use abstract concepts to create new events in the reality it perceives. Transforming perceived events into ideas and ideas into new events generates power.

Figure I.1 defines inductive thinking as the process of constructing ideas from experience. It also defines deductive thinking as the process of applying general ideas or concepts to specific problems in experience. Inductive thinking involves making meaning, through purposeful scanning of experience, categorization, and theory building. Deductive thinking involves the application of ideas to experience, in prediction, plan-

**FIGURE I.1   The Thinking Wheel:
A Graphic Organizer for This Book**

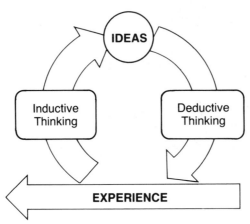

ning, and problem solving. Learning in most subject areas depends on inductive and deductive processing. Inquiry in subject area learning proceeds in a widening spiral, with new experience supporting the development of new ideas and those ideas being further developed and tested in the endless stream of new experience. Induction and deduction work together to turn the wheel of the mind.

In this Introduction, the Thinking Wheel can also be used to express the more specific relationship between thinking and teaching. The first chapter in this section develops a perspective on thinking; the second chapter develops a related perspective on teaching. Figure I.2 shows how thinking and teaching can relate to each other. Essentially, Figure I.2 suggests that we can base part of our approach to teaching on ideas we develop by watching our students think.

How we teach should depend on what we can see of how our students think. The figure may also be expressed in a series of related propositions:

- Thinking involves converting experience to ideas, as well as ideas to experience.
- Teaching involves converting ideas to experience, as well as experience to ideas.
- Teaching may change thinking (by shaping experience).
- Thinking may change teaching (by shaping ideas).

FIGURE I.2 Section I as a Wheel Relating Thinking to Teaching

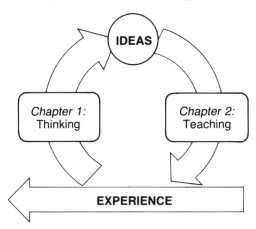

All of this is fine, in the abstract, but what is *not* being suggested by the metaphor of the wheel?

- Classroom teaching cannot directly convey or control thinking; it can only shape experience.
- Classroom experience cannot transport ideas to students; ideas are always reconstructed by student "thinking."

None of us can teach students to think. We can, however, create experiences for students that will cause them to think and develop ideas. None of us can set thinking as our "terminal objective." Our obligation to the profession and to our students is to help them turn the wheel of their own minds with increasing power and ever clearer direction as they grow and learn.

At the concrete level, Figure I.2 reflects the chapters of Section I. Chapter 1 of this book introduces a way of looking at thinking that may allow teachers to intervene in support of refined thinking skills. Chapter 2 suggests an approach to teaching that relates to the definition developed for thinking. Both chapters propose that we can use graphic organizers to show students patterns of thinking in the content they are studying and to help them control their thinking about subject area content.

This book is based on four assumptions about teaching in the subject areas.

ASSUMPTIONS

1. *The primary goal of subject area instruction is to help students control the work of their minds in that content.* Each of the subject areas is in a continual state of revolution; it is this instability that makes learning to process information so important. Learning facts, concepts, procedures, rules, and relationships must be secondary. The sciences offer the easiest examples: Physics has become submolecular in the last twenty years, and biology has moved from describing genetic codes to splicing genes in the last decade. History, needless to say, changes by the minute. Mathematics is being transformed by the computer revolution. Certainly, students need to know something about all the subject areas. They cannot think about nothing. More important, however, they need to learn how to apply what they know to an expanding universe of knowledge. They need to know how to learn and think.

2. *The classroom teacher has the best vantage point for developing a specific approach to the teaching of thinking.* A number of programs have been tested that develop thinking skills independent of content and without involving classroom teachers. (See Nickerson, Perkins, & Smith, 1985 or Costa, 1985 for some program descriptions.) Thinking skills programs and individual therapies face a number of limitations. They all require "adding on" to the existing curriculum, an entity already overburdened, fragmented, incoherent, and wildly expensive. For these reasons, a thinking skills curriculum outside of the content areas must be, by necessity, short term. In contrast, learning to manage one's mind is clearly a long-term endeavor. It takes a lifetime. If separate instruction in thinking skills and the process of transfer do not include the subject area teacher, then the skills taught are not likely to be reinforced during subject area teaching. Without reinforcement, they are likely to perish.

Without content on which to operate, general strategies may appear meaningless to students. Students want to succeed in their regular content courses where they associate meaning with an organized body of facts and concepts. Under ordinary conditions, they accept guidance from the person who is teaching the content course (and grading the tests). If the subject area teacher is also trying to help students learn to manage information, the students are more likely to include managing information as part of their purpose in school learning. Specific content knowledge and strategic thinking must develop simultaneously, through instruction which helps students think about the content (Perkins & Salomon, 1989; Alexander & Judy, 1988).

3. *The conventional curricular subjects offer students the most promising medium for learning to direct and refine strategies for thinking.* Each of the central subject areas—such as history, language arts, mathematics, and science—is based on an organized body of knowledge in the academic disciplines and established processes of inquiry. Thinking about organized subjects invites the application of specific kinds of organized thinking processes. Looking at literature can easily become an exercise in inductive thinking, as students find relationships between different parts of the text and generalize from those pieces. History can offer opportunities to practice causal analysis, as students trace the origins of one event through a sequence of preceding events. Science can emphasize concept modeling. Problem solving in mathematics can emphasize procedural thinking. The link between the disciplines and some specific patterns of thinking is almost a matter of common sense. Using a pattern of thinking from one discipline to pry into content from another can sometimes yield surprising insights.

4. *The K–12 curriculum offers the most supportive framework for the teaching of thinking.* Learning to think is not the kind of thing we do once, then move on to other things. We need the entire span of formal schooling for the developing of thinking patterns and strategies. Adopting more complex and flexible approaches to thinking is rooted to some extent in developmental processes of growth. Learning to think also depends on the slow acquisition of knowledge in increasingly complex forms. In the area of thinking, there is no ladder of skill acquisition. Advanced and intricate kinds of thinking are only simple forms made more elaborate through practice and refinement. Learning to think occurs in a circular or recursive pattern in which essential skills are established early, then challenged by increasingly complex kinds of experience. For many reasons, learning to think well takes a lifetime.

One central belief guiding the recent movement in thinking across the disciplines is that we should base our approach to teaching on what we know about how the mind works. Psychological research has discovered much about intellectual processes over the last ten years. Jones and colleagues (1987) have summarized this research in six propositions for teachers of the content areas, included as Figure I.3. The approach to thinking skills instruction described in this book applies these principles and related research on learning and thinking to classroom teaching of subject area content.

FIGURE I.3   Research-Based Statements about Learning

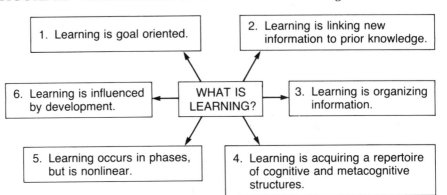

B. F. Jones, A. S. Palinscar, D. S. Ogle, and E. G. Carr, *Strategic Thinking and Learning: Cognitive Instruction in the Content Areas* (Alexandria, VA: ASCD Publications, 1987). Reprinted with permission of the Association for Supervision and Curriculum Development and B. F. Jones. Copyright © 1987 by the Association for Supervision and Curriculum Development. All rights reserved.

MAKING ROOM FOR DIFFERENCES

Learning to think does not occur in a uniform pattern for all individuals. Some factors that influence the way we think, such as speed of processing and depth perception, are probably based in physiology (Travers, 1982). Others are deeply seated in personality, such as willingness to suspend judgment, to tolerate ambiguity, to persist, and to challenge. Other attributes of character, like impulsivity and the sense of personal efficacy, are learned early in life and changed only with the greatest effort. As we learn and grow, each of us takes on a particular learning and thinking style, an approach to information based largely on patterns of earlier success in thinking (Keefe, 1979).

With differences in experience, we grow increasingly different. Psychologist Arnold Gesell observed early in this century, "All present growth hinges on past growth." Neither genetics nor the environment influences the process of growth as much as the continuous, self-conditioning process of growth itself (Vygotsky, 1986, p. 125). In learning to think, we do not all come out the same, yet continuous progress is essential for each of us. We all need to learn to manage the problems we encounter. Perhaps the most important outcome of learning to think is learning how to monitor and control our own thought processes so we can meet increasingly complex challenges.

Both chapters in Section I will prepare the subject area teacher to assume an expanded role in thinking skills instruction and to join with other teachers in helping students learn to manage the work of their minds. The responsibility for supporting thinking skills development must lie with all of us, in all the content areas—throughout the years of formal education.

REFERENCES

Alexander, P. A., & Judy, J. E. (1988). The interaction of domain specific and strategic knowledge in academic performance. *Review of Educational Research*, 58(4), 375–404.

Clarke, J. H., & Hood, K. (1986). School improvement in a rural state. *Educational Leadership*, October.

Costa, A. (1985). *Developing Minds: A Resource Book for Teaching Thinking*. Alexandria, VA: ASCD Publications.

Jones, B. F.; Palincsar, A. S.; Ogle, D. S.; & Carr, E. G. (1987). *Strategic Thinking and Learning: Cognitive Instruction in the Content Areas*. Alexandria, VA: ASCD Publications.

Keefe, J. W. (1979). *Student Learning Styles: Diagnosing and Prescribing Programs*. Reston, VA: NASSP.

Nickerson, R. S.; Perkins, D. H.; & Smith, E. E. (1985). *The Teaching of Thinking*. Hillsdale, NJ: Lawrence Erlbaum.

Perkins, D. N., & Salomon, G. (1989). Are cognitive skills context bound? *Educational Researcher*, 18(1), 16–26.

Travers, R. M. W. (1982). *Essentials of Learning: The New Cognitive Learning for Students of Education* (5th ed.). New York: MacMillan.

Vygotsky, L. (1986). *Thought and Language*. (A. Kozulin, trans.). Cambridge, MA: MIT University Press. (Original work published 1926)

1

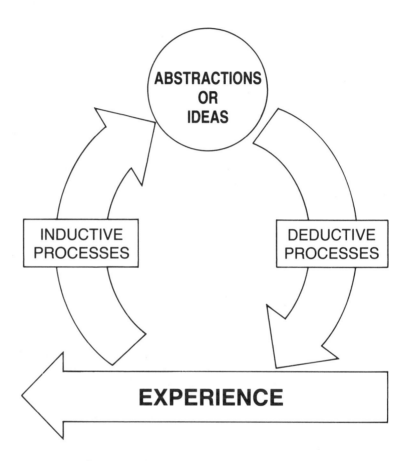

Consciousness is reflected in a word as the sun in a drop of water. A word relates to consciousness as a living cell relates to a whole organism, as an atom relates to the universe. A word is a microcosm of human consciousness.
—LEV VYGOTSKY, *Thought and Language*

Thinking

WHAT IS THINKING? THIS CHAPTER WILL BEGIN WITH A story rather than a definition. The story will include six kinds of thinking that depend on different patterns of mental organization. After the story and its explanation, the chapter shows how students can learn to recognize and apply these patterns to learning in school subjects.

AN EXPERIENCE IN THINKING

The Red Ball

Imagine for a moment that you are driving down a street in a residential neighborhood, heading home. Your speed is constant. Music from the radio washes in and out of hearing.

But please don't—step on my blue suede shoes . . .

Suddenly, your head snaps to the left—a red blur, in motion, uneven trajectory. Eyes focus. Red ball. Bouncing. Up down knee jerk. Foot to brake pedal, softly first. Scan again, behind bushes. Focus. Eyes fix on running child. Boy, six years. Hit the brakes! Hammer down right knee. Lock brakes. Tires shriek, drifting right. Adjust wheel to fit drift. Steady the slide. Boy, bent to ball, looks up. You watch boy startle at sudden shriek, eyes like two round questions, flashing quickly to the left. No thud. Passed. Done.

Your knee lets up. The force you bring to the pedal decreases. As your brakes unlock, the wheels track again. You center the car in the road. Through the mirror over the dashboard, you watch the boy, now appearing to be seven or eight years old, retrieve his ball from the gutter and run back again to the game in his front yard. Your foot returns pressure to the gas pedal. And the radio plays again.

You can do anything but lay off of my blue suede shoes . . .

A representative of the Vermont State Police has assured me that this entire episode could transpire in less than four seconds. Figure 1.1 represents this story as a chain of events in experience. As our eyes see them, events seem to happen in linear order. We cope with experience one event at a time.

Let us return to the episode with the red ball. This time we will take it more slowly and look not only at the experience, but at some of the mental processes involved in working through the experience without hitting the boy.

FIGURE 1.1 Thinking as Experience

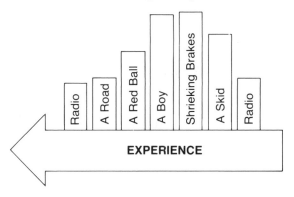

Six Aspects of Thinking

If we focus less on the events in the story of the red ball and more on the mental processes necessary for coping with those events, we can derive a different picture of the story. Figure 1.2 represents the story of the red ball, interpreted as if thinking were a circular process or wheel, and reduced to six basic components. This figure depicts the work of the mind as a circular process where perceptions of the situation trigger elaborate mental processes which then allow us to take control of the actual situation.

What has the graphic representation in Figure 1.2 done to the story? It has stripped the story of detail and reduced it to six large chunks. The graphic has converted the story from a description of experience to an abstract model. Each chunk or phase in the model involves a management skill for thinking:

1. *Scanning and focusing*: purposefully searching for meaningful information
2. *Creating categories and classes*: using grouping techniques to increase mental efficiency and power
3. *Inducing propositions from facts*: using what the senses know to create new ideas
4. *Activating conceptual knowledge*: hypothesizing relationships between concepts and events
5. *Predicting and planning*: using mental models to predict, plan, or decide on the future
6. *Developing procedures*: creating problem-solving steps appropriate to a specific decision or plan

FIGURE 1.2   An Interpretation of Thinking in One Short Episode: The Red Ball

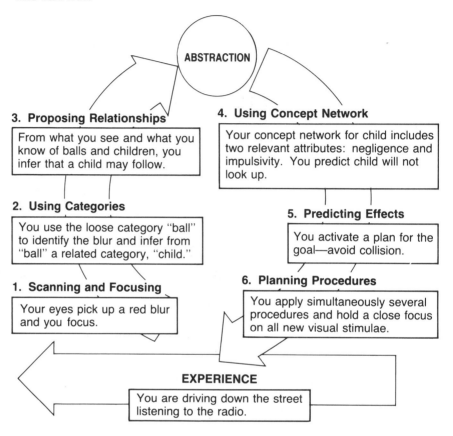

These six steps can help us understand how the driver avoided hitting the boy. They can also give us a way to think about learning in conventional subjects.

To work on problems in experience, the human mind has to reduce everything to symbols or ideas—like images, words, rules, principles, and concepts. The use of abstract symbols, in place of physical objects and actions, gives the human mind exceptional power and speed. The mind can work through its construction of symbols in a few seconds, or again and again over a lifetime, adding in new perceptions, finding new relationships, trying to assert general rules or laws. Using symbols, the human mind constructs elaborate models of how things work. Mental models allow the mind to return to experience and to learn more or to solve problems (Gentner & Stevens, 1983). The conventional school subjects also depend on abstract symbols to create models that describe how things work.

The mind is built to help us manage our experience. Each of the six kinds of thinking listed in Figure 1.2 is part of a management system. Each kind of thinking plays an important role, not only in driving a car, but in learning to manage anything—even school subjects. The six management skills of thinking described in Figure 1.2 begin to define the term *thinking* as it is used in this book. It is a definition derived in part from recent theory and research in thinking skills, tailored to fit the need for a design framework in classroom teaching. The six management skills can give us a fresh view of the episode of the red ball.

SCANNING AND FOCUSING
Your eyes pick up a red blur and you focus.

Under normal conditions, experienced drivers do not apply reasoning to the task of driving home. Most of the mind's work in driving is automatic rather than consciously controlled. Hands hold the wheel, adjusting pressure to the vibrations and jolts coming in from the road; eyes scan ahead, feeding a constant stream of images to a part of the mind that is not quite conscious but surely not unconscious either. From those images, the mind creates short-term mental icons, checks them for meaningful associations, then lets them go in order to attend to the steady flood of new perceptions. The ear is scanning, too, creating short-term memories or echoes from wheel sounds, engine sounds, and the wind, then filtering all of it away if the sounds have no meaning (Letteri, 1983). The foot adjusts the gas pedal to hold constant speed, using calculations that require no algebra. Under normal conditions the complex job of driving has been reduced to a set of automatic responses.

How much of the school day can be managed on automatic pilot? Paradoxically, the same school walls built to protect learning can also seal off students from compelling reasons to learn. Under normal conditions, students may see no need to direct the work of their minds to fit the purpose of schooling. Teachers have no way of determining which students in a classroom full of faces are thinking purposefully and which are simply flying through time on autopilot. Working on automatic pilot, the mind is not ready to learn. Teachers and students need to develop ways to turn off automatic pilot and turn on other cognitive processes that can help them think their way through the content.

USING CATEGORIES
You use the loose category "ball" to identify the blur and infer from "ball" a related category, "child."

In the episode of the red ball, the sight of the red blur tells you that it is time to control the thinking process. A question arises: What is this red blur? Such a question can activate higher mental processes. The mind checks the blur for specific attributes, tying it to a larger class of objects, all with similar features and expected patterns of behavior, but none with the same patterns. Feature analysis reveals that the blur is a member of the general class called "ball." Tying the red blur to the idea of "ball" makes the blur more predictable. The mind uses its knowledge of the general category called "ball" to make specific predictions about the red blur it has seen. Unlike a blur, a bouncing ball moves in a predictable pattern. In a millisecond, the mind has traced a path for the ball into the future—into the car's grill near the headlight.

In school learning, categories also make new events or ideas comprehensible. If we can tie new information to a larger class of information we already understand, the new information is no longer completely new. It is simply a variant of what we already know. Teachers and students need to see the development of categories and concepts as a way to lend efficiency to the mind's work. Each of the subject areas offers teachers this opportunity because each consists of a limited number of concepts and categories. The classroom is a place where we can practice applying categories to experience, looking for those with the greatest explanatory and predictive power.

INDUCING PROPOSITIONS FROM FACTS

From what you see and what you know of balls and children, you infer that a child may follow.

Recognizing a problem situation, you also call up higher-level reasoning abilities, several at once. You begin drawing inferences from the flow of sensory data. From the motion of the ball and from prior knowledge, the mind infers that a child may be following the ball. It sets a probability estimate for that inference. That a child may follow the ball becomes a kind of hypothesis. To check its hypothesis, the mind focuses the eyes on a place behind the ball where it would predict the appearance of a following child. Sure enough, the eyes pick up a young boy, following the path of the ball. The driver is able to create new information—a prediction—based on current fact. Our minds are built to induce new ideas from older information. The new ideas we create ourselves can have as much influence as those we absorb from experience.

School learning often presents students with a flood of diverse and even unrelated facts. It is the relationship between facts, rather than the facts alone, that bring us meaning. Inductive reasoning is the process of making connections between facts and then creating a generalization based on the facts. Teachers and students need to develop ways to make connections between facts so they can create new ideas, develop hypotheses, or propose theories that they want to test. Each of the subject areas gives teachers an opportunity to teach inductive thinking. The classroom context lets us slow experience so we can help students link facts and make inductive inferences.

USING CONCEPT NETWORKS

Your concept network for "child" includes two relevant attributes: negligence and impulsivity. You predict the child will not look up.

The driver of the car understands the boy, to some extent, even without actually knowing him. The mind can relate the running boy to a network of concepts related to children that are already stored in the mind. By relating this boy to the general concept of boys that it has developed, the mind can deduce the age of this particular ball player—and a number of other features. With the boy in view, the driver's mind starts tapping into what it already has stored as propositions about six-year-old boys. The driver knows that six-year-old boys may be impulsive and negligent while playing. Working deductively, the driver then predicts that this boy may not look up from the ball he is chasing. In this story, the deduction proves correct. The boy may be hit. A concept network processed deductively can let us see the future in time to change it.

School subjects also include a great deal of information we can use to think deductively. The subject areas offer rules, laws, theories, and causal propositions that teachers and students use to examine facts or solve problems. Often, students begin to enjoy learning when they see how deductive thinking creates a view of the future. Teachers and students need a way to represent relationships between facts and concepts that supports deductive reasoning. Representing concept networks can give them a medium that supports the examination of abstract ideas in light of specific events and lets them deduce answers to difficult questions.

PREDICTING EFFECTS AND PLANNING THE FUTURE

You activate a plan for the goal—avoid collision.

From years of experience with motion, with cars, and with children, you are able to predict that the boy will follow his ball out into the road, and you can plan a response to that eventuality. Through exposure to experience, each of us develops general expectancies or models for the way the world works. Our minds have reduced particular experiences to organizing schemata or models of the world as we think it works. Our general models include specific scripts for different kinds of situations. A causal model lets the driver predict that the car will hit the boy unless quick steps are taken. Causal models also let the driver imagine ways to avoid the boy. When we can predict an accident, we can prepare to avoid it. With the ball and the child on collision course with the car, the mind activates a plan to meet the goal: avoiding collision.

Much of school learning also amounts to "model making." What conditions are "causes" for other conditions? What rules or principles prevail? When one event occurs, what are the chances that a second event will also occur? Cause/effect thinking is always hypothetical and a bit risky, but the payoffs to thinking can be enormous. If we can interrupt the causal chain, we can shape the future. Teachers and students need a vehicle for describing cause/effect relationships, making predictions or plans and assessing the risks of those plans. Schematization of cause/effect relationships can support prediction, planning, and problem solving in school projects.

DESIGNING PROCEDURES

You apply simultaneously several procedures and hold a close focus on all new visual stimulae.

Almost without conscious effort, the driver of the car executes an elaborate set of simultaneous procedures. As the knee snaps up and down, the mind is projecting further steps necessary to avoid collision. Ears hear the brakes lock. The car starts a controlled four-wheel drift; the mind corrects, recalculates, replans, and continually resets the steps necessary to avoid hitting the child, using perceptions to evaluate and revise its procedures. The eyes bring a steady flow of assessment information. All of this is blended into a seamless flow of actions, information, and reaction. When the boy looks up at last, passing to the left of the car, the driver's knee relaxes. A new goal and new plan emerge: keeping the car on the road. Finally, the wheels track normally again. Then, somewhat changed, you are again driving down the road listening to the radio.

In school learning, there are many intellectual and behavioral routines. When students do them well, we can leave them alone. If students make errors in defining their approach to a problem, however, we can show them how to design a new procedure. Before procedures can be reduced to automatic responses, they must first be designed, planned, tested, and revised. The classroom is an excellent place for designing procedures for use outside—where the stakes are considerably higher. Teachers and students need a vehicle for designing and revising different kinds of intellectual procedures so they can be stored away as reliable and called up again when needed.

The Mind as Manager

The six steps described here take place in the "Red Ball" within a few seconds. In an experienced driver, most of them occur automatically. What allows the human mind to work through such a complicated process so quickly?

Compression of thought and action is possible for several reasons. First, the mind appears to be built to think in certain ways, *to create images*, for example, or *to draw inferences*. Experience adds specific content to these natural capabilities. Second, the mind can *operate its sys-*

tems simultaneously. Even if the mind has focused attention temporarily on shrieking brakes, the hand still guides the wheel and the eyes still watch for new information while the mind manipulates its mental model for speed, mass, and change—all at once. Third, through practice, the mind can *reduce elaborate reasoning procedures to simple routines* often called *scripts* (Galambos, 1986). Much of what the mind knows is stored as schemata—complex networks of related knowledge—which include preprogrammed responses to certain kinds of situations (Rumelhart, 1984). The braking response at the appearance of a red ball has been reduced to a script in the minds of most drivers. Fourth, in addition to scripted knowledge, the mind can *activate more flexible "models"* of how the world works, including generalized patterns of behavior for objects like bouncing balls (Holland et al., 1986) and people like six-year-old boys (Brewer & Nakamura, 1984). Mental models allow the mind to think deductively, predicting what will happen on the basis of a previously learned pattern. Fifth, all of its prior knowledge allows the mind to *create things that do not, in fact, exist.* The mind can create its own perceptions, imaging a six-year-old boy being hit by a car, for example, or a car avoiding the boy. Sixth, the mind can *apply higher-level reasoning to information* in any of its systems, including information it invents for itself. It can begin avoiding the boy before he appears (Perkins, 1986). Seventh, and most important, the human mind can *control its own processing.* It can shift attention among several kinds of simultaneous mental activity with remarkable speed, all in pursuit of purposes it has developed (Sternberg, 1985). Using all of these capabilities, the human mind constructs an internal environment that it can understand and manage. *Management of the internal world where the mind does all its work translates into management of the external world (where boys chase balls).*

   With all that work going on at once in the mind, strong management is required—and can be learned. Psychologists have created the term *metacognition* to describe the mind's management system (Sternberg, 1985; Gagne, 1980; Flavell, 1985). Metacognition includes two linked capabilities: the ability to focus awareness and the ability to control or direct mental processing to achieve goals (Presseisen, 1985). Metacognitive awareness monitors activity in all the layered systems of the mind, but allows attention to be focused on one thing at a time. Timing, sequencing, recognizing checkpoints in a process, aiming for effects, evaluating errors, choosing and adapting strategies, and checking output against goals—such is the work of metacognition. Metacognitive control directs the work of the mind toward purposes, rather than just letting things happen.

   What relationship does any of this have with thinking and learning in school? The point is that all minds—lined up in rows in our classrooms—have the innate ability to think with precision, ingenuity, or foresight about the subject being studied. Our students also have the potential of learning to manage the way their minds are working on those subjects. It is not likely that they will refine their thinking skills in relation to academic subjects or learn to focus their abilities unless we ask them to do so, show them some different approaches, and then give them plenty of practice and feedback. The subject areas are much too large and diverse to be memorized. They are nicely organized, however, as a practice ground for purposeful thinking. Working within school subjects, teachers can help young people use organizing patterns to manage the work of their minds (Presseisen, 1988).

A Pattern for Thinking in School Subjects

In order to include a focus on thinking in school subject content, teachers need an organizing pattern they can use to contemplate the processes of thought. The components of thought have been described in a number of ways. Ennis (1985, 1987) has developed a useful taxonomy from a philosophical perspective. Sternberg (1985) has developed a comprehensive theory of intelligence, based broadly in psychological research. Marzano and associates (1988) have created a conception of thinking as both process and skill which is directly applicable to curriculum design for content teaching. Bloom's (1956) taxonomy long ago created a perspective on thinking which has been built into a large portion of U.S. education. In Figure 1.3 and throughout these chapters, I have adapted a model of think-

FIGURE 1.3   The Wheel as an Inquiry Process

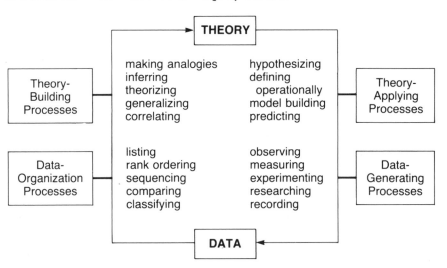

From Art Costa (Ed.), *Developing Minds* (Ben Strasser, designer). Alexandria, VA: ASCD Publications, 1985, p. 167.

ing proposed by Costa and colleagues (1985, p. 167) as a pattern of inquiry learning. Costa's circular model is consistent with recent research and theory in thinking skills. It is also consistent with the intellectual demands of most school subjects. Costa's circular model gives teachers a simple framework for understanding thinking within the subject areas and for developing instruction that will help students use different patterns of thinking. (Costa's model has been adapted slightly in Figure 1.3 to fit the purposes of this book.)

To think about inquiry learning, one may start anywhere in the cycle. Costa and associates identify two main starting points for inquiry in a problem area: data and theory. I use the term *data* to mean anything the mind brings in through the senses, even abstract ideas from books. *Theory* is the mind's abstraction of what the senses have brought. When the senses bring data suggesting that a problem may exist, the mind may set two processes in motion. "Data Organization Processes," such as recording, sequencing, or classifying, simply put the information into a form that the mind can handle independently of what the senses have perceived. "Theory-Building Processes," such as analogy, inference, or generalization, create new ways of explaining events, utilizing not only the original data, but a much larger array of events as well. Data, verifiable with the senses, have been reconstructed as theory, which is no longer directly verifiable but is much more powerful as a source of explanation and control.

The emergence of a potential theory triggers "Theory-Applying Processes," attempts by the mind to extend its mental model into the future. Will the emerging theory explain future data, or confirm a model of how things really work? Theory-Applying Processes generate questions that can only be answered by further data. "Data-Generating Processes" return the mind to the senses again. Can a predicted effect be observed and measured? What happens when the mind introduces one of its "solutions" to the world of problems? What happens if the human mind creates something new? Whatever the mind creates becomes part of the data it experiences. The hands are there to make new events for the mind to ponder. Of course, data-generating processes start the cycle again.

Costa's cycle explains the close relationship between two kinds of thinking, one usually called *induction* and the other called *deduction*. Inductive thinking transforms small bits of information (facts, observations, or excepts from texts) into broader ideas (categories, generalizations, or theories). Deductive thinking, in contrast, uses abstract theories to make judgments about specific events, predict future occurrences, or plan an approach to the future—to solve problems. The differences between these two kinds of thinking can be demonstrated by dividing Figure 1.3 in half vertically. On the left side, induction moves from data (derived from experience) toward theory. On the right, deduction tests theory with experience (data).

In Costa's model, induction includes all the processes the mind uses to organize data and then develop concepts or theories; deduction includes all the processes the mind uses to model the world around it and create solutions to problems. Together, induction and deduction are what Sternberg termed "fluid abilities"—the abilities laypersons identify with problem solving (Sternberg, 1985, p. 131). Both Kolb (1977) and Gregorc (1979) have developed learning style inventories based on a similar conception of thinking and experience. Through experience, each of us learns to rely on different patterns of thinking. Confronted by different kinds of content, we each prefer to start thinking from different places in the cycle and rely on different learning processes.

Although different subject areas utilize different kinds of thinking, success in most subjects requires both data management (bottom-up induction) and application of principles (top-down deduction). A cycle in which induction and deduction support each other provides a simple framework for teaching thinking in the content areas. The two processes, induction and deduction, Vygotsky explained, can give birth to different kinds of ideas. Some ideas we have to discover inductively, whereas other ideas must occur first in our minds and then slowly gather specific examples. A child probably develops the concept of "exploitation" deductively, first as a category or word in the mind and then as a set of recognized experiences with people or groups. In contrast, the child's concept of "brother" probably develops inductively from a set of experiences with brothers toward the development of a loosely organized concept (Vygotsky, 1986, p. 193).

Some ideas, called *Roschian concepts*, can never by fully defined through induction. They remain aggregate words standing for a mass of specific examples (see Flavell, 1985, p. 252; Piaget, 1964). Some skills, like the skill of tying one's shoes, would defy being taught deductively as an application of principles. They do not follow principles. To work well with academic content, we need to develop inductive and deductive abilities as appropriate to the task. A teacher's task includes designing a process for thinking about the content which may include both inductive and deductive processes.

Together, induction from experiences and deduction from subjectively established concepts and rules combine powerfully to let us understand and then control our environment (Gagne, 1980; Rumelhart, 1984, p. 171). In the objective world of experience, all five senses are busy collecting information. Daily experiences give us *data*; so does classroom instruction. In the subjective recesses of the human mind, our interpretive processes transform data to concepts we use to build abstract models showing how we think the world works. Data from the senses are momentary, but become enduring in the mental models we devise to represent our world. Thought is the process of working back and forth between observation and reflection. It is also the process of working from analysis of past events toward planning for future events (Bruffee, 1986). The relationship between induction and deduction lets us create experience for our own senses to perceive. We control the element of our own learning process.

When psychologists argue that we construct the world in which we live, they are not arguing that the human mind can operate independently of the material universe or others who inhabit that universe. The two worlds, internal and external, interact constantly. The senses supply the mind with a constant flow of potentially useful raw materials from "the world." The thinking processes of the mind use some of those materials, along with materials previously in place, to reconstruct a mental model. The senses are there to ensure that we do not become so absorbed in our thinking that we lose track of the external world where our survival hangs in the balance. Each sense is continually scanning for information worth processing. Inductively, we process some new information to further build a world view and then act in accordance with that view. If our world view is partly wrong, which is likely, our senses are there to bring us corrective information—usually quickly and sometimes quite painfully. Thankfully, most of us are granted many years in which to refine and test our constructions of a world view.

Controlling the Mind's Work

The central assumption of this book is that students need to be aware of their own mental processes in order to learn to control them. The wheel in Figures 1.2 and 1.3 gives teachers a metaphor for the workings of the mind. Using this metaphor and others, teachers can stop or slow thinking long enough for students to see some part of how their minds are working. Of course, the mind has no wheels, but the wheel (or cycle or circle) is a useful two-dimensional image, letting us see a great deal in little space. The form of the wheel lets us see different aspects of the thinking processes as they reinforce each other, and offers an integrating view of thinking skills that are often treated as if separate. Figure 1.4 illustrates the general plan put forth in this book as a wheel on which six kinds of thinking can become visible. Although not an expression of the ultimate purpose of thinking skills instruction in the content areas, the six management skills in the figure constitute one way teachers can imbed an organized approach to thinking skills in conventional content instruction. This book converts each skill into a visible form, a graphic organizer for that thinking process. Students can use patterns of thinking in simplified chunks and in graphic form to practice managing the work of their minds.

Figure 1.4 provides a simple organizer for thinking skills instruction across the subject areas, grades K–12. As Resnick (1987, p. 8) has argued,

FIGURE 1.4   The Wheel as a Plan, Using Graphics to Teach Six Aspects of Thinking Skills

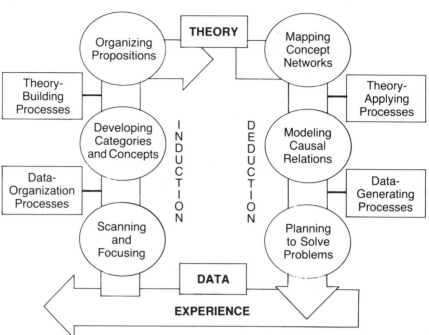

The most important single message of modern research on the nature of thinking is that the kinds of activities traditionally associated with thinking are not limited to advanced levels of development. . . . In fact, the term higher order skills is probably misleading, for it suggests that another set of skills, presumably called 'lower order,' needs to come first. . . . Research suggests that failure to cultivate aspects of (higher order) thinking may be the source of learning difficulties even in elementary school.

In the chapters describing graphic frames for thinking skills (Sections II and III), I have deliberately mixed examples of similar approaches from all the grades and many subjects areas. The patterns of thinking used by the mind to manage information keep the same basic structure from the beginning. It is mainly the content that begins in relatively simple forms and grows toward complexity. Students should see that the nature of thinking does not change as they progress through school, but adapts to increasing challenge in all the subject areas.

In setting out to teach students to manage the work of their minds, with a particular focus on higher-order reasoning, what kinds of capability are we trying to encourage? Resnick (1988) has focused much of her attention on the kind of thinking required for success in modern life, and sees a need for thinking skills adaptable to different demands. From her perspective, the thinking we seek:

- Is nonalgorithmic; the path of action is not fully specified in advance
- Is complex; the total path is not mentally "visible" from any single vantage point
- Often yields multiple solutions, each with costs and benefits, rather than unique solutions
- Involves nuanced judgment and interpretation
- Involves uncertainty; not everything bearing on the task is known.
- Involves the application of multiple, sometimes conflicting, criteria
- Involves self-regulation of the thinking process, not regulation by others
- Involves imposing meaning, finding structure in apparent disorder
- Is effortful

In pursuit of this kind of thinking, teachers in the content areas cannot just plug in a few exercises or run their students through a short program. Resnick is describing outcomes for teaching that can be achieved only if their attainment is a purpose of the entire educational process.

Left to its own devices, the human mind may not be inclined to refine its own strategies. It can reason automatically, but it can also dispense with reason automatically. It can ignore the facts, fail to recall, infer incorrectly, leap to unreliable conclusions, get the wrong idea, fail to set goals, devise shoddy plans, endlessly repeat a fruitless procedure, and carry out an approach without checking for accuracy. If it fails to find a purpose for processing information, the mind sinks quickly to boredom. It turns to other interests. It wanders, seeking other pleasure. It can work better—to a greater number of purposes and with greatly increased power—if we teach our students how to control the work it does by nature. How can teachers of subject areas help their students to switch off their autopilot and learn to monitor and control the work of their minds?

REFERENCES

Beyer, B. (1987). *Practical Strategies for the Teaching of Thinking*. Boston: Allyn and Bacon.

Bloom, B. S. (Ed.) (1956). *Taxonomy of Educational Objectives. Handbook I: Cognitive Domain*. New York: McKay.

Brewer, W. F., & Nakamura, G. V. (1984). The nature and functions of schemas. In R. S. Weir & T. K. Krull (Eds.), *Handbook of Social Cognition*. Hillsdale, NJ: Lawrence Erlbaum.

Bruffee, K. (1986). Social construction, language, and the authority of knowledge: A bibliographical essay. *College English*, 48(8), 773–790.

Costa, A.; Hanson, R.; Silver, H. F.; and Strong R. W. (1985). Other mediative strategies. In A. Costa (Ed.), *Developing Minds: A Resource Book for Teaching Thinking*. Alexandria, VA: ASCD Publications.

Ennis, R. H. (1985). Goals for a critical thinking curriculum. In A. Costa (Ed.), *Developing Minds: A Resource Book for Teaching Thinking*. Alexandria, VA: ASCD Publications.

Ennis, R. H. (1987). A taxonomy of critical thinking dispositions and abilities. In J. B. Baron & R. M. Sternberg (Eds.), *Teaching Thinking Skills* (pp. 1–26). New York: W. H. Freeman.

Flavell, J. H. (1985). *Cognitive Development*. Englewood Cliffs, NJ: Prentice-Hall.

French, L. A. (1985). Real world knowledge as the basis for social and cognitive development. In J. Pryor and J. Day (Eds.), *Development of Social Cognition*. New York: Springer-Verlag.

Gagne, R. M. (1980). Learnable aspects of problem solving. *American Psychologist*, 15(2), 84–92.

Galambos, J. A. (1986). Knowledge structures for common activities. In J. A. Galambos, R. P. Abelson, & J. B. Black (Eds.), *Knowledge Structures*. Hillsdale, NJ: Lawrence Erlbaum.

Genter, D., & Stevens, A. L. (1983). *Mental Models*. Hillsdale, NJ: Lawrence Erlbaum.

Gregorc, A. F. (1979). Learning/teaching styles: Their nature and effects. In *Student Learning Styles: Diagnosing and Prescribing Programs* (pp. 19–26).

Holland, J. H.; Holyoak, K. J.; Nisbett, R. E.; & Thagard, P. R. (1986). *Induction: Processes of Inference, Learning and Discovery*. Cambridge, MA: MIT Press.

Kolb, D. (1977). *Learning Style Inventory* (Manual). Cambridge, MA: McBer and Associates.

Larkin, J.; McDermott, J.; Simon, D. P.; & Simon, H. A. (1980). Expert and novice performance in solving physics problems. *Science*, 208(20), 1335–1342.

Letteri, C. (1983). An introduction to information processing: Cognitive controls and cognitive profiles. Unpublished manuscript.

Marzano, R. J.; Brandt, R. S.; Hughes, C. S.; Jones, B. F.; Presseisen, B. Z.; Rankin, S. C.; & Sohor, C. (1988). *Dimensions of Thinking: A Framework for Curriculum and Instruction*. Alexandria, VA: ASCD Publications.

Nisbett, R. E.; Fong, G. T.; Lehman, D. R.; & Cheng, P. W. (1987). Teaching reasoning. *Science*, 238, 625–698.

Perkins, D. N. (1986). *Knowledge as Design*. Hillsdale NJ: Lawrence Erlbaum.

Piaget, J. (1964). *Judgment and Reasoning in the Child*. Patterson, NJ: Littlefield.

Presseisen, B. (1985). Thinking skills: Meanings, models, materials. In A. Costa (Ed.), *Developing Minds: A Resource Book for Teaching Thinking*. Alexandria, VA: ASCD Publications.

Presseisen, B. (1988). Avoiding battle at curriculum gulch: Teaching thinking and content. *Educational Leadership*, April, 7–10.

Resnick, L. (1987). *Education and Learning to Think*. Washington, DC: National Academy Press.

Resnick, L. B. (1987). Learning in school and out: The 1987 presidential address. *Educational Researcher*, 19(9), 13–19.

Rumelhart, D. (1975). Notes on a schema for stories. In D. G. Bobrow & A. D. Collins (Eds.), *Representation and Understanding: Studies in Cognitive Science*. New York: Academic Press.

Rumelhart, D. E. (1984). Schemata and the cognitive system. In R. S. Weir & T. K. Krull (Eds.), *Handbook for Social Cognition*. Hillsdale, NJ: Lawrence Erlbaum.

Sternberg, R. M. (1985). *Beyond IQ: A Triarchal Theory of Intelligence*. Cambridge/New York: Cambridge University Press.

Vygotsky, L. (1986). *Thought and Language*. (A Kozulin, trans.). Cambridge, MA: MIT University Press.

2

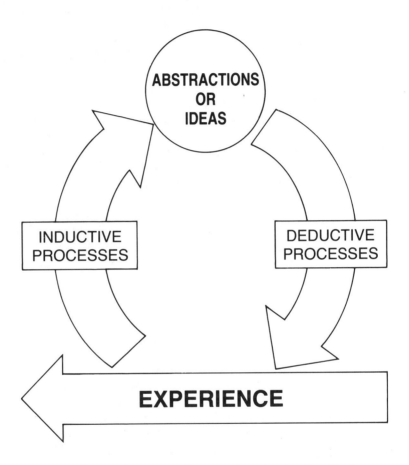

ABSTRACTIONS
OR
IDEAS

INDUCTIVE
PROCESSES

DEDUCTIVE
PROCESSES

EXPERIENCE

*The most important single factor influencing learning is what the learner
already knows. Ascertain this, and teach him accordingly.*
—DAVID AUSUBEL, *Educational Psychology: A Cognitive View*

Teaching

T O DIAGNOSE THE LEARNING NEEDS OF STUDENTS AND TO plan appropriately, teachers must be able to see how students are thinking about the content. How can we see thinking? I don't really think we can. The things children do in school, their writing, pictures, tests, and talk, can give us a sense of *what* they know. Such artifacts are a bit less useful in letting us see *how* they know what they know. This book will show how graphic organizers, as representations of content knowledge, can give teachers a vision of how students are managing their learning and thinking and how learning and thinking can be made more manageable.

Graphic organizers are words on paper, arranged to represent an individual's understanding of the relationship between the words. Whereas conventions of sentence structure make most writing linear in form, graphic organizers take their form from the presumed structure of relationships among ideas. Different kinds of relationships—like parts to the whole, cause to effect, or evidence to conclusion—suggest different kinds of graphic representations. Graphic organizers can be used as a facsimile of student knowledge. In working with graphic organizers, students struggle to find a form that fits the content they are learning. The struggle for form is a struggle for control over an idea. When we ask students to represent graphically what they think, we are asking them to extend control over the subject of our questioning. Graphic organizers aim to show students how they are thinking about a subject.

LET'S SEE HOW THEY THINK

Suzanne LaRocque, a third-grade teacher in the town of Swanton, Vermont, asked her students to write a journal entry about thinking. "Thinking!" she stated, "What does thinking mean to you?" After a period of startled silence and a few exclamations of concern about the "right answer," the children settled down to the task. The third grade wrote for two or three minutes in a short journal entry. The students struggled with the question with varying degrees of confidence. Figure 2.1 is a sample of what some students wrote, using different patterns of thinking. I have drawn a graphic illustration of each journal entry, hoping to get a clearer view of "thinking" in the eyes of these third-grade students. The graphic illustrations may also show how graphic organizers may be used to try to see *how* students are thinking about a subject. Such graphics may help us to assess the way their minds are managing what they know and how they know it.

We'll start with Christopher, whose example raises some questions about thinking and about graphic ways of representing it:

FIGURE 2.1   Third-Graders Thinking Inductively about Thinking

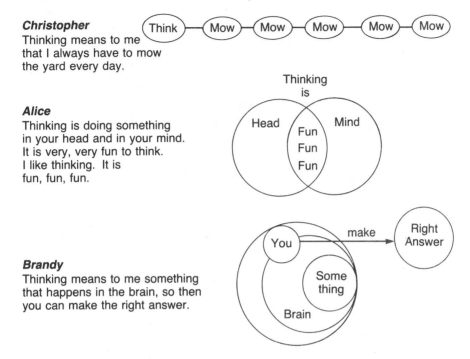

Christopher
Thinking means to me
that I always have to mow
the yard every day.

Alice
Thinking is doing something
in your head and in your mind.
It is very, very fun to think.
I like thinking. It is
fun, fun, fun.

Brandy
Thinking means to me something
that happens in the brain, so then
you can make the right answer.

      CHRISTOPHER: Thinking means to me that I always have to
mow the yard every day.

Let's take Christopher at his word and assume that what he wrote is what
he thought about thinking—at that moment.

    At the word *thinking*, Christopher has turned his mind toward the
endless task of mowing the lawn. It is possible that Christopher was so
absorbed with what he had to do when he got home that any question
we might have asked would have provoked the same answer. It is also
possible that he was depressed about the prospect of going home because
the job seemed so big. From a different perspective, it is possible that
Christopher could not separate the "what" of thinking from the "how"
of thinking. Can he distinguish "thinking" from the other daily acts it
supports?

    To Christopher, thinking may be just one more demand in a long
series of demands. Is thinking the same as action for him? In writing, did
he see his mind as separate from its contents or from physical action?
Are thinking and mowing equivalent? If not, what diverted him from
looking at differences? Fear? Anger? Lack of opportunity? Could we imag-

ine ways to help Christopher see his mind working in different ways? Could we devise ways to help him think about how to direct the energy in his mind? It is possible that his "thinking" does not separate itself from the endless tasks of his days. It may not be a separate concept; it may not yet be under his control. The graphic can help him and his teachers formulate questions about his thinking—and consider different patterns.

Alice may have enjoyed thinking about thinking more than Christopher did. Once she started to think, the process gained its own momentum:

> **ALICE:** Thinking is doing something in your head and in your mind. It is very, very fun to think. I like thinking. It is fun, fun, fun.

Let's take Alice at her word, too, and assume that what she wrote is a facsimile for what she thought. She first tried a definition of thinking as "doing something in your head." It almost worked for her, but she had to add, "and in your mind." Suddenly two ideas, "head" and "mind" were fighting for the same turf. Did the word *mind* achieve new meaning in contrast to the word *head?* Where does thinking come from, anyway? Who is in charge here, body or mind? Unlike her classmate, Christopher, she seems not at all depressed by the failure of easy answers. In fact, she may have gotten a bit carried away with the hilarity of getting stuck between two options—"Fun, fun, fun." The graphic may support her exploration of the relationships between head and mind.

Brandy took a slightly different tack. She first noticed a product of thinking, "the right answer."

> **BRANDY:** Thinking means to me something that happens in the brain, so then you can make the right answer.

Thinking helps you produce things—"right answers." By inference, some process must account for the production. Between product and process, however, Brandy was far more confident about the product—the right answers. Working backward from "the right answers," she began to struggle. What is this "something that happens"? Is it in the "you" or in the brain? She came up against the problem that the "you," the "brain," or the "something" produces right answers. But which one can take responsibility. Which one is in charge? How does it work? The question is large indeed. To answer the question, she would need a broader base of observations or facts from which to induce the relationships she seeks. Still, the graphic creates a stable version of the problem while questions take form.

All of these third-graders were struggling to think well about a difficult topic. Their journal entries and the graphic representations give us a way to assess what they were thinking and how they were managing the process of thinking. I believe these third-graders were all using a similar approach—a reliance on induction. They each juxtaposed two ideas or experiences and then tried to derive a generalization from the juxtaposition. They succeeded to different degrees. Christopher made little progress juxtaposing "thinking" and "mowing the lawn," but he also made no effort to exploit the comparison. Alice saw the fun of trying to link her "head" with her "mind," but she never fully worked out that juxtaposition, either. Brandy tried to use one idea—the product of thinking—as a basis for inducing the process. These third-grade students did not know they were working inductively. Their short journals were simply an attempt to let words organize their thinking. Potentially, the graphics would let us—and them—think about how they were thinking and then develop the ideas represented there.

Other students in Suzanne LaRocque's class wrote differently about thinking. They tended to think deductively about the question. They used an organizing definition to develop or test specific instances of that definition. Figure 2.2 includes their written response with a graphic I have drawn of their ideas.

Joe saw thinking as a fairly nonspecific function.

> **JOE:** Thinking helps you do things. Thinking helps you make things.

Still, if we accept this graphic representation of what he wrote as an artifact of his thought, we can see a concept forming. "Thinking helps" is an organizing concept for the two subordinate ideas, doing things and making things.

For Joe, the concept of thinking formed tentatively around the idea of what thinking does for people. At the time he wrote, thinking was helpful in only two ways: toward "doing" and "making." The possibility of a relationship between doing and making was not developed. Specific instances did not appear. Still, this simple structure—one concept with two categories of example—could allow the addition of further functions. "Solving problems" could be added, or "painting." Joe worked through two examples of the idea he had developed. Then he let it go.

Stacie was moving on the same track.

> **STACIE:** I think thinking helps you do your work. It also lets you draw amazing pictures. You need to think about whatever you want to do.

Initially, Stacie and Joe had similar ideas. But Stacie went on to propose something much larger: "You need to think about whatever you want to do." She opened vast horizons with that sentence. What would happen if Joe and Stacie drew a graphic of thinking together? Would Joe be willing to

FIGURE 2.2   Other Third-Graders Thinking Deductively

Joe
Thinking helps you do things.
Thinking helps you make things.

Stacie
I think thinking helps you
do your work. It also lets you
draw amazing pictures. You
need to think about whatever
you want to do.

Beth
Thinking means if you need
some ideas about making a
birdhouse or a house. You
need to think when you ski
or sled and if you don't think
you could ram into a tree.

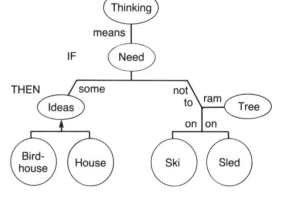

Andrew
Thinking means to me that you
are thinking of something to do
and if you do think of something
to do you do it... say you are
thinking of something to eat.

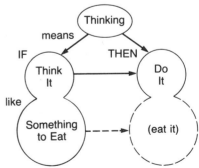

entertain "amazing pictures" as a third category? Would they decide that "painting" is another kind of "making" that the mind can do? How many things might they "want to do"? How much thinking might they discover? The graphic can help us imagine their thinking processes. If they work together, they may refine and elaborate their ideas.

Beth did not get stuck at all in defining a position or in testing it against experience. With almost shocking aplomb, she worked through two different stages of a deductive process, once to assert a positive definition of thinking and the second time to test her definition against its antithesis.

> **BETH:** Thinking means if you need some ideas about making a birdhouse or a house. You need to think when you ski or sled and if you don't think you could ram into a tree.

Beth worked systematically from the idea of needs. If you needed a birdhouse, or by association, a real house, then you needed ideas and that is the work of thinking. That was easy. Round one goes to Beth. Let's try it again, this time in the negative. Let's say you need to ski or sled. If you need to think but you don't think, you ram into a tree. From the concept of need, Beth was able to work deductively through positive and negative instances.

Andrew proved as artful in deductive thinking as had Beth. Andrew asserted that thinking has something to do with "if/then" sequences, what some researchers in artificial intelligence like to call "rules" (Holland et al., 1986; Bobrow & Collins, 1975).

> **ANDREW:** Thinking means to me that you are thinking of something to do and if you do think of something to do you do it . . . say you are thinking of something to eat.

Thinking produces something to do, Andrew proclaimed. Once you think it, you do it. He carried this abstract statement all the way to the concrete level, the level of eating. "Say you are thinking of something to eat . . ."; he need go no further. The completion of the example is obvious from his original proclamation.

Which of the deductive thinkers is right? Again, each of these students is right. Each of them has given his or her teacher a vision of the starting point for further practice in thinking. For all of them, inductive and deductive thinkers alike, the problem is that *all* of their definitions are necessary to a full understanding of mental activity. None of them, in itself, is complete and sufficient. Left to their own devices, these students might go on to develop more fully the specific approach to thinking with which they began. Would all of them develop skill in a full array of approaches to thinking? Why can't they develop and share one full definition among themselves—a definition that would be, in combination, far richer than any of them could achieve singly? What would happen if all of these children had a chance to try inductive thinking in their regular class work? If they worked together, could they develop a more reliable or more flexible approach? Would they all grow to share Christopher's practical concern for procedures, Alice's delight, or Beth's flare?

Suzanne LaRocque used these statements as a beginning. Over the next few months, her students used many different patterns of thinking, working with various kinds of subject area content. In fact, they each wrote a book called "ME" in which they used many different patterns of thinking to look at themselves in different ways. As Suzanne LaRocque introduced different kinds of graphic frames, she and her students had fresh opportunities to assess what they knew and then to add or change content or organization. Graphics became a mediating vehicle for an exploration of themselves.

LOOKING AT GRAPHIC ORGANIZERS

Should we give our students a chance to "see" what they think? Should they also "see" what we think as a way to understand our purpose? Can we use graphic organizers to diagnose problems and plan a program of study for students? A graphic organizer or thinking pattern creates a simplified version of these highly complex intellectual skills. In correspondence during the development of this book, Art Costa called this use of graphic organizers "displayed metacognition." Graphic organizers bring some of the control mechanisms of the mind's work to the surface—in visible form—where they can be discussed, practiced, and refined. Finally, as the processes they represent become automatic, graphic organizers can be discarded as superfluous. In teaching, the purpose of displaying aspects of metacognitive process is to increase the students' awareness of how their minds can work and increase their control over different ways of thinking.

A graphic frame is an organizing pattern students can use to represent relationships in the information they confront in school (Jones, Pierce, & Hunter, 1989). Perkins (1987, p. 47) suggests two metaphors that help define the uses and the limits of any frame for thinking:

> *As any photographer knows, the frame of the viewfinder organizes the image within it, creating a visual statement where, without the frame, one might see only clutter. And, as any builder knows, the frame of a building supports its totality. Both metaphors highlight a crucial feature of thinking frames: They support and organize thought, but they do not do the thinking. They are guides, not recipes.*

Graphic organizers are simultaneously a medium for assessment of student learning and a medium for constructing new ideas. Students and teachers can use a graphic frame to analyze how they are thinking, or, within a graphic organizer, students can collect information, draw inferences, propose hypotheses, or plan (diSessa, 1979). As Perkins points out, frames of any kind are guides to a process, rather than statements of outcome for teaching.

Part of the recent interest in graphic organizers results from studies that show how experts use patterns to store and manage vast quantities of information. When researchers compare expert and novice performance in solving problems, they notice a number of differences between the two groups. Experts see problems in terms of organizing patterns. Remarkable feats of memory and skill in problem solving may rely in part on our ability to "chunk" information and to use a perceptual pattern or general schema to hold the information (Simon, 1974). Studies of master chess players, for example, suggest that the experts may be using 50,000 to 100,000 perceptual patterns to understand the organization of a chess game (Chase & Simon, 1973). The patterns described by Chase and Simon are interlocked within a vast network of ideas about chess. "This large set of perceptual patterns serves as an index, or access route, not only to the expert's factual knowledge, but also to his or her information about actions and strategies" (Larkin et al., 1980, p. 1336). Beginners have to reconstruct a chess game one piece at a time—without reference to organizing patterns.

Graphic representation of basic thought processes can be used to mediate between a student's experience of subject area content and manipulation of more formal systems of expression (see Figure 2.3). Graphic

FIGURE 2.3   Graphic Organizers as a Mediating Language for Teaching Thinking

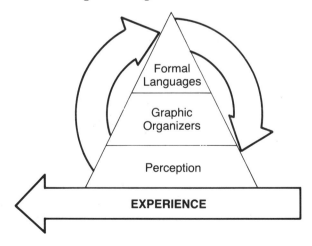

organizers constitute a "spacial language" students can use to explore and express basic relationships in content (see Holley & Dansereau, 1984). The formal languages of mathematics (arithmetic, algebra, geometry), science (chemistry, physics), language studies (logic, rhetoric, grammar), and even musical notation all employ specialized languages to express relationships. Most of those languages require great precision in expression. Graphic organizers, in contrast, let students explore more elementary relationships, with considerably less precision, as they struggle to gather information or solve problems. The graphic organizers in this book can be part of the formative process of thinking, just as imaging and planning are part of the process of developing final forms of prose writing (Fulwiler, 1987). In the formative stages of learning, students discover purpose, structure, and potential meaning of the content.

To the extent that our classes ask students to use words or other symbols in an organized fashion, we all teach thinking. Any symbol system organizes mental work. Graphic organizers provide another medium for the same purpose. A graphic "language" representing aspects of thinking has the purpose of mediating the learning process:

1. Describing *simple* steps for procedures that can evolve toward more *complex* forms
2. Creating an *objective form* for a *subjective process* so students can practice managing basic tools with guidance
3. Showing students *manageable procedures* for thinking which they can then *adapt flexibly* to novel situations
4. Creating a *social context* for sharing and refining a *personal perspective*

The purpose of a graphic language is to initiate basic questioning. What is the nature of the material I am confronting? Am I looking at a step in a process? An instance of a concept? A way of explaining a series of event? One cause or one effect? What is the frame or organization that holds all this together? With the basic structure of the content identified, the student can be more efficient in developing a purpose for learning, deciding what to remember, and planning how to respond to the material (Dansereau & Holley, 1984).

Graphic organizers or frames are the primary design, teaching, and assessment medium for all of the thinking strategies included in this book. Graphic organizers have the advantage of integrating the diagnostic stage of teaching with the treatment phase, and potentially with the assessment phase as well. A diagnostic map can be revised continually over the course of a unit until it comes to represent a more complete and accurate representation of the subject. Within conventional teaching methods for conventional subjects, graphic organizers also have the purpose of describing simple steps for mental procedures that can evolve toward more complex forms. On small notebook paper or on giant roles of wrapping paper, graphic organizers create an objective form for a subjective process so students can practice managing basic tools with a teacher's guidance.

The purpose of showing students manageable procedures for thinking is to help them develop methods that they can then adapt to novel situations. Perhaps most important, a graphic organizer establishes a vehicle for interaction between teachers and students, creating a social context for sharing and refining personal meaning. In this interaction, assessment and teaching can become one. The following assumptions underlie the use of graphic organizers in teaching:

1. Direct experience—in the classroom and in the world at large—is full of clutter; *graphic frames help students make basic connections.*
2. The spoken word moves at great speed through the mind, often scattering its meaning; *graphic frames give greater control to students and teachers who are searching for relationships in the content.*
3. The formal languages of science, mathematics, and written English are all abstract; *graphic representation allows students to manipulate ideas as if they had some properties of things.*
4. Formal languages tend to be linear in structure; *graphic frames capture a whole idea in relation to its assembled parts.*
5. It is hard to talk about an invisible process; *graphic frames create an objective form for a subjective thinking process.*
6. Thinking is considered an individual enterprise; *graphic frames make thinking a social (enjoyable) occasion.*
7. Prolific detail can obscure the central organizing purpose of learning or thinking; *graphic organizers tend to bring purpose to the surface.*
8. Assessment and teaching lose power when conducted separately; *graphic frames unify both in a single medium.*

In effect, the point of using graphic organizers in teaching is to give students an overview of the learning process where a clear purpose can be easily inferred. As teachers, we need to be able to slow the speed at which the students are processing. By letting students reflect on how they are thinking about the content we present, we can aim to increase the control they exert over the work of their minds.

USING GRAPHIC ORGANIZERS IN TEACHING

If only for the sake of consistency, I have chosen to see teaching as just another kind of thinking. Figure 2.4 is a graphic representation of the teaching process, with the same basic structure as Costa's thinking proc-

FIGURE 2.4   Teaching as a Thinking Wheel

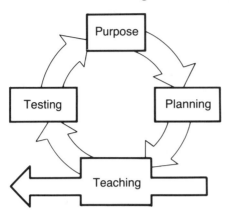

ess in Chapter 1, or Kolb's (1977) learning styles. If we begin at the most abstract level, teaching relies on some clear statement of general purpose for the students—which can be called *mission*, *goal*, or *objective*, depending on the scope of the effort. Second, the teacher has to convert that goal into a plan for herself or himself and the work of her or his students. Third, the teacher has to put that plan into action through classwork and homework. Finally, the teacher has to gather up information from what students have done that lets her or him know whether the original goal has been met. With a revised purpose in view, the teacher can replan. The wheel turns.

Purpose, plan, teach, and test—the pattern is well established in teaching, albeit with different expression, as in Hunter's instructional process (1982) or Beyer's direct instruction (1987). Teaching within different structural frameworks can create different kinds of effects, as described by Joyce and Weil (1986). I have used the same circular pattern to manage the process of designing lectures, discussions, and writing instruction (Clarke, 1980, 1987, 1989). How do graphic organizers for patterns of thinking relate to this conception of teaching process?

Purpose

Learning and thinking are purposes that require mutual agreement. Graphic organizers give teachers a way to express a purpose for learning in collaboration with their students. A graphic organizer includes an outline of the content; it also contains an expression of the kind of thinking that can be applied to that content. Consequently, a graphic organizer often gives teachers and students a way to talk about the purpose for learning. Students cannot be made to learn or made to think. Teachers and students must reach a natural consensus as to why they are in a classroom together (Marzano et al., 1988). Unless the students are able to verbalize or otherwise represent the purpose in their learning, it is not likely that they will put much energy into carrying out our plans.

Increasingly, research has confirmed the importance of academic content in the development of thinking skills (see Gagne, 1980; Larkin et al., 1980; Nisbett et al., 1987). We may first develop a new way of thinking within a narrow portion of a subject. Slowly, we practice and refine that skill within similar content. Gradually, as we confront content of increasing complexity, our ability to adapt teaching skills to new content increases. Glaser (1984, pp. 97–98) states:

> What can be interpreted as abstract pervasive changes in the child's reasoning and learning abilities are repeated as knowledge is gained in various domains. These changes come about with the acquisition of specific knowledge and these knowledge structures comprise theories that enable different kinds of thinking. . . . The acquisition of knowledge in some domains is more broadly applicable than in others.

As a child progresses through school, what is most desirable appears to be a sharpened awareness of fit between certain approaches to thinking and certain kinds of situations, with the ability to adapt patterns of thinking to fine nuances in a given situation. As students gain experience with different patterns of thinking, they should also grow more able to express their own thinking with relation to specific content.

Planning and Design

Instructional design is the part of teaching that happens before we walk into the classroom. From a sense of student needs and the learning goals those needs imply, the "teacher-as-designer" designs sequences of activities that involve students in learning new content and using new techniques. The two most important questions the teacher-as-designer has to ask are: What is the most promising pattern of exposition for the facts, concepts, procedures, or rules in this content area? and What kind of thinking is required by this content? Each of the academic disciplines puts emphasis on different basic patterns of thinking (Donald, 1983). Most of the time, a design for instruction has to begin with simple concepts and work toward more complex forms (Reigeluth, 1987, p. 247). Learning in most subjects requires a process of gradual elaboration.

In designing instruction, teachers can (1) develop graphic organizers to express their own thinking or (2) develop graphic organizers that engage students in thinking about the content. Each of the chapters that follow includes a few examples of graphic organizers expressing a teacher's view of a subject. The vast majority of examples, however, were exercises designed by teachers to engage their students in thinking about the content. What a teacher knows and how he or she knows it can be useful as a model to students. What is more important in learning to think, however, is being able to represent and explain one's own processes. As designers, teachers need to think about the knowledge and techniques their students already have. They need to think about the content itself—its structure, shape, and the problems it presents. Then, as part of classroom activity, discussions, small-group activity, reading assignments, projects, field trips, and examinations, teachers can design graphic organizers that help students struggle with the content and make sense of it. When students have completed such an exercise, it is important that they look at what they have done and evaluate it. How well does this structure express what I think? Where else in school or in life might I use this kind of thinking?

Teaching and Learning

Beyer (1987) has described a process for the direct teaching of thinking skills. In his conception, the teaching of any thinking skill can be managed through six stages:

1. *Introduction* of the skill
2. *Gradual practice* of the skill, with plenty of demonstration
3. *Individual application* in a familiar context
4. *Transfer and elaboration*, exportation to new contexts and more complex forms
5. *Guided practice* in new situations
6. *Autonomous use*

This approach pertains to the use of graphic organizers to teach thinking, particularly at the point when students first try a graphic organizer. Careful introduction may prevent the format of the organizer from confusing students. Through practice and demonstration, students can be shown the rules for a graphic organizer, as well as opportunities for creative adaptation. Successive uses of organizers in other content areas and grade levels may support long-term transfer and elaboration. When students use a graphic organizer developed for one subject area in another content area, perhaps in a new form, we can be fairly sure that some learning has taken place.

Graphic frames can be used to support many kinds of learning. They have been used extensively to teach purposeful reading and study skills such as test preparation (Holley & Dansereau, 1984). You will find examples in this book of graphic organizers used to help in unit planning, test design, independent research, and whole-class inquiry projects. The most common use, however, is in small-group discussion or cooperative learning groups where graphic organizers help students recognize a learning task, adopt a particular kind of cognitive purpose, and also define the realm of applicable knowledge (Slavin, 1983; Johnson & Johnson, 1986). Most important, well-designed organizers elicit more than pat answers. As frames for thinking, they make students think their way through the content. Discussions of how to complete an assignment within a collaborative group of 3 to 5 students can get quite heated. Because graphic organizers provoke discussion, they make students work hard to clarify their ideas.

Evaluation

The final chapter of this book includes some discussion of evaluation strategies for thinking across the disciplines. When students use graphic organizers to think, write, study, prepare projects, or collaborate in learning, they are also producing artifacts for evaluation. Assessment criteria and standards can be built into assignments with graphic organizers. Teachers can provide a list of concepts that should be included, a blank graphic for students to use, or a set of questions that should be answered within the graphic. The chapters that follow include additional assessment methods. I do not believe that what students produce in fact reflects the working structure of their brains. I cannot provide a comprehensive approach to "reading" these products diagnostically. I do believe that we have a professional obligation to try to "see" how students are thinking and to devise methods to help them think more effectively. This book is dedicated to that purpose.

I have been unable to locate any solid research on the effects of graphic organizers on teaching effectiveness. In classroom teaching of content subjects, what are the effects of graphic organizers on the development of cognitive skill? What are the effects on content acquisition? On long-term memory? On satisfaction with schooling? Does an emphasis on thinking about the content interfere with the flow of content information from teacher to student? These questions are surely important ones. Part of my hope is that this book will help organize investigations of questions such as these.

GETTING STARTED

I have found that the best way to begin using graphic organizers in content teaching is to try a few. Look for an objective in your teaching that clearly implies a need for thinking. Do you want your students to look carefully at an array of facts and begin to question their relationship? A web diagram might help. Do you want your students to acquire a new concept that will let them understand a number of different events? Circle diagrams could frame the process of their learning. Do you want them to develop a theory or hypothesis? They could build an inductive tower. Concept maps might help them organize their reading or prepare for a test. A causal map might help them analyze events. A flowchart may help them design a procedure. The trick is not in the technique; the trick is finding "fit" between a body of content, the need to think clearly about that content, and a technique for organizing inquiry.

Does a graphic organizer help a student or teacher clarify basic relationships in the content? That is the question that should separate good graphic organizers from poor ones. Consequently, Figure 2.5 should not be considered a prescription for graphic expression. In fact, it is the flexibility of graphic languages that distinguishes them from more formal languages. Cartoons, sketches, imaginative symbols, and snatches of formal language can all find a place in a graphic organizer. In introducing graphic organizers as a medium for thinking, teachers should start with simple diagrams and few rules. As students gain confidence in the medium, they usually also see the need for refinement.

For most classroom applications, teachers make no distinction between circles, boxes, and triangles. When distinctions are important, however, as in flowcharting for computer programming, circles can be used to set off concepts, propositions, or similar idea clusters; boxes can represent steps in a process; and diamonds can represent decisions or questions. Arrows usually represent relationships, often with a verb, preposition, or conjunction as a label (see Figure 2.5). Arrows pointing right can indicate positive causal relationships, as in chemistry. Arrows pointing left can represent negative causal relations: problems, constraints, or restrictions. Arrows pointing down usually suggest illustration or exemplification. Arrows pointing up indicate an implication or inference drawn from facts. Novak and Gowin (1984) suggest that the top portion of a map be reserved for abstract concepts and the bottom portion contain data and illustrative material. Similarly, the left side of a map may be reserved for causes (or past events) whereas the right side is held for effects (or outcomes or future events). These simple symbols are related to the symbols emerging to support the development of artificial intelligence and to describe the formal properties of language in general (Young, 1983; Chomsky, 1972, pp. 115–160).

All of the graphic organizers included in this book have been used throughout grade levels K–12. That is not to say that all of the graphics will be equally effective with students of all ages or with all content areas. Different groups and individuals prefer different patterns of organization. Unless graphic organizers are being used widely in a school, it is

FIGURE 2.5   A Representational Language for Teaching Thinking Skills in Content Instruction

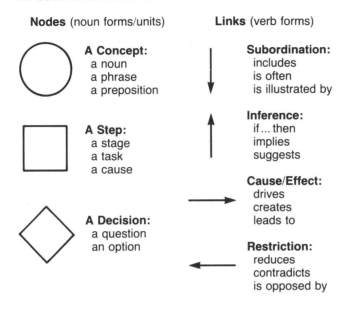

likely that a teacher will have to introduce simple graphics before more complex forms.

Graphic organizers give students a field organized to help them find meaning in the content. Helping students use graphic organizers is similar to any other approach to teaching a skill. Jones, Pierce, and Hunter (1989) have suggested five guidelines for teaching students to develop graphic organizers:

1. Present at least one good example of a complete graphic organizer representing the type you want students to use.
2. Model how to construct either the same graphic organizer or the one to be introduced.
3. Provide procedural knowledge.
4. Coach the students.
5. Give the students opportunities to practice.

In general, they suggest teaching only one organizational form at a time. There are many organizational frames, only some of which are included in this book. Once students have seen an example and tried to use a frame with teacher support, they can apply the frame elsewhere. After working with some forms, it is not uncommon for students to start designing their own, organized to support a specific purpose.

Once graphics have entered common usage, they become part of the language we use to teach and learn: "In your small groups, I want you to create a circle diagram that shows the difference between communism and socialism," we might say.

Or, we can assign homework: "As you read the chapter on swamp ecology, create a concept map that includes both mammals and reptiles and shows their relationship."

Graphics can begin a class discussion: "To help us talk about McCarthyism, I would like each of you to draw a causal map of the five most important events leading up to the Red Scare after WWII."

Graphic organizers in teaching are a medium for managing thinking. They are a practice field. The task of teaching thinking is much larger than the display represented by a graphic organizer. Glaser (1984, p. 103) states:

> *The task is to produce a changed environment for learning—an environment in which there is a new relationship between students and their subject matter, in which knowledge and skill become objects of interrogation inquiry and extrapolation. As individuals acquire knowledge, they also should be empowered to think and reason.*

Graphic organizers may play an important part in the realization of that vision.

REFERENCES

Armbruster, B. B., & Anderson, T. H. (1984). Mapping: Representing informative text diagrammatically. In C. T. Holley & D. F. Dansereau (Eds.), *Spacial Learning Strategies: Techniques, Applications and Related Issues*. Orlando, FL: Academic Press.

Ausubel, D. (1968). *Educational Psychology: A Cognitive View*. New York: Holt, Rinehart and Winston.

Beyer, B. (1987). *Practical Strategies for the Teaching of Thinking*. Boston: Allyn and Bacon.

Bobrow, D. G., & Collins, A. (Eds.) (1975). *Representation and Understanding: Studies in Cognitive Science*. New York: Academic Press.

Chambers, J. H. (1988). Teaching thinking throughout the curriculum: Where else? *Educational Leadership*, 45(7), 3–4.

Chase, W. G., & Simon, H. (1973). The mind's eye in chess. In W. G. Chase (Ed.), *Visual Information Processing* (pp. 215–278). New York: Academic Press.

Chomsky, N. (1972). *Language and Mind*. New York: Harcourt Brace Jovanovich.

Clarke, J. (1980). The learning cycle: Frame of discourse for paragraph development. *New England Association of Teachers of English Leaflet*, 79(3), 3–11.

Clarke, J. (1987). Building a lecture that works. *College Teaching*, 35(2), 56–58.

Clarke, J. (1989). Designing discussion on the inquiry cycle. *College Teaching*, 37(2), 3–6.

Costa, A. (1988, November). "What human beings do when they behave intelligently and how they can become more so." Paper presented at "Creative Thinking," Vermont ASCD Conference, Burlington, VT.

diSessa, A. (1979). On "learnable" representations of knowledge: A meaning for the computational metaphor. In J. Lockhead & J. Clement (Eds.), *Cognitive Process Instruction* (pp. 239–266). Philadelphia: Franklin Institute Press.

Donald, J. (1983). Knowledge structures: Methods for exploring course content. *Journal of Higher Education*, 54(1), 31–41.

Fulwiler, T. (1987). *Teaching with Writing*. Upper Montclair, NJ: Boynton/Cook.

Gagne, R. M. (1980). Learnable aspects of problem solving. *American Psychologist*, 15(2), 84–92.

Glaser, R. (1984). Education and thinking: The role of knowledge. *American Psychologist*, 39(2), 93–104.

Holland, J. H.; Holyoak, K. J.; Nisbett, R. E.; & Thagard, P. R. (1986). *Induction: Processes of Inference Learning and Discovery*. Cambridge, MA: MIT Press.

Holley, C. T., & Dansereau, D. F. (1984). *Spacial Learning Strategies: Techniques, Applications and Related Issues*. Orlando, FL: Academic Press.

Hunter, M. (1982). *Mastery Teaching: Increasing Instructional Effectiveness in Secondary Schools, Colleges and Universities*. El Segundo, CA: TIP Publications.

Johnson, D. W., & Johnson, R. T. (1986). *Learning Together and Alone*. Englewood Cliffs, NJ: Prentice-Hall.

Jones, B. F.; Pierce, J.; & Hunter, B. (1989). Teaching students to construct graphic representations. *Educational Leadership*, 46(4), 21–25.

Joyce, B., & Weil, M. (1986). *Models of Teaching* (3rd ed.). Englewood Cliffs, NJ: Prentice-Hall.

Kolb, D. (1977). *Learning Style Profile*. Cambridge, MA: McBer and Associates.

Larkin, J. J.; McDermott, J.; Simon, D. P.; & Simon, H. A. (1980). Expert and novice performance in solving physics problems, *Science*, 208, 1335–1342.

Marzano, R. J.; Brandt, R.; Hughes, C.; Jones, B. F.; Presseisen, B.; Rankin, S.; & Suhor, C. (1988). *Dimensions of Thinking: A Framework for Curriculum and Instruction*. Alexandria, VA: ASCD Publications.

Nisbett, R. E.; Fong, G. T.; Lehman, D. R.; & Cheng, P. W. (1987). Teaching reasoning. *Science*, 238, 625–698.

Novak, J. D., & Gowin, D. B. (1984). *Learning How to Learn*. Cambridge/New York: Cambridge University Press.

Perkins, D. N. (1987). Thinking frames: An integrating perspective on teaching cognitive skills. In J. Baron & R. Sternberg (Eds.), *Teaching Thinking Skills: Theory and Research*. New York: W. H. Freeman and Sons.

Perkins, D. N. (1988). Thinking frames. *Educational Leadership*, 43(8), 4–11.

Reigeluth, C. M. (1987). *Instructional Theories in Action*. Hillsdale, NJ: Lawrence Erlbaum.

Resnick, L. (1987). Learning in school and out. *Educational Researcher*, 119(9), 16–19.

Shuell, T. J. (1986). Cognitive conceptions of learning. *Review of Educational Research*, 56(4), 411–436.

Simon, H. (1979). How big is a chunk? In H. A. Simon (Ed.), *Models of Thought*. New York: Yale University Press.

Slavin, R. E. (1983). *Cooperative Learning*. White Plains, NY: Longman.

Slavin, R. E. (1987). Cooperative Learning and the cooperative school. *Educational Leadership*, 45(3), 7–12.

Sternberg, R. M. (1987). Questions and answers about the nature and teaching of thinking skills. In J. Baron & R. Sternberg (Eds.), *Teaching Thinking Skills: Theory and Research*. New York: W. H. Freeman and Sons.

Vobeija, B. (1987). A mathematician's research on math instruction. *Educational Researcher*, 16(9), 9–11.

Young, R. M. (1983). Surrogates and mappings: Two kinds of conceptual models for interactive devices. In D. Gentner & A. Stevens (Eds.), *Mental Models*. Hillsdale, NJ: Lawrence Erlbaum.

SECTION II

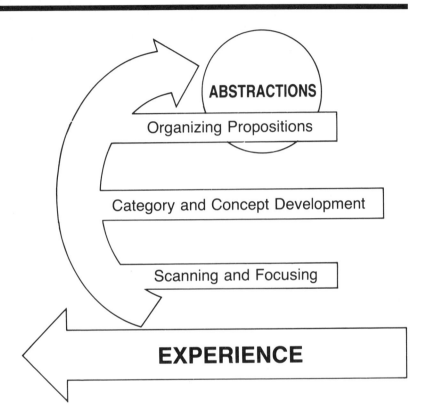

ABSTRACTIONS

Organizing Propositions

Category and Concept Development

Scanning and Focusing

EXPERIENCE

Frames for Inductive Thinking

3

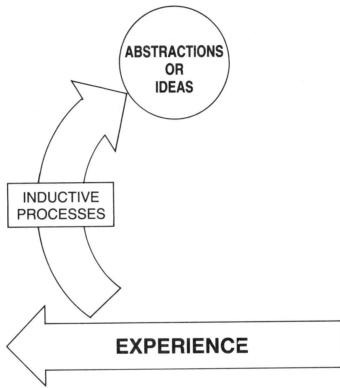

An infant watches her hands and feels them move. Gradually she fixes her own boundaries at the complex incurved rim of her skin. Later she touches one palm to another and tries for a game to distinguish each hand's sensation of feeling and being felt. What is a house but a bigger skin, and a neighborhood map but the world's skin ever expanding?
—ANNIE DILLARD, *An American Childhood*

Inductive Frames in Teaching

IMAGINE THAT THE HUMAN MIND LIVES IN A HOUSE CALLED the brain. In the house of brain, there is always plenty to do. The mind can stay inside, particularly if the day is drab, and do what it likes. It can turn on the TV and watch movies—any movie it would want to produce. It can listen to music, changing the tune and composition to suit its fancy. It can sing to itself, earning wild acclaim from an imaginary audience. It can invent wonderful machines that carry out its wishes, or play baseball and always win.

The walls of the mind's house are covered with old photos to peruse. The mind can rehash ancient disputes until it comes out on top. Or it can simply clean up from yesterday, moving an old idea to the side and trying something fresh in its place. It can set out steps to a plan, then set them again for better effect. It can wrestle on the rug with its old enemy "Boring" or any of Boring's friends. The human mind can stimulate itself. It does not depend entirely on the senses. It can choose to focus on any of its many interests.

Tired of working inside, of course, the mind can open the doors and walk out on the porch to take a look around. From the porch of the brain, there is plenty to observe. There are usually other houses in the neighborhood, some exciting to look at, some not. Neighbors walk by; some stop and sit, some want to play. Cars roar along the street. Birds fly. A scrap of paper skitters along the walk. Sirens scream. The roadway radiates heat; the wind is cool. There are leaves and twigs to touch in the yard and plenty of things need fixing. The mind can let impressions filter in and work with them at its pleasure, or it can focus its energy narrowly on certain kinds of events, asking questions and looking for answers.

Inductive thinking is the process of fusing small bits of information from memory or perception into generalizations. By collapsing smaller bits of information into broader abstractions, we slowly assemble a view of the world that explains how things happen. Knowing how things happen gives us creative and analytic power.

As every teacher knows, the mind does not have to come out at all. It does not have to focus on anything in particular from the porch of its senses. It does not have to step down into the street to find new information or to assemble a coherent view of the world around it. The teaching profession has assumed responsibility for helping students use content knowledge to construct a world view. We help young people learn to think inductively. We can help them use the subject areas to:

1. *Focus and scan* for meaning in the content areas
2. *Create categories and concepts* that explain events
3. *Construct propositions* that describe a theory of the way things really work

These are all aspects of inductive thinking. The task of the skillful teacher is to help students recognize the value of what they already have in mind, focus purposefully on new information available, and go out to bring it home so it can be put to use in building a world view. Part of teaching involves helping perpetually active yet invisible young minds, usually 20 to 30 at a time, get out the door and off the porch to gather and bring home new information. Reassembling that information so it is more compact and more powerful is the work of inductive thinking.

INDUCTIVE THINKING AND LEARNING

"Every time we move from some specific observations about the world to a generalization, we have made an induction; thus, much of what we call learning is really induction" (Nickerson, Perkins, & Smith, 1986, p. 119). In this section, techniques will be introduced that can help students make generalizations from specific observations in the content areas. The three chapters in this section are arranged to reflect information gathering and inductive thinking in three phases of information processing:

- *Focusing and scanning:* Free writing, free drawing, web diagrams, time lines, story lines, and graphs or grids can be used to help students *select and organize information* for processing.
- *Creating categories and concepts:* Circle diagrams, lapped circles, and matrices can be used to help students *develop categories and concepts* as the basic tools of complex thinking skills.
- *Proposing relationships:* Inductive towers can be used to help students *generate and organize propositions* to represent a view of the world based on perceived facts.

Inductive learning is recursive; improvement takes practice. Right answers can prove evasive; perfection is impossible. Still, helping students learn to process information flexibly is clearly a purpose for classroom teaching.

From the information we obtain from the senses and through contact with the larger culture, we construct a model of the world in which we then attempt to live (Norman, 1983). Experience and subject-based knowledge provide us with some basic materials; the work of the mind transforms those materials to create a model that reflects, but does not replicate, the world of experience. The way we inductively transform new information is regulated to a large extent by what we already know. In a sense, the structure of what has already been built in the mind determines the way new information can be used in further construction.

The human mind is not built to absorb all the information carried in through the senses. To allow inductive thinking to occur, the mind must first filter the tumult of impressions. Knowledge acquisition requires *selective* sifting of information, *selective* combination of elements, and *selective* comparison of new information with related information in prior knowledge (Sternberg, 1985, p. 107; my italics). The mind is built to construct from selected bits of information a model of the world that conveys meaning, suggests value, allows creative planning, and supports problem solving (Costa, 1985). Generally speaking, the more closely the "constructed," inner world view in the mind reflects the actual workings of the universe, the more likely the individual is to survive and flourish. Each human mind, independently, is built to pursue a single purpose: *to construct a view of the world that empowers the individual to actively engage that world.*

We use inductive thinking to construct a world view. Using induction, we gather pieces of information through our senses. By inference, we identify common elements or links between bits of information, creating meaning for each bit and for both together. Inductive reasoning can be applied to events in serial order—events that share certain attributes by analogy or events that share a common classification (Sternberg, 1985, p. 135). When several meaningful inferences line up, we infer again; we generalize, creating ideas that we hold as true, not only for the contributing facts and inferences, but also for similar events in the future. Using generalizations as a base, we assemble an internal model of our universe—a world view. Our world view includes more than the present. Based on individual construction of past experience, the mind creates imaginings, a blueprint for the future—the way it may turn out to be and the way it should be. Using induction, we create value positions and a sense of ongoing process, the groundwork for skill in planning, prediction, and problem solving.

In terms of memory, there are two ways we can know a subject. We can remember events themselves, as if they happened yesterday, or we can subordinate events to larger categories that we find meaningful. Recounting the chain of events as they occurred and explaining the chain of events as they convey meaning may depend on different kinds of memory. Some experts say that we use *episodic memory* to capture a visual and auditory record of the specific events we experience, and we use *semantic memory* to capture the meaning of events in relation to each other and more abstract concepts (Tulving, 1983). Some researchers believe that these two ways of knowing have two different structures. Inductive reasoning can convert episodes or other bits of evidence into semantically meaningful concept structures.

Most of us hold long strings of early childhood events in episodic memory, loosely held by a pattern of images, themes, or sounds. We can recite them as if they occurred yesterday. We can "sing" episodic nursery rhymes forever, a facility with ancient lineage in our cultures. Episodic memory tends to arrange itself in serial order, in visual or auditory form. If you ask someone about *Gone with the Wind*, for example, you may have to sit through a long recitation of episodic memory. Before writing became the vehicle for knowledge in our culture, we used to "sing" the wisdom of the tribe as formulaic episodes. Homer's epics, *Beowulf*, and even much of the *Old Testament* represent episodic memory captured first by ancient singers, and then transcribed (Lord, 1969). Rap songs are a current example of episodic strings, street wisdom tied together by rhythm. Recitation of episodic strings, however, is usually not the purpose of learning in the content areas (see Figure 3.1).

FIGURE 3.1 Comparison of Episodic and Semantic Memory Structure (*Gone with the Wind*)

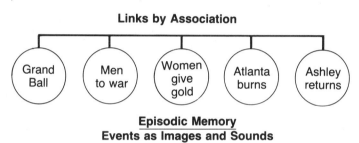

Links by Association

Episodic Memory
Events as Images and Sounds

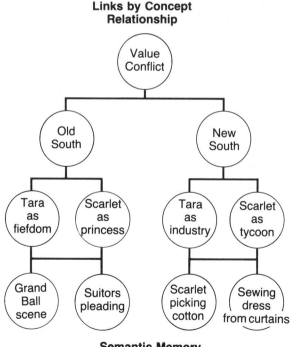

Links by Concept
Relationship

Semantic Memory
Events as Examples of Ideas

Semantic memory is more useful in school learning. It holds events not by their relation in time, but their relation to each other through organizing ideas and concepts (Reed, 1973). Semantic memory tends to arrange itself in hierarchical order, with superordinate concepts serving as organizing nodes for related concepts and related details. Serial order is incidental to semantic memory. If you ask an adult about *Gone with the Wind* who has seen it six times, you are likely to receive an exposition built around governing ideas, with only those scenes described that reflect the organizing concepts. To reduce a long string of episodes to a more concise (and powerful) semantic structure, a person has to be able to (1) select details on the basis of some purpose and (2) express the details in a simplified abstraction (Kay & Black, 1986).

Inductive thinking reduces linear strings of events to more efficient concept hierarchies. By drawing inferences from evidence, then drawing inferences from our inferences, we construct more abstract propositions which increase our powers of explanation, prediction, and control over future events. The human mind is built to think inductively. We infer automatically (Travers, 1982). Our inductive reasoning, however, is not automatically reliable. We do not always control the process of building a view of the world. In school, students may treat the entire day as a series of episodes and fail to see the concepts or ideas we put there to tie the day together. The chapters in this section describe ways teachers in the subject areas can help students develop greater control over the inductive procedures they automatically use so they can find meaning in school subjects.

ERRORS IN INDUCTION

We are born with the inductive equipment we need to collapse information from the senses into compact forms we can then manage as symbols. That doesn't mean we all use inductive thinking without error, however. In fact, the process of inductive thinking guarantees a margin of error. Inductive thinking involves probabilities. Since we can never have all the information available, we are always susceptible to error. New information, unexpected events, or a bewildering array of unpredictable forces intervene and change what we see and the way we think. The process itself opens the door to error. When students see that they can manage, in part, the risks involved in reasoning from probabilities, the risk of error can bring excitement to learning.

Errors in inductive learning generally result from failure to "sample" adequately, to assess probabilities adequately, to abstract to the right level, or to discard unlikely hypotheses (Nickerson, Perkins, & Smith, 1985, p. 111). Considerable practice may be necessary to reduce the margin of error (see Sternberg, 1986, pp. 91–108). Let us assume, for a moment, that we want our students to be able to predict the temperature for tomorrow. Right now, it is 58 degrees Fahrenheit, the wind is blowing from the west, and it rained this morning. In addition to this information, we have supplied our students with weather maps for the entire hemisphere and with 24 years of weather history.

1. *Sampling:* How much of this information makes the "right" sample? In many regions of the world, the present temperature often seems to suggest more about what will not be true tomorrow than what will be true. Temperatures at several locations to the west are often a better indicator. How far west? Which direction? What weather systems will impinge? Where are the prevailing winds? While there may be enough information in our sample, the problem is selecting the information that will prove important and reliable. Inadequate search and/or faulty selection cause errors in induction.

2. *Estimating probabilities:* What are the probabilities for tomorrow's temperature suggested by the facts? Even with a vast sample of verifiable facts, we still struggle with probabilities. Temperature will probably tend to hold steady. The air mass 120 miles south/southeast will probably begin to move this way. Probably, a low pressure system will create a cloud cover. Maybe the prevailing winds will die down. Error is built into our assessment of probabilities.

3. *Abstracting to a reasonable level:* When looking at probabilities, it is tempting to leap at generalities along the way. "Our weather always comes from the west; there's no way it could rain." A torrent may follow such a proclamation. To use induction well, we need to move from verifiable information to a supportable level of generalization. Error results from jumping past information or wallowing among narrow inferences and failing to generalize at all.

4. *Maintaining hypotheses:* We usually start inductive thinking with a goal in mind that implies some purpose. For example, in trying to predict the temperature, we may really be trying to decide whether to go to the beach. Therefore, in working through information and inferences, we may try to protect our original purpose and favor a line of reasoning that gets us to the beach. Flexible induction may require that we maintain several hypotheses simultaneously, but our tendency to favor our own predispositions allows error. Expert thinkers in a subject may keep five or more hypotheses active as they sift through information.

In helping students practice inductive thinking, our aim cannot be to eliminate error and arrive at "right answers." The goal of inductive thinking must be *probable* answers, based on defensible reasoning from available facts. In learning to control their inductive thinking, students are also learning to recognize sources of error and to tolerate ambiguity. It is the risk of error, with differences in interpretation arising among students, that makes inductive learning and thinking exciting in the classroom.

"It is going to be 75 degrees tomorrow," one student may say.

"No, not with the rain coming in. Make it 40 degrees and you'll be close," another may respond.

"Forty degrees? Where do you see rain for tomorrow?"

There is no such thing as cold reasoning. As we work inductively, we can come to believe in our own discoveries and grow hot in their defense.

CHANGING MINDS IN THE SUBJECT AREAS

If each of us had to create from raw sensory experience a unique view of the world, human progress would be an impossibility. We would move backward with every new birth. Schools, among other institutions, are there to make sure that young people have access to more information than the stuff pouring in from immediate, sensory experience. Methods introduced in this section have the purpose of slowing automatic tendencies in the human mind either to dismiss information if it doesn't promise sensory excitement or to process it impulsively, increasing the risk (and pain) of error. Students cannot make sense of information in the content areas unless they control the process of making sense. In showing students inductive processes and introducing content from the subject areas, teachers are showing students how to use established knowledge to change their own minds.

In constructing a view of the universe, students can use fresh building blocks provided by their own experience or "tried and true" blocks from the subject areas. Organized knowledge in the subject areas, however, does not have the same structure as raw experience. Often it is not quite as exciting to students. Experience is linear in structure; it is often unpredictable and it usually activates all the senses at once. Young people like the relentless unpredictability of experience. The subject areas, by contrast, may have some features that are linear—stories, procedures, and processes—but the subject areas usually assume that knowledge, in part, is hierarchical in form. A layer of "reliable facts" organized into categories represents higher-level ideas or concepts which the subject areas use to make propositions at an abstract level (Bruner, 1975; Donald, 1983). Experience tends to reinforce episodic "knowing," whereas the content areas are usually organized in semantic hierarchies.

For teachers, the problem is that experiential knowledge and subject area knowledge both have to arrive in the human mind through the senses. Sensory knowledge and academic knowledge are built quite differently, but both must arrive through the same door. The human mind is built to filter out perhaps 95% of the sensory impressions it receives. There are "buffers" between the senses and the brain that filter out the clutter. As every teacher knows, the mind is just as well prepared to filter out 95% of the organized information coming from the subject areas. Converting classroom episodes into semantically structured long-term memory takes a deliberate effort on the part of teachers and students. The challenge is to shape the learning experience so as to support knowledge restructuring. Frames for inductive thinking can give us a way to manage part of that task.

GRAPHIC FRAMES FOR INDUCTIVE LEARNING

When used to support information gathering and interpreting, graphic organizers may help students reduce the extent to which inference is automatic and increase their conscious control—thereby reducing the risk of error. By reducing the tendency of the mind to infer without having a clear purpose or sense of alternative options or some control over its own processes, we may increase the degree to which students direct the work of their own minds and benefit from working with content in the subject areas.

Graphic frames provide a practice field; the game itself can take many forms. Chapters 4, 5, and 6 each cover one of the three stages of inductive thinking (see Figure 3.2), reflecting current concepts of how the mind processes information from the senses to develop causal propositions (Sternberg, 1986; Travers, 1982; Letteri, 1988). Working through stages of inductive process, we try to develop "causal" explanations for the effects we see through our senses.

The idea of "stages" should not imply that inductive skill is dependent on age or class level in school. The evidence suggests that these stages apply to learning new content areas at any age. For example, first-grade teaching should not confine itself only to scanning and focusing, leaving propositions to high-school teachers. First-graders need to learn to focus and search simple stories for critical events, develop explanatory

FIGURE 3.2   Inductive Stages of Information Processing

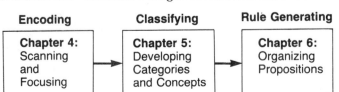

concepts, and generate thematic propositions in the same way that medical students need to learn to search a patient history to create symptom lists and generate diagnostic propositions. The process is the same. The complexity of content varies.

The degree of organization in prior knowledge in the learner also varies, often by age, but age is not the determining factor. Over time, we become more efficient learners, but not necessarily because we have learned a system of learning. What is most notable in research on thinking skills is that training in one subject does not easily transfer or generalize to other subjects or even to the same subject at higher levels. Students can learn to control their inductive processes, to activate them appropriately, and to assess their reliability—if they are applying similar skills across the content areas throughout their school experience. Our students need recursive practice in induction throughout the curriculum.

The three stages of information processing reflect a simplified version of a much more complex process. (Actually, learning to think inductively proceeds over a lifetime in an infinite number of stages.) The graphic organizers presented can be adapted flexibly to different content areas and different grade levels. Figure 3.3 includes graphic representations of three kinds of inductive thinking, each of which is related to teaching in the chapters that follow. It also includes a list of some thinking skills associated with each kind of processing.

1. *Scanning and focusing:* We see (hear, feel, taste) something and liken it to things we have experienced before.
2. *Developing categories and concepts:* We create an abstract idea— a category or concept—that gives us a fresh understanding of both the new experience and the older experience.
3. *Organizing propositions:* We use the category or concept to propose more abstract relationships of cause and effect (McGuigan & Black, 1986, p. 237).

Simple graphics have been used to illustrate teaching methods for these three stages of inductive learning. Drawings, web diagrams, graphs, circle diagrams, and inductive towers are all special learning strategies, allowing students and teachers to see and manipulate information. The graphic frames all support inductive thinking, working from parts to a new whole, from the bottom to the top, from concrete information to abstract conceptualization (Dansereau & Holley, 1984, p. 7).

If you develop and use graphic organizers with your students, you should also consider devising a way to help them "transfer" the use of that organizer to different subject areas, to careers, or to life in the larger community. Your efforts to help your students "transfer" or "bridge" the skill will also help them *see* the organizer as separate from the content and to gain more control over its use. The representation of a "bridge" at

FIGURE 3.3   Frames for Inductive Thinking: Bottom-Up Teaching

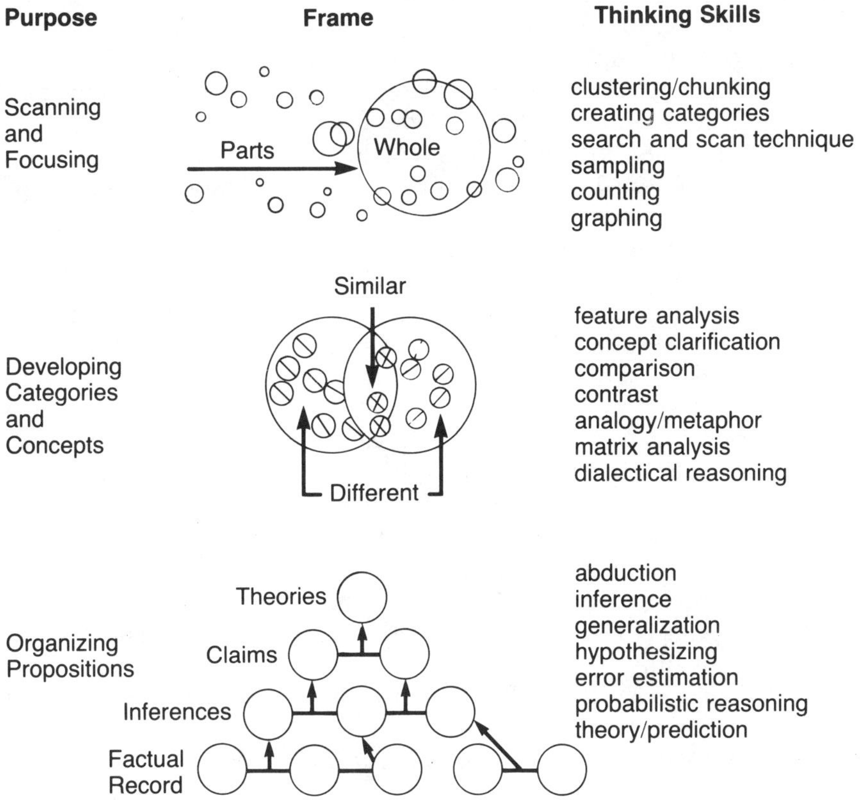

Purpose	Frame	Thinking Skills

Scanning and Focusing — Parts → Whole

clustering/chunking
creating categories
search and scan technique
sampling
counting
graphing

Similar / Different

Developing Categories and Concepts

feature analysis
concept clarification
comparison
contrast
analogy/metaphor
matrix analysis
dialectical reasoning

Theories
Claims
Inferences
Factual Record

Organizing Propositions

abduction
inference
generalization
hypothesizing
error estimation
probabilistic reasoning
theory/prediction

the end of each chapter is there to raise the question: Do my students have an objective sense of the cognitive skills they have just applied? Do they see the "frame" as a tool?

Graphic frames for inductive thinking give students and teachers a way to talk about what they know and how they came to know it. They are not the purpose of teaching, but only stations on the road to improved learning and teaching in K–12 classrooms.

REFERENCES

Bruner, J. S. (1975). *Toward a Theory of Instruction.* Cambridge, MA: Harvard University Press.

Costa, A. (1985). Toward a model of human intellectual functioning. In

Developing Minds: A Resource Book for Teaching Thinking. Alexandria, VA: ASCD Publications.

Dansereau, D. F., & Holley, C. (1984). *Spacial Learning Strategies: Techniques Applications and Related Issues*. Orlando, FL: Academic Press.

Donald, J. G. (1983). Knowledge structures: Methods for exploring course content. *Journal of Higher Education, 54*(1), 31–41.

Kay, D. S., & Black, J. B. (1986). Explanation driven processing in summarization: The interaction of content and process. In J. A. Galambos, R. P. Abelson, & J. B. Black (Eds.), *Knowledge Structures*. Hillsdale, NJ: Lawrence Erlbaum.

Letteri, C. A. (1988). The NASSP learning style profile and cognitive processing. In J. W. Keefe (Ed.), *Profiling and Using Learning Style* (chap 2). Reston, VA: NASSP Publications.

Lord, A. (1969). *A Singer of Tales*. Cambridge, MA: Harvard University Press.

McGuigan, S., & Black, J. B. (1986). Creation and comprehension of arguments. In J. A. Galambos, R. P. Abelson, & J. B. Black (Eds.), *Knowledge Structures*. Hillsdale, NJ: Lawrence Erlbaum.

Nickerson, R. S., Perkins, D. N., & Smith, E. E. (1985). *The Teaching of Thinking* (chap 5). Hillsdale, NJ: Lawrence Erlbaum.

Norman, D. A. (1983). Some observations on mental models. In A. L. Stevens & D. Gentner (Eds.), *Mental Models*. Hillsdale, NJ: Lawrence Erlbaum.

Reed, S. K. (1973). *Psychological Processes in Pattern Recognition*. New York: Academic Press.

Sternberg, R. J. (1985). *Beyond IQ*. Cambridge/New York: Cambridge University Press.

Sternberg, R. J. (1986). *Intelligence Applied: Understanding and Increasing Your Intellectual Skills*. San Diego: Harcourt Brace Jovanovich.

Travers, R. M. (1982). *Essentials of Learning*. New York: MacMillan.

Tulving, E. (1983). *Elements of Episodic Memory*. New York: Oxford University Press.

4

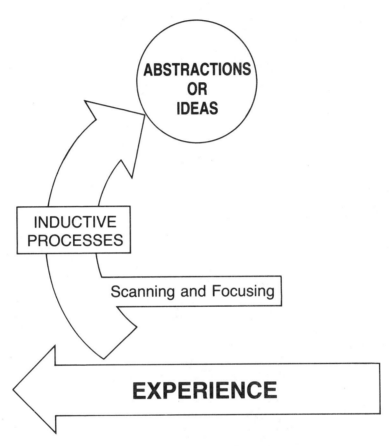

ABSTRACTIONS
OR
IDEAS

INDUCTIVE
PROCESSES

Scanning and Focusing

EXPERIENCE

God is visible in the details.
—STEPHEN JAY GOULD, *Urchin in the Storm*

Scanning and Focusing

THIS CHAPTER DESCRIBES METHODS TEACHERS CAN USE TO improve the ability of their students to seek, gather, and store information from text, film, or other sources of content.

Focusing: With a clear purpose in view, looking at information from the senses

Scanning: Searching through information for pieces that fit the purpose

Storing: Reassembling new information in light of old information in patterns that assist recall and allow later application.

Each of these learning activities implies strategic purpose on the part of students. After all, it is the student who finally must decide to set out in search of new information. The teacher's job is to help students develop a strategic purpose for learning—with skills of information gathering that can fulfill that purpose.

AN EPISODE IN FOCUSING

"Look!" I shout over my shoulder toward the back seat. "Deer! Two deer!"

I take my foot off the gas and touch the brake to give the kids a chance to see. Looking in the mirror, I see my six-year-old son snap his head up from make-believe mayhem among the gang of plastic cowboys in his lap. He looks out the left-hand window, the one next to where he happens to be sitting. I see his eyes fix on a herd of guernsey cows. He frowns. Wrong side. Wrong animal. Wrong instructions.

At the word *deer,* my eight-year-old daughter and her eight-year-old friend both sit bolt upright. Their heads rotate right to left, left to right, eyes wandering in middle distance. They are focused. They are scanning. I decide to start with them. My chances are better with practiced sight.

"Right-hand side." I point to get their eyes up from the trampled feed lot by the side of the road to the forest edge beyond a far pasture. "At the edge of the pasture by the treeline," I say, hoping to capture the location in a crisp phrase. Silence follows.

"Where, Daddy?" I suddenly sense two more mistakes. Neither one of them can tell a pasture from a cornfield. Neither one, having missed Vietnam by twenty years, recognizes the word *treeline.* The girls have no reference point for their eyes. They are lost in space. I dread the looming prospect of frustration. The car is moving toward woods, which will block their view.

"Look for two brown dots at the end of those trees over there, where one field starts and another stops. Look in the shadow of the trees—a doe and a fawn. The doe is standing." Silence again. My son has shifted his blank gaze in the right direction. Initial interest has turned to competition between the girls. Who will be first to see the deer? Soon, their eyes fix on a narrow band near the right spot.

The car has slowed to a crawl. In the rear-view mirror, I see a loaded logging truck round the corner and come up fast behind us. I also see the furrow creasing my son's forehead, which says he is moving quickly past attention into the torture of unmet expectation. I prepare myself for his howl.

"A mommy and baby deer," I say to pump him up again. His eyes are pasted to a bright red silo a few feet from the roadside. "Look where the mountain comes down to meet the field way over there. You'll see a tree there with fluttering leaves. The deer are under that tree."

The car is creeping toward roadside woods, which will block our view completely. In the rear-view mirror, the logger has seen the deer, too. He is happy enough to wait for us.

"I see them!" my daughter's friend shouts with glee.

"Me, too," my daughter says quietly. The pause tells me she is still scanning.

"The doe is looking right at us." Ah, she's got them. She grabs my son by the arm and pulls him toward her. We pass the blind wall of the woods. I step on the gas again.

"Did you see them, Ethan?" I ask. "Yep," he says in a noncommital voice. I see his head bow and hear the plastic cowboys renew their dispute in his lap.

This brief episode can illustrate three skills of information gathering, under the separate direction of a central, executive control for each of the children. My son, Ethan, has staged a showdown among his cowboys, a rough crew who nevertheless act under his absolute authority. The girls are talking about friends, their favorite subject. As the "teacher," I try to break into the happy routine of their own thinking. Still, they all agree to refocus at the word *deer*, an animal they already admire as a movie hero. They redirect their activity to a new purpose.

With the new purpose active, they are ready for information. They start scanning impulsively. I try to break the field down into components. Unfortunately, I fail to relate new information to the existing structure of what they already know. They cannot focus because they have no referent. They cannot tell the figure from the field. For them, the field is a blur and the task is initially hopeless.

I struggle to tie my guidance to what the girls already know of farms, leaving my son a victim of frustration, temporarily I hope. If he sees the girls scanning, he may scan, too. My daughter's friend scans most skillfully, piece by piece, setting apart what she sees as familiar from what she wants to see as new. Suddenly, an image in the field matches the general expectation in her mind. She checks the seen deer against the idea of deer in her mind. A fit! She feels the rush of success. My daugher mimics her, hoping to capture some part of victory. My son mimics both, having seen nothing.

"How was your trip?" my wife asks at home.

"We saw two deer in a field," the girls answer. My son looks vacantly at his plastic horses.

PURPOSEFUL SCANNING

The ability to attend emerges early in infancy. Studies of infant perception suggest that human beings may be predisposed to attend to both familiar and unfamiliar patterns in what they see. Distinguishing the figure from the field is the eye's first challenge (Flavell, 1985, p. 169; Witkin et al., 1977). Early on, babies may show a preference both for familiar impressions, like a mother's voice, and unfamiliar objects, like a moving pattern of striped lines. Soon, of course, an infant begins scanning not just for novelty or stimulation, but to meet some recognized need, such as food or a favored toy. With age and experience, the expanding bank of what is remembered exerts an increasing influence on what a baby scans to see. Children learn early to scan for familiar objects that meet their needs and for unfamiliar objects that may bring new pleasure. What is most familiar to the child apparently becomes an anchor for the examination of what is changing or unfamiliar (Reed, 1973).

Scanning is a highly trainable skill (Travers, 1982, p. 40). Newborn infants do not scan skillfully; usually they scan and then fix their gaze on something distinctly novel or something desired. Children refine their skills in purposeful and systematic scanning throughout the grade-school years. Older children can direct their attention, search systematically for information, and monitor their search patterns better than younger children (Flavell, 1985, p. 201). With increasing knowledge, the embedded pattern of what is already known begins to influence that which is newly seen. The ability to use patterns to augment both scanning skill and memory or recall occurs largely as a function of knowledge and experience in a subject rather than age. As what is known achieves a recognizable pattern in a specific domain, the ability to remember in that specific area increases dramatically. Purposeful scanning for things "the same as" and for things "different from" becomes the basis for other kinds of directed thinking—for "reconstructive" and semantic memory and for critical thinking.

Learning to focus, to scan purposefully, and to store efficiently require the development of metacognitive control, an executive function in the house of the mind which directs the mind's work. Metacognitive control allows the mind to be aware of its own work and to change its approach to achieve better results. The best plans for thinking are general at first, large enough to accommodate a whole purpose. People who develop a global strategy for approaching a problem show greater "intelligence" than those who adopt specific strategies for problem parts (Sternberg, 1985). Some psychologists believe that the flexible, executive controller must evolve slowly with intelligence and experience (Derry & Murphy, 1986). Others argue that teachers and others can intervene directly to make students aware of how they think, and how to think more productively (Glasser, 1987; Paris, Lipson, & Wixson, 1983). Teachers can encourage the development of cognitive control through use of focusing, scanning, and storing for retrieval if they help students clarify purpose and search for patterns in the content they are trying to learn (Gagne & White, 1978).

STRATEGIC FOCUSING

All the teaching tactics that follow aim to help students construct knowledge from episodic classroom experience. Graphic organizers for scanning and focusing help students seek out new information for a purpose and then reconstruct what they know so the meaning is clear.

Focusing

Free drawing: Creating a visual image of something known as a medium for processing new information

Journaling: Using focused writing in short blocks to activate and organize prior knowledge

Webbing: Using circles and lines to make connections between new information to known information

Scanning

Time lines: Selecting and linking critical events in series from the flow of information

Story frames, themes lines, and trend lines: Mapping events in serial order as they lead to a specific end

Storing for Use

Gridding: Establishing a pattern to guide the search for new information

Graphing: Creating a medium for measuring selected events in experience

Graphic organizers can be used to guide the process of scanning. Teachers can use the frames illustrated in this chapter to help students filter the flow of information through the senses and to select a smaller number of impressions for processing. In classroom teaching, teachers can use graphic frames to help students process new information, from lectures, films, books, or raw observation.

Over the longer term, patterns supporting focusing and scanning can become part of a large repertory of more elaborate management patterns that let us control the way we see the world. "As children acquire story and scene schemas, scripts for everyday routines, categorical knowledge and innumerable other 'mental templates,' they automatically use those templates to constructively process inputs at storage and to reconstruct them at retrieval" (Flavell, 1985, p. 216). When students use patterns to examine new information, they can create the basis for complex causal analysis, prediction, and planning (Reder, 1980). In any event, success in school subjects depends on being able to scan large volumes of information and use a purpose to select certain items for more careful processing. Helping students scan, sift, and select is the purpose of graphic organizers described in this chapter.

DRAWING AND LABELING

Some psychologists argue that the mind is always intentional, planned, and focused in its work (Sternberg, 1985). For teachers, the problem is that 20 students may enter the room with intentions, plans, and a focus that have absolutely nothing to do with each other or the subject at hand. The first step in classroom teaching, and in classroom learning, is often to narrow the focus of inquiry to the subject, a task that may take 10 seconds or waste 30 minutes. In focusing a class, and in teaching students to focus, teachers need to look for an approach that also activates what students already know about the subject, inspires goal formulation, and helps students begin to scan for new information.

Drawing pictures can give teachers a way to highlight all of these purposes in a manner that attracts and holds student interest. When teachers ask students to draw, they are asking for a representation of what students already know. Particularly in the lower grades, student drawings are likely to represent "episodes." Student drawings can also reveal what students understand of relationships in a subject, including parts to the whole relationships, summaries of sequenced events, illustration of concepts, and even causal explanation. By introducing new labels for what students have drawn, teachers can help students see what they know in a new light. When students begin to label their own drawings, they add "semantic" meaning to their visualizations.

Lynn Currier, a middle-school language arts teacher, uses student drawings to anchor her vocabulary program. Students first draw what they know; what they represent then becomes the basis for more difficult concepts. Student drawings become individual study guides both for her vocabulary program and for the themes her class is studying. By orienting her vocabulary instruction to larger themes and asking students to draw a picture of what they need to learn, she also motivates their learning. Figure 4.1 is a picture of a castle drawn by one of her students during a unit on medieval times.

All her students were able to draw a castle. Slowly, however, the students began to add labels to the pictures they had drawn. The first labels probably existed in their prior knowledge, like the words *gatehouse* and *flag* in Figure 4.1. Other words related to the theme of the content unit, like the words *buttress* and *pointed arch*. They were added as the students studied medieval architecture. An additional set of words, like *lexicographer* and *emissary*, were added weekly from Currier's vocabulary list. By using student pictures to add vocabulary incrementally throughout the unit, she linked the new information to the old and forced a certain amount of rehearsal. The pictures her students draw give immediate assessment information. She can see—as can her students—how many vocabulary words have been included and how many concepts represent the theme. When their pictures are complete, her students use them as study guides.

FIGURE 4.1   Student Drawing as an Organizer for Thematic Concepts and Vocabulary

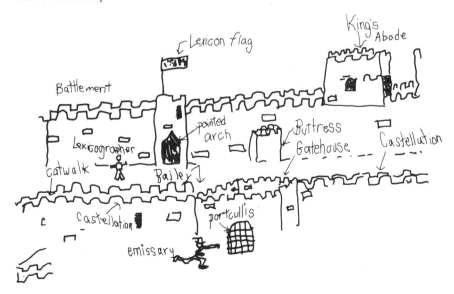

FIGURE 4.2   Student Drawings as Illustration for a Lecture

A Bit	**Grainy Blob**	**A Bunch**	**A Solar Bundle**	**The Modern Atom**
Aristotle	Democritus	Dalton's Molecules	Rutherford 1911	Einstein Bohr Hawking

Student pictures need not be used solely as individual study guides. Because they evoke what students already know, drawing a picture can be a good way to start any class in which students will struggle with new ideas. Mike Strauss teaches a chemistry course for college freshmen. To understand how molecules form, students need to know something about subatomic physics, an arcane subject with which few are familiar. Rather than bombard them with a welter of recent ideas about subatomic matter—quarks, leptons, photons, gluons, and varieties of antimatter—Strauss asks them to spend three minutes drawing the best picture they can of an atom as they know it. He creates transparencies of a few representative drawings and uses the transparencies to illustrate the history of thought about atomic structure from Aristotle to modern physicists (see Hawking, 1988).

Figure 4.2 includes a few drawings typical of those he might get from his students. Some students see the atom as Aristotle did, a small bit with the same composition as larger bits of the same substance. Most see the atom as a very small solar system, as physicists did early in this century before Quantum Theory. As he goes through student drawings, Mike Strauss can point out aspects of student drawings still considered to be accurate. He uses the transparencies to revise student knowledge slowly until it approximates a modern view—a view almost impossible to represent in a drawing. What students know provides the focus for what they learn as new.

FREE WRITING AND WEBBING

In the "writing across the curriculum" movement, free writing and other journal activities give teachers a medium for focusing student attention and activating prior knowledge—using only two or three minutes of the class period. Free writing and journaling evolved from process-oriented composition classes. Because they also serve to focus student attention, they have found application in "thinking across the curriculum" as well (Fulwiler, 1987). In free writing, students are asked to write without stopping for two or three minutes about a specific question provided by the teacher. Free writing can start off a class, gathering student perceptions and thoughts around a single topic. It can also be used during class to sample student questions or identify points of confusion. It can wrap up a class, forcing students to look reflectively at a whole period to identify main ideas or to generate further questions among the bits they remember. Used at the beginning, middle, or end of class, student free writing can be excerpted on the blackboard to give the whole class a sense of the focus that moment.

The teacher sets the guidelines: Write as fast as you can; don't worry about spelling and punctuation; write without stopping for two (or three) minutes. To begin a class, the focusing question for a free write usually relates to the theme of the day. For example, to lead off a class on French history from 1775 to 1790, the teacher might ask: What does it take to start a revolution? A question can also focus narrowly on part of the homework. What bothers you most about word problems? can lead off a class on close reading in math. At the end of class, or at any point when discussion has been heavy or information has come in a burst, a teacher can help students organize their minds by asking for a free write. At any point in the class period, free writing has the advantage of shifting responsibility for learning and thinking from the teacher (or film, or book, or experiment) to the student—where it belongs. A free write gives control over learning to the students. It gives them a chance to identify organizing patterns and ideas.

Teachers can use student free writes within a class period to assess what students understand. Students can do a free write at the beginning and end of a lecture, then note the changes in their beliefs or knowledge and raise new questions. Students can exchange their free writes with each other to get a sense of other points of view. A teacher can read a few pieces of student writing to the class, or ask that they be read, to get a sense of the base of student knowledge available in the room. Over the course of a unit or a year, free writing and other in-class journals can become a medium for communication between teachers and students and a regular part of class discussions.

Gail Bottiggi, a social studies teacher, asked her eighth-grade students to read a chapter on the American West, 1865–1880. To get a sense of what the class understood from the reading, she opened the next class with an imaginative free write: Imagine that you are the S&K Steam Engine in 1880. Tell us about yourself. Comparing the response of student #1 to student #2 gave her a sense of the span of knowledge among her students.

> STUDENT #1: I'm the S&K Engine . . . sh, sh, sh. I'm in the most important part of the development of the wessssst. I link the east to the wessst. I carry—pull—supplies from one end of the country to the other. But my most important job is to pull the cars that carry the supplies that feed the wesssst. I'm the main attraction in my timeees. I also create a lot of jobsssss. I developed the country all by mysellllf.

This student clearly understood the place of the train in the opening of the West. Other students had not read the chapter the same way, or had not read it at all.

> STUDENT #2: Hi. My name is Joe the train engine. You people need us to have more transportation and without us you would have no form of transporting cargo except for your feeble old horse and buggies. And if you were going up a hill, gravity would pull you down again.

By asking students to read their free writes and listing aspects of the engine's contribution to the West on the board, Bottiggi could capsulize the information from the homework necessary to take the class further. She could also galvanize the historic imagination of each student in the group and ensure involvement, even if they had not understood the chapter. The free write exercise makes each student focus. When displayed on overheads, they also provide focus for the whole class. *The Journal Book* (Fulwiler, 1989) provides many additional examples of journaling to support content understanding.

Student journals can bring to light ideas a teacher can use later to focus discussion, provoke questions, or introduce new ideas. Students, however, may not be aware of the structure of relationships embedded in their own writing. They may not have "seen" what they thought. One way to get them to focus on their ideas is to ask them to circle the most important words in what they have written and to link those words with lines, creating a web diagram of their thinking. A web diagram forces students to seek out isolated ideas and to look for linkage.

Gail Bottiggi asked for a free write with web analysis from her eleventh-grade students (see Figure 4.3). The circles and lines of a web diagram helped her students scan what they had written themselves, this time from greater reflective distance (Holley & Dansereau, 1984). The result was a set of questions from students to the teacher or each other: Did all slaves pick cotton? Did they all know the Civil War could end with their freedom? What did they do about hate? Students can use a web to scan their own thoughts or the thoughts of others. The questions or insights developed through webbing can be used to begin class discussion or to guide further study.

FIGURE 4.3   From Free Write to Web Diagram

Question: What would you be like if you lived as a slave in 1863?

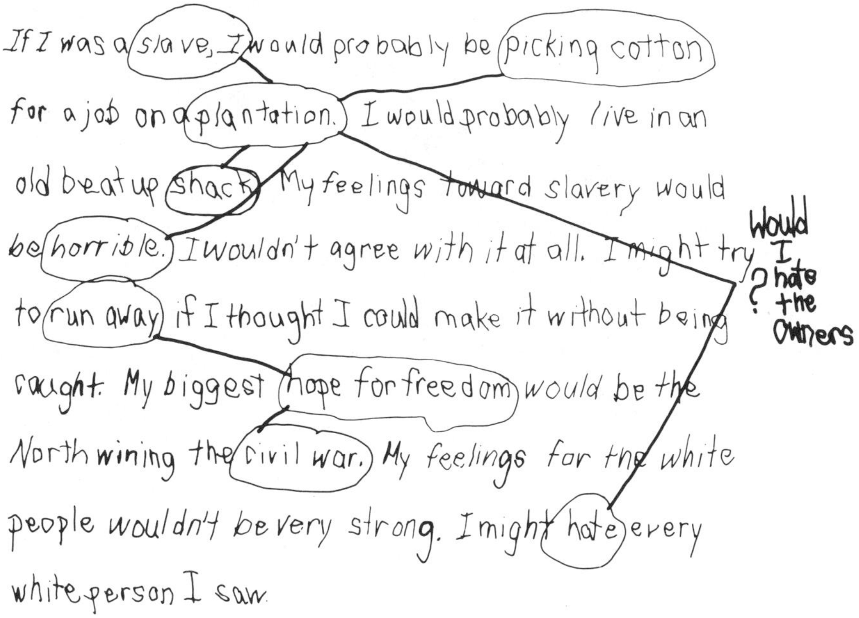

Webbing a text has become a focusing and scanning technique in "reading across the content areas." The technique is particularly useful with difficult prose text to which students need to bring active inquiry, persistence, and a good deal of prior knowledge. Figure 4.4 is a student's web diagram of the introductory sentences of the Declaration of Independence. These sentences are both familiar and forbidding; students find them easier to recite than to understand.

Webbing a piece of text, like the first sentences of the Declaration of Independence, helps students isolate relationships and generate questions for further examination. Webbing a text can evoke prior knowledge, like the "us/them" distinction in the first two lines of Figure 4.4 and the link between King George and "destructive" forms of government at the end of the passage. Webbing also evokes further questions, particularly if the teacher asks each student to use their webs to raise questions. In this example, the student is beginning to ask: In the Declaration, who gets to be equal? Women as well as men? Are the laws of nature the same as God's laws? Transferred to the blackboard, such questions can generate a productive discussion. They can also encourage further scanning, perhaps a search of all the "transgressions" listed by Jefferson in the body of the Declaration of Independence as reasons to break from England. Fo-

FIGURE 4.4   Webbing to Search and Scan

First sentences: Declaration of Independence

Focusing Question: Why did the colonists split from England?

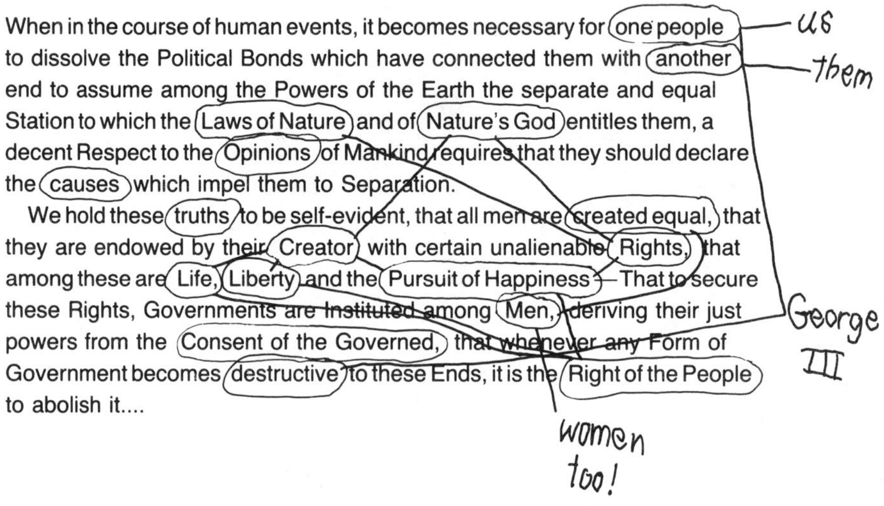

When in the course of human events, it becomes necessary for (one people) — *us*
to dissolve the Political Bonds which have connected them with (another) — *them*
end to assume among the Powers of the Earth the separate and equal
Station to which the (Laws of Nature) and of (Nature's God) entitles them, a
decent Respect to the (Opinions) of Mankind requires that they should declare
the (causes) which impel them to Separation.
    We hold these (truths) to be self-evident, that all men are (created equal,) that
they are endowed by their (Creator) with certain unalienable (Rights,) that
among these are (Life,) (Liberty) and the (Pursuit of Happiness) — That to secure
these Rights, Governments are instituted among (Men,) deriving their just   *George*
powers from the (Consent of the Governed,) that whenever any Form of   *III*
Government becomes (destructive) to these Ends, it is the (Right of the People)
to abolish it....

women too!

cused minds are apt to have more questions the more they see and know.
Webbing a text is a way to move students from a surface reading to deeper
understanding. With further refinement, web diagrams can become concept maps—a graphic organizer that is described more fully in Chapter 8.

TIME LINES AND STORY FRAMES

Time lines offer teachers another technique for focusing student attention on the question of how events take place. Unlike web diagrams, time
lines are a graphic organizer that represents events in serial order, the
natural order of events, and the usual order of episodic memory. Unlike
episodic strings, a time line isolates events related to some purpose or
theme. To make a time line, students have to decide that certain events
are worth selecting and others are not. A teacher might ask, "Create a
time line of the plot in this short story," or "Create a time line that shows
what happens to plants in springtime." In response, students create a visual that represents the order of events. When students represent the flow
of events in a time line, they begin the process of abstraction that evolves
toward trend analysis, causal analysis, and prediction.
    At the simplest level, a time line is a mnemonic that allows stu-

dents to "see" and remember facts in relation to other facts, in serial order. Judy LaRose used a time line to anchor her second-grade unit on Ancient Egypt. Each child started the unit with a blank time line of Egypt. At the beginning, it is not likely that any student could have a clear idea of what 3000 BC means, for example, or what Western calendars mean by "0." Throughout the unit, a large time line made of brown wrapping paper (shown in Figure 4.5) hung on the wall. As the children read their book, saw filmstrips, found books in the library, and looked at photographs, they pasted something to the wall. Slowly, the time line became a record of their observations and thoughts, a facsimile of "time" between 4000 BC and the present day. As the class read and observed, their time line filled out, decorated with pictures from magazines and illustrated with student drawings. The time line held the unit in Egypt together.

Used with a slightly different purpose, a time line can provide the basis for theme analysis, an exercise in which students try to connect certain events on the time line to an idea larger than the facts themselves. The idea of "theme" is often difficult to convey to young people. Teachers can express the difference between theme and plot by separating the theme from the time line, as shown in Figure 4.6.

Sally Kaufman wanted her third-grade students to read fables, not only for the story effect but for theme. She asked them to create a time line that would show the reader what the story means. Kaufman put her students in cooperative groups of three students, both to increase the depth of the search and to provoke the kind of discussion likely to clarify the theme. Her students constructed a time line of critical events, then tried to figure out what the events meant. She hung different time lines on the wall, which represented different ways the same story could be interpreted by different people.

After her students had become skillful at scanning a time line, Sally

FIGURE 4.5 Basic Time Line for Facts on Ancient Egypt

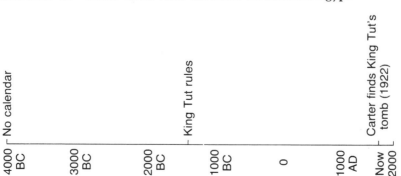

FIGURE 4.6 Time Line for Theme: The Fox without a Tail

THEME
: Before accepting advice, besure it's for your own good.
PLOT
Neil got his tail caught in a trap
He was frightened so he cut it off
Neil was embarrassed
He held a meeting Saturday Night
He asked the other foxes to cut off their tails
They gasped when they saw his tail
They were sorry for him, but kept their tails
Time Line

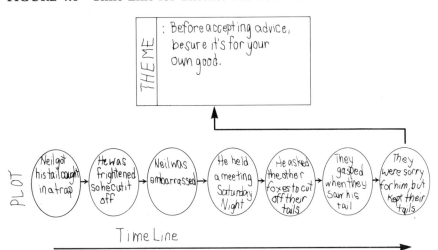

Kaufman increased the challenge by splitting the story line. She asked her students to scan fables for critical events for two characters separately, creating a story frame with two theme lines (see Figure 4.7) (Alverman, 1987). A story frame provides students with a visual summary. In looking at two lines separately, they have to consider two perspectives on theme. Should you, the fox, take advantage of someone else? How do you, the goat, know whom to help? With two possible interpretations of theme, which one is more important?

FIGURE 4.7 Story Frame for Two Themes: "Fox and the Goat"

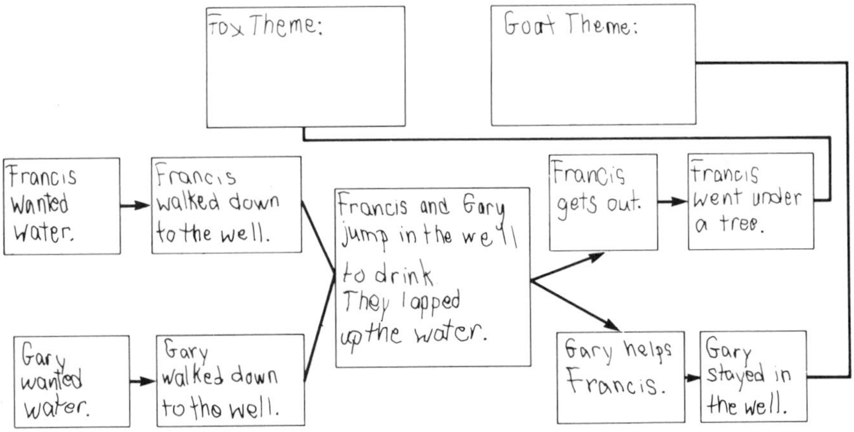

Fox Theme:
Goat Theme:
Francis wanted water.
Francis walked down to the well.
Gary wanted water.
Gary walked down to the well.
Francis and Gary jump in the well to drink They lapped up the water.
Francis gets out.
Francis went under a tree.
Gary helps Francis.
Gary stayed in the well.

With his eleventh-grade history students, Larry Trombley created a time line of European history from 1720 to 1975. On a roll of brown wrapping paper, the line finally stretched completely around the classroom, 60–75 feet. Each country was represented in a different color. At the beginning, Trombley used the time line to focus student attention on events occurring simultaneously in different European countries. Readings, film, lecture, and discussion all added critical events to the line. At the end of the unit, he asked his class to predict the future. Which country would dominate? Which countries would experience turmoil? Which governments would collapse? Who would fight a war? Which economies would expand? Which ideas would catch on? In order to predict the future, the students had to analyze the past, country by country. He assigned student essays on predicting the future to wrap up the unit. They also became the basis for the next unit, which included the French revolution, Spain's collapse, England's rise, and turmoil in Germany. During the next unit, his students wanted to see their predictions verified in fact, but they were also better prepared to revise their predictions as new events changed the picture. Simple story lines as summary take the same form as abstract frames in causal analysis, prediction, and planning (see Chapter 9.)

GRIDS AND GRAPHS

When students are focusing their attention on what they observe, they begin to notice regularities in the pattern of events. History may or may not repeat itself, but certain kinds of events do recur—in all the disciplines. Keeping a count of events that recur can help students "see" patterns. As a technique, keeping count lies at the heart of the sciences and social sciences. By asking students to keep count of recurring events and measuring the regularities, science pries at the invisible laws of cause and effect which apparently govern our experience. Keeping count of recurring events on a grid or graph requires the most disciplined kind of focused observation. Using a numerical count of recurring events is a formal sampling procedure, more rigorous than simply selecting critical events for a time line.

In the early grades, *Mathematics Their Way* (Beratta-Norton, 1976) has given teachers a medium for focusing student attention so that they want to "count" what they observe. Jodi Raine teaches a combined first/second-grade class in which students regularly draw what they see and then use their drawings to make simple graphs. After her class visited an apple orchard and saw how hard it was to pick apples, they drew the apples they picked and made a graph comparing stemmed to stemless apples. Apparently, it is pretty hard for a first-grader to pick an apple and keep the stem on (see Figure 4.8).

FIGURE 4.8   Counting and Graphing Recurring Events, Grade 1

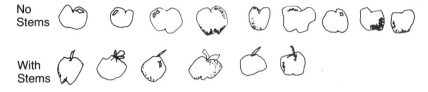

Picking Apples
Drawn from 1st–2nd Grade Orchard Trip

Jodi Raine's classroom walls are covered with such measurements: a comparison of student and parent preferences for the stories of Leo Lionni in which students prefer "Swimmy" and parents favor "The Alphabet Tree"; a graph composed of student self-portraits on the first day of school, arranged to show that students new to the class are almost as numerous as returning students. The students draw what they see, then use what they have drawn to measure differences. Measuring similarities and differences lets them "see" ideas that are more abstract; kids and their parents look for different things in stories. It also provokes further questions; for example: What is it like to be a new kid in school?

Mary Heins uses graphs and grids to focus student attention throughout her sixth-grade science and social science units. She introduced graphing at the beginning of the year by involving the students in opinion surveys. On the first day of class, she asked her students what they like to do with their time. From a list of things they mentioned, she created a simple data collection frame, a bicycle with data grids as wheels. With this grid on a bulletin board, her students then signed their names in appropriate areas. Student signatures became the unit of measure. Some activities drew many signatures (pizza, rock music, and TV); others drew fewer signatures. With student signatures converted to numbers, the sixth grade was ready to make comparative graphs (see Figure 4.9). To make a meaningful graph, Hein's students had to scan "Big Wheels" carefully for themes, like food, music, and entertainment. They created histograms simply by pasting signed pictures to a large sheet of paper. Why did sixth-graders prefer pizza to hot dogs? Why did rock music outstrip singing? The students could see several hundred different comparisons in the pattern of student signatures on the "big wheels" grid. Which comparisons were important? As the students scanned for meaningful comparisons, they were identifying themes and using the themes to organize an approach to measurement.

Stewart Clark uses a similar technique with his twelfth-grade physics class. To understand physics, his students must see the relationship between abstract propositions, stated as mathematical formulae, and

FIGURE 4.9   Converting Grid Data to Graphed Comparisons, Grade 6

A Data Collection Grid

Big Wheels in Grade Six
What We Like to Do

**A Graph Comparing
Preferences**

Hot Dogs versus Pizza

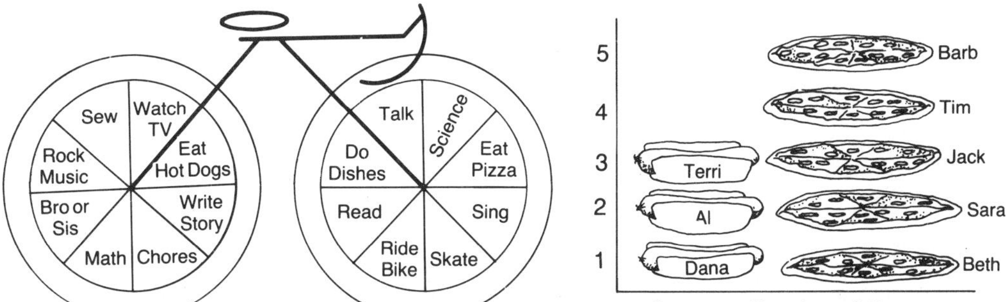

Write Your Name Under Any Activity That Fits

Create a Graph and Convert
Numbers to Percentages

events occurring regularly in their experience. How can students "see" ideas like nonuniform motion? Their eyes are not calibrated to measure nonuniform motion. They can see velocity, but not its cousin, acceleration (see Holland et al., 1986, pp. 209–219). They can, however, tape a rock to a strip of ticker tape. They can drop the rock with the ticker tape attached through a ticker tape printer that will print dots at equal time intervals. With a pair of scissors they can then cut the ticker tape into strips at every dot and past the strips to graph paper. Their strips of paper cut off at the markings can become a graph that lets them "see" both acceleration and velocity. Every time they drop a rock, they get a fresh sample on tape of distance traveled for rocks of different types. As Figure 4.10 shows, if the students tape the pieces next to each other they can see that acceleration is a constant. If they tape the pieces corner to corner, the get a picture of increasing velocity.

"This is the best so far," one student comments. "Nah," her partner asserts, "Somebody spit on it. What if we try different sized rocks?" Her friend pauses. "What the heck, let's try it." As students paste up tape bits, they are not sure where to draw the line representing change in velocity.

"Let's average," one says. A dot in the middle of each tape piece becomes an average. Dot to dot, the pattern of speed during "free fall" becomes clear. "What patterns do you see?" Stewart Clark asks the teams. If the tape pieces are pasted next to each other, they show a constant rate of acceleration. If the tape pieces are pasted corner to corner to represent "real time," they show the rapidly changing rate of speed.

**FIGURE 4.10   Two Graphs of Motion from Pieces of Ticker Tape,
Grade 12**

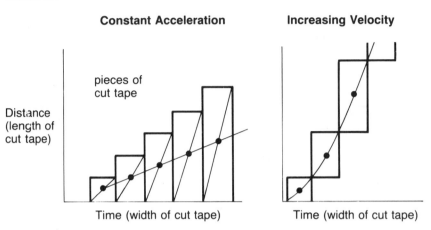

A CASE STUDY: THE LONG STREAM PROFILE
_____

Ninth-grade students are no better prepared to look carefully at the world
in which they live than the rest of us. Like most people their age, ninth-
graders surely do not look closely enough to "see" the patterns of abstract
forces like "energy" in ordinary events (Gray, 1979). Stewart Clark
wanted his ninth-grade earth science students to recognize the effect of
energy, stored in water on the land where they lived. He wanted his students to "see" the effects of energy on the land and then induce some
general principles from their observations. He designed the Long Stream
Study as a way to encourage his students to observe carefully and draw
inferences from observation. At each stage of the study, his students:

1. Looked around and *drew a picture* of what they saw
2. *Wrote a description* of what they saw and looked for patterns
3. Took *samples* they could use to *measure*
4. *Graphed* their samples and *inferred* rules from patterns

As a basis for his unit plan on water and energy, Clark applied these steps
to one stream. Recursively, his students took the same four steps in focusing, scanning, and measuring, from the headwaters of the stream in
the Green Mountains, through the meandering channel in the valley to
a small pond near the end of the river.

To begin the study, Clark drove the students in a bus to the ravines
of Ripton, Vermont. Heading down toward the valley, he stopped the bus
six times. At each stop students clambered down into the creek bed and
drew a picture of the valley around them. The completed short free writes

described the valley around them. Then they collected samples of the stones in the river. Finally, they dropped wood chips in the water and used a stopwatch to time the velocity of the chips between two points. They climbed back to the bus carrying pictures, free writes, samples, and measures of stream velocity at six points along the river.

The journal entries had the purpose of forcing students to scan the larger environment before they took specific measures. Clark had to focus the students' attention on the larger context, away from each pebble lining the stream bed. One student's free write can demonstrate this larger view, in addition to some conjecture on causes.

UPSTREAM "FREE WRITE"
Upstream, the speed of the stream is fast because the gradient is steep. The sediment size is mostly boulders and a few cobbles. There is little sand. So, the sediment is poorly sorted upstream. The channel shape is basically straight, because the stream moves faster upstream so it cuts down through the valley floor. The valley is narrow and V shaped because as the stream erodes sediment from the bottom of the stream, it leaves the steep sloping banks of the mountains behind.

Back in the classroom, the ninth-graders superimposed their pictures to get a visual profile of the river from the mountains to the valley. As represented in Figure 4.11, they could get a "picture" of the effects of water energy on the valley by holding all six pictures up against a strong light.

FIGURE 4.11   Six Superimposed Drawings of the Stream Bed

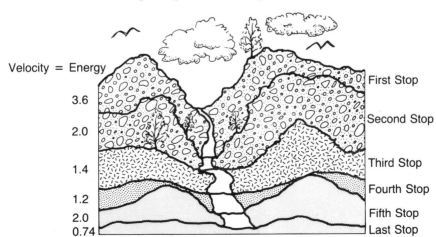

Their superimposed drawings allowed them to "see" energy leave the river as it entered the lowlands in the valley.

To encourage careful observtion, Clark had asked the students to measure stream velocity, as an indicator of energy in the water. Measuring the stream bed at a regular interval and timing wood chips floating from one point to the next gave them a numeric value for energy they could put on a graph. They collected samples of "average" sediment from each site. Collecting samples of stones, sand, and mud gave them a physical measure of erosion (see Figure 4.12). Their samples of sediment from the stream bed and their measures of velocity varied considerably from student to student, giving the class a clear vision of "error" in scientific research. Even with variation among samples, the students could see the pattern in sediment size from the mountains to the valley.

Stewart Clark's students easily saw the pattern in their perceptions. In the mountain ravines, water energy was high, sorting was uneven, sediment size was large, and the land was steep. They had to struggle with simultaneous causes: The high-energy water was making little rocks out of big ones and also carrying the smaller rocks down toward the valley. As it ran out of energy, it dropped heavier rocks. As one student wrote in her final report on this phase of the stream profile, "Once the river levels out, it slows down. It has less energy because it is not moving as fast. Now it cannot carry the bigger rocks that it did before, so it just drops them on the bottom and carries the lighter stuff. When the lighter stuff gets too heavy, it drops that, too, and eventually only carries sand."

With experience in observation and data collection, the students grew increasingly capable with more indirect observation and inferential reasoning. During the pond study, the final phase, students mapped the bottom of a small valley pond, perhaps half a mile in diameter. They could not "see" the bottom they way they had "seen" the river. Again, they drew pictures and wrote descriptions of the pond area. Then on a

FIGURE 4.12   Samples of Sediment from Stream Bed

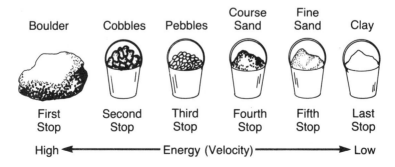

cold winter day, three teams of students walked out on the ice with ice drills, reels of marked rope, and data collection grids. Each team traversed the pond on a straight line running from different points, shoreline to shoreline. Their lines and measures are represented in Figure 4.13.

With descriptive free writes, drawings, and depth data in hand, students returned to the high school, distressed that they had spent half a day running only three lines of measurement. Looking at their measures, they felt they knew little of the underwater topography. "How would you find the rest from what you now know?" Stewart Clark asked. The students discovered that they could draw lines between any two known points, including the shoreline, and then divide by 2 to get an average depth midway between those points, an estimate based on their real measures. They worried that their interpolated depths were less reliable than their known depths. Suddenly, they were dealing with probabilities. Their concern led to the discovery of a principle of scientific measurement:

1. **The greater the distance between two points, the greater the risk of error in the average.**

By marking the half-way point between known depths, they could guess at the unknown.

FIGURE 4.13   **Real and Interpolated Measures of Depth**

Monkton Pond (at 50' Intervals)

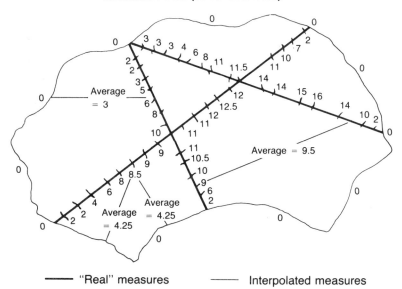

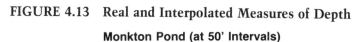

When the students had interpolated a large number of average depths between known points, their maps became a mass of depth calculations, some directly observed and some inferred. Using both types of measure, they could map the bottom of the pond. They could connect dots with equal depths—dot to dot—to profile the pond's bottom (see Figure 4.14). Separately, each student constructed a map of the pond bottom, then added labels from the written descriptions to make a map of the pond. Students with a large number of dots to connect drew profiles slightly different from students with fewer dots. Having more dots took the guesswork out of drawing and gave rise to a second principle of measurement:

2. Having a large sample reduces the risk of error.

The two principles of measurement raised further questions. When is precision desirable? What is the "right" sample size? Can you ever eliminate the chance of error?

Their maps, with their initial journal entries, led the students further toward inference. They could guess that the town built the beach at the safest point, a shallow slope. They saw that the cliff on the west side kept dropping, even below water level. Those cliffs and the hills to the

FIGURE 4.14   Using Induction to Map the Pond and Question Further

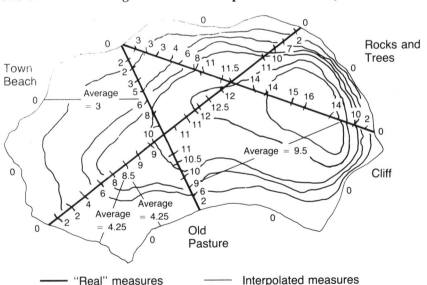

north probably blocked water from running out to the river and created the pond. From their observations and measurements, they could begin to tell the story of the pond.

Focusing and scanning must be considered the basic skills of thinking, if only because they force the mind to consider new information and then reconsider old ways of seeing in light of the new. If the academic subjects have anything in common, it is their requirement that we look carefully at some aspect of the world around us and resist leaping backward toward foregone conclusions. The mind may have many reasons not to venture off its own porch to see the world it inhabits. Fear, habit, and the awful momentum of what is already known can cut short any exploration. Teaching should lead the mind out in confidence from what it knows now to new knowledge and new ways of knowing. To have permanent effect, teaching must lead the mind out not just once, but many times in a widening circle of inquiry.

Focusing, scanning, and storing for later use become intellectual habits only when they are used recursively across the domains of knowledge and experience. Breaking into the mind's work to ask for "directed thinking" sacrifices some of the mind's delight with unfocused thinking and with its own sense of direction. Graphic organizers from scanning and focusing may open the mind's eye without sacrificing either delight or the sense of personal control that drives inquiry.

SUGGESTIONS FOR TEACHERS

1. Make a list of the vocabulary necessary for success in a unit you plan to teach. Consider different drawings or other visual organizers that would include all the words on the list:
   a. Develop a large drawing to hang in your room and add the words one at a time.
   b. Have students draw a picture that will anchor the word as they progress through the unit.

2. Develop a focusing question for a class you plan to teach. Use a two- or three-minute free write that asks the students to look at the question and assess what they already know about the subject. Consider each of the following processing possibilities:
   a. To begin a class, have students read their free writes and record what they know on a transparency or blackboard.

    b. To begin a class, have students read their free writes to each other and identify similarities and differences so they can explain them to the class.

    c. After the free write, introduce new information through lecture, film, or reading. Then ask the students to revise what they first wrote to accommodate the new information.

    d. At the end of a class period, ask students to free write their questions and comments. Make transparencies of a few and use them to open the next class.

    e. Show students how to "web" a free write by circling the most important words. Then, organize groups of two or three to interview each other and clarify connections between circled words.

3. For any text handout, show students how to "web" a text. Ask them to identify a major idea in the next and to trace that trend or theme by circling words and connecting them with lines. Can they use webbed words to generate questions?

4. Ask groups of students to extrapolate a trend or theme from a chapter, put it on separate paper as a time line, and then explain it to the rest of the class.

5. For any aspect of content that falls in serial order, pin a roll of paper on the wall and show students how to map out critical events in a time line.

    a. As the time line grows, ask them to make connections between events with a pen. Can they label the connection?

    b. Use colored pens or crayons to label different trends, themes, or causes.

6. Cut a story, fable, myth, or other short narrative into small pieces. Give each student one piece. Ask the group to reconstruct the narrative by taping pieces to a wall. Can each member of the group explain how he or she did it? What ideas give coherence to a story?

7. Are there recurring events in any unit you teach? Would counting and graphing clarify important issues? Redesign a unit plan to emphasize focused scanning and organizing information for analysis. Design graphs or grids that will help students organize and measure recurring events.

Helping Students Reflect on Their Thinking

Even when your students experience success in using a graphic organizer for understanding the subject area, they will not automatically see wider usage for the technique they employed. They will need your help in finding other situations where the same technique would work as well. When your students are using a graphic to think about some part of content, make some effort to let them: (1) review the process they used to think and (2) look for other situations in or out of school where the same process might work. We can call the transfer of a thinking process a "Bridge."

A Bridge for Thinking

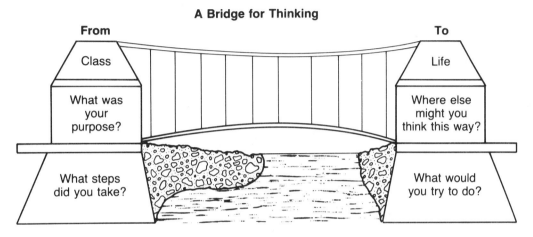

- What careers or jobs require careful scanning and focusing?
- What are the risks in making a mistake?
- When you are in a situation requiring scanning for a distinct purpose, what tricks have you learned?

REFERENCES

Alverman, D. (1987). Strategic teaching in social studies. In B. F. Jones, A. S. Palincsar, D. S. Ogle, & E. G. Carr (Eds.), *Strategic Teaching and Learning: Cognitive Instruction in the Content Areas.* Alexandria, VA: ASCD Publications.

Beratta-Norton, M. (1976). *Mathematics Their Way.* Menlo Park, CA: Addison Wesley.

Derry, S. J., & Murphy, D. A. (1986). Designing systems that train learning ability. *Review of Educational Research, 56*(1), 1–39.

Flavell, J. H. (1985). *Cognitive Development.* Englewood Cliffs, NJ: Prentice Hall.

Fulwiler, T. (1987). *Writing to Learn.* Upper Montclair, NJ: Boynton Cook.

Fulwiler, T. (1989). *The Journal Book.* Upper Montclair, NJ: Boynton Cook.

Gagne, R. M., & White, R. T. (1978). Memory strategy and learning. Review of Educational Research, 48(2), 187–222.

Glasser, W. (1987). *Control Theory in the Classroom*. New York: Harper and Row.

Gray, R. L. (1979). Toward observing that which is not directly observable. In J. Lockhead & J. Clements (Eds.), *Cognitive Process Instruction*. Philadelphia: Franklin Institute Press.

Hawking, S. W. (1988). *A Brief History of Time: From the Big Bang to Black Holes*. New York: Bantam.

Holland, J. H.; Holyoak, K. J.; Nisbett, R. E.; & Thagard, P. R. (1986). *Induction: Processes of Inference Learning and Discovery*. Cambridge, MA: MIT Press.

Holley C. D., & Dansereau, D. F. (1984). *Spacial Learning Strategies: Techniques, Applications and Related Issues*. New York: Academic Press.

Kay, D., & Black, J. D. (1986). Explanation driven processing in summarization: The interaction of content and process. In J. A. Galambos, R. P. Abelson, J. B. Black (Eds.), *Knowledge Structures*. Hillsdale, NJ: Lawrence Erlbaum.

Paris, S. G.; Lipson, M. Y.; & Wixson, K. K. (1983). Becoming a strategic reader. *Contemporary Educational Psychology*, 8, 293–316.

Reder, L. M. (1980). The role of elaboration in the comprehension and retention of prose: A critical review. *Review of Educational Research*, 50(1), 5–54.

Reed, S. K. (1973). *Psychological Processes in Pattern Recognition*. New York: Academic Press.

Simon, H. A. (1979). The information storage system called the "human memory." In H. Simon (Ed.), *Models of Thought*. New Haven, CT: Yale University Press.

Sternberg, R. J. (1985). *Beyond IQ*. Cambridge/New York: Cambridge University Press.

Travers, R. M. (1982). *Essentials of Learning*. New York: MacMillan.

Witkin, H. A.; Moore, C. A.; Goodenough, D. R.; & Cox, P. W. (1977). Field dependent and field independent cognitive styles and their educational implications. *Review of Educational Research*, 47(1), 1–64.

5

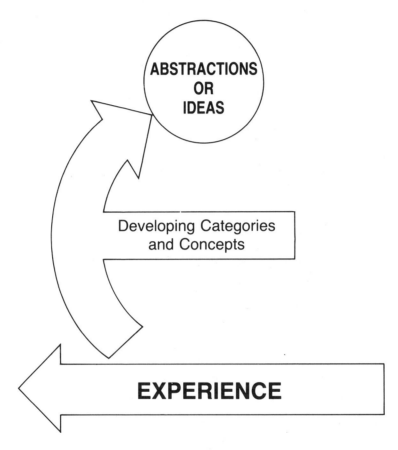

To divest ourselves of categories is to divest ourselves of thought.
—NICKERSON, PERKINS, AND SMITH, *The Teaching of Thinking*

Developing Categories and Concepts

GIVE AN INFANT A SHOE BOX TO PLAY WITH, AND SHE WILL try to put it in her mouth. A toddler will see the same box as a hat and put it on his head. A kindergartner may search the local area for anything that might fit in the box and load it up. Toys, food, buttons, and broken glass may all find a place in a kindergartner's box. By the beginning of grade school, a child begins to search for similar things to put in one box, all of Barbie's clothes, for example, or stuff she gathered on the beach last summer. A fourth-grader is apt to keep lots of boxes, one for Barbie's old clothes and others for the button collection, precious jewelry, and shiny river stones. By the time she starts off to middle school, the child may put away all of her boxes. They no longer serve to hold the things she feels important. Instead, she uses "boxes" her mind has built to hold her ideas together and organize her world. Now more metaphoric than material, "boxes" give the mind increased carrying capacity, inferential power, and the ability to predict. These hypothetical boxes—groups for objects, categories for groups, and concepts for related categories—are the basic tools for the work of the mind (Wilson, 1963).

A FAILURE OF CATEGORIES

"This is a cheat," my third-grade daughter comments, scanning the cereal box propped in front of her breakfast.

"How is it a cheat, Jess?" I ask.

"My friend Marvin sent away for this toy motorcycle. It never came," she says.

"What happened?" I ask, always on the alert for fraud.

"He sent twenty-five cents and the box top to this address in Chicago, the way it says. Then he wrote his box number here and Bristol on these lines, here."

"Oh," I said. "I thought he lived in our town, not Bristol."

"Right, but Bristol is bigger."

"Yes, it is bigger."

"He thought Bristol would be easier to find 'cause it's so much bigger."

With the school bus pulling up outside, I decided to hold back my explanation of Marvin's problem. It was bigger than I could handle at the moment.

Marvin was missing the fundamental classification system that undergirds the entire postal service. The postal service functions because it has created a vast grouping system that ultimately includes every citizen in this country. We are all linked to our street or box numbers. Our street numbers are linked to postal zones for a city, region, and state. By seeing each citizen as a member a hierarchical system of grouped houses, the postal service can send plastic motorcycles around the country with remarkable efficiency. The postal system has the power to move motorcycles. Marvin, with a simpler classification system, does not.

The two classification systems in Figure 5.1 reflect different ways of thinking about time and space. In Marvin's system, motorcycles are most often attributes of big cities like Chicago, where you can find almost anything. Small towns like ours lack motorcycles and in fact have little of anything. To raise your chances of getting a plastic motorcycle in a small town, it's best to look bigger. Marvin probably shares some important concepts with the postal service. Both understand how distance creates problems and how two places, however similar, may not be the same. Marvin shares a goal with the postal service—some general assumptions about how the country looks and how far it may be from here to there. Without the classification scheme of the postal service, however, he cannot satisfy his desires.

Groups, categories, and concepts built by each human mind can give it remarkable power. The human mind has no hands. It cannot solve problems directly. To work well, it has to reduce what it sees to a language it can manage. In Howard Gardner's (1983) view of intelligence, the mind has at least seven languages it uses to express itself, including verbal and mathematical languages common in school learning, but also languages for sound, movement, color, and emotional relationship. By grouping sounds, the mind can imagine and create chords for a piano. By grouping colors, the mind can create shades and light on paper which we then may mistake for a landscape. By grouping items or numbers, the mind can add or subtract. By grouping movements, the mind can imagine a ballet and then actually dance it. By grouping words, of course, the mind can create

FIGURE 5.1 Simple versus Sophisticated Categorical Systems: Marvin versus U.S. Postal Service

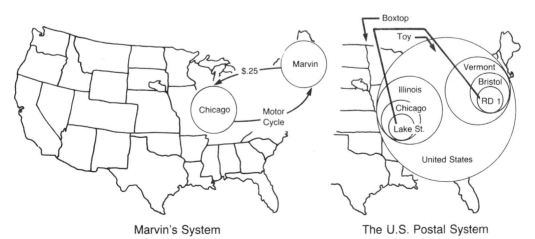

Marvin's System   The U.S. Postal System

ideas—sentences that describe experience, define abstractions, explain causes, predict consequences, or propose solutions. All these languages help the mind organize its work. All depend on a system of classification, using symbols as labels for groups, categories, and concepts. All the languages of the mind are abstract. That is, they can operate independently from the physical universe where events actually occur. As it develops its full power, the human mind needs to experiment with grouping different kinds of language symbols, just as it experiments with the physical universe, to gain increasing control over both realms.

REVOLUTION AMONG CONCEPTS

Teaching essentially amounts to promoting gradual revolution in the thinking of individuals. We are in the business of changing minds. Thomas Kuhn (1970) has shown how a revolution occurs in scientific thought—a process that may be repeated endlessly in the process of learning. First, nearly all the evidence available supports the truth and utility of a simple concept. The few events or facts that do not fit the concept are usually ignored or dismissed. Further experience produces more evidence supporting the concept—and more evidence that does not fit. Suddenly, the evidence that does not fit the old concept itself begins to fall into a pattern. A revolution in thinking occurs and a more powerful idea rises to prominence. During the last 1000 years, Copernicus, Galileo, and Einstein each caused a revolution in the way we think about the structure of the universe, by explaining anomalies in existing information with a new theory. Our idea of "intelligence" has evolved from a simple concept to a more elaborate construct through a similar process (Sternberg, 1985). At one time intelligence was viewed as one monochrome, general category; now it is more often seen and measured as multifaceted. The same kind of revolution can occur during encounters with subject area content (Hill, 1986).

With guidance, students can learn how to group and regroup evidence to form new classes, categories, or concepts essential to each subject area. As contrary evidence mounts, students can be shown how to reclassify and assemble more powerful concepts. At any grade level and in any discipline, part of a teacher's job is to help students build mental boxes that will let them organize, understand, and control the widening sphere of their world. Creating groups and categories may be a natural tendency in the human mind. Even ten-month-old infants have been observed creating nonspecific categories to organize the impressions from their senses (Husaim & Cohen, 1981). Between the second and sixth grades, students begin to prefer grouping strategies over simple repetition when they try to memorize information (Justice, 1985). Categories play an essential role in higher-level thinking, as in science, where shared concepts guide the work of scientists who may never actually meet (Gould, 1987).

In developing reliable classification schemes and useful concepts in a subject area, novice learners work through stages toward sophistication (Vygotsky, 1986; Piaget, 1964; Lingle, Altom, & Medin, 1984):

> *Grouping by surface attributes:* A dog and a horse both have four legs; the mind will infer that both probably share additional surface attributes.
>
> *Grouping by deep attributes:* Hydrogen sulfide can be found in coal-burning smokestacks and in raindrops; the mind can infer that the stacks may cause acid rain.
>
> *Grouping across multiple categories:* Both astrology and astronomy make scientific predictions from the stars; the mind can infer that "science" does not always predict reliably.

As the final example suggests, categories may open the door to misconception. Teaching has the purpose of helping students develop more elaborate classification schemes to help them manage subject area content.

SUBJECT KNOWLEDGE AS A CATEGORY SYSTEM

Each discipline or subject area can be considered an elaborate construction of interactive "boxes" or categories. Returning to the anecdote at the beginning of this chapter, Marvin cannot gain efficiency by memorizing the classification system in a discipline, any more than he can get his plastic motorcycle by memorizing the ZIP codes that lend efficiency to the postal service. He can be led to explore the the structure of what he already knows, experiment with new concepts or classification schemes, and test what he has organized in his mind against real experience. The task of the student is to construct and manage language for the work of the mind and to test that abstract language against concrete experience. As students build elaborate classification schemes to manage their thinking, they gain increasing control over a widening sphere of experience itself.

Like any large bureaucracy, each of the subject areas uses a classification system to work efficiently. Some subjects, such as mathematics and physics, use classification schemes for both objects and operations which are both highly elaborate and inflexible. Clearly defined categories of classification allow the mind to work with precision. Other subject areas like literature and social studies employ more flexible categories and are much less rigid. More loosely arranged categories allow the mind to explore experience to find hidden relationships. Some verbal categories, like the words *chair* and *intelligence,* may have few if any clear attributes. These categories are filled only with specific examples (Nickerson, Perkins, & Smith, 1985, p. 16). Other categories, like the words *witchcraft* and *fairy,* may have firm boundaries and fixed attributes, but lack any but imaginary examples. The mind can create categories to manage the physical world, as well as worlds that may not exist at all.

Because classification plays such an important role in all mental activity, from early concept formation to the intricacies of scientific research, most thinking skills programs include categorization exercises (Marzano et al., 1987). "Chunking" disparate elements, like random numbers, into recognizable categories or groups appears to extend short-term memory (Travers, 1982, p. 112). Grouping words from a list into classes, then providing a label for the class has been used to train students to consciously apply categorization strategies (Feuerstein et al., 1980; Nickerson, Perkins, & Smith, 1985; Kinnison & Pickens, 1984). Matching exercises using geometric graphics have been used to help students identify criterial attributes and form classes as they approach an academic task (Letteri, 1982).

REPRESENTING CATEGORIES IN TEACHING AND LEARNING

Graphics have an advantage in teaching categorization because they are representations of "boxes for kids to put stuff in." Circle diagrams, as we will call them, also provide the basis for more sophisticated graphic techniques. As Figure 5.2 shows, a circle diagram is a visual way to express relationships between ideas (Winocur, 1987; Halpern, 1984). Circle diagrams can represent simple ideas in a simple form (Neimark, 1987, p. 148). Venn diagrams, which use lapped circles to represent logical arguments, can also represent thinking of the most complex sort. In using circle diagrams to teach categorization in the content areas, it is best to move from simple to complex forms.

Circle diagrams, like other graphic representations of thinking, can meet four kinds of instructional purpose:

1. *As a diagnostic medium,* circle diagrams can be used to assess what students know, and how they organize what they know, prior to the introduction of new information.

2. *As a teaching medium,* circle diagrams can be used in presentations of an organized body of new information, as in:
   a. Handouts before lectures
   b. Overhead transparencies

FIGURE 5.2   Ways to Represent Categories in Content Subjects

Circle diagrams can be used to show that:

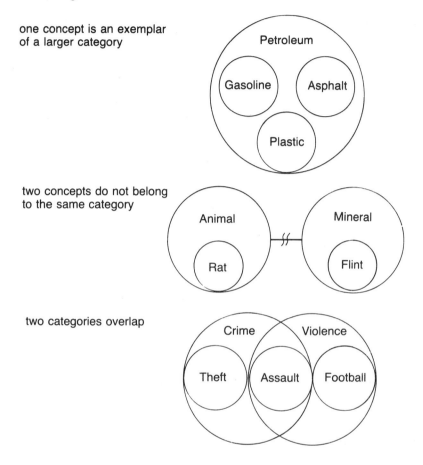

one concept is an exemplar
of a larger category

two concepts do not belong
to the same category

two categories overlap

    c. Chalk talks on the blackboard
    d. Reconstructions of ideas from class discussion

3. *As a medium for student learning*, circle diagrams can provide
a medium for small group discussions and individual projects,
guiding:
    a. Collaborative groups
    b. Small group discussions or debates
    c. Individual reading, research, and expository writing
    d. Metaphoric thinking and creative writing

4. *As a testing medium*, circle diagrams can be used to measure the
depth of student learning from a unit or lesson, including:
    a. Concept acquisition

b. Discrimination between concepts
c. Relation of facts to ideas

TESTING FOR CONCEPT ORGANIZATION

Since most subject areas depend on a system of related category labels, giving students a list of active categories or concepts in random order and asking them to rearrange the list can reveal how much prior knowledge students have in a particular concept area. Students with no categorical knowledge in the area represented by the list will tend to rearrange it by personal association or by some criteria other than meaning. Students with surface knowledge will tend to group items to larger categories based on physical features. Students with elaborate knowledge will use several alternative systems, some based on deep features or hypothetical relationships.

Teachers use tests for several purposes—to find out what students know before they start a new unit, to find out how students are doing as the unit progresses, and to find out what they have learned when the unit ends. Used before starting a unit, a circle diagram represents what students know and how deeply they know it, giving the teacher a baseline for beginning the unit and a way to measure progress. Used in the process of teaching, a circle diagram can illuminate the gaps in student understanding that restrict further learning. Used in a final unit test, a circle diagram can represent the students' comprehension of relationships. When students use circle diagrams in all three phases of teaching, they are being invited to think about categories and relationships within the content and develop management systems for the subject matter.

Diagnostic Tests A circle diagram as a diagnostic device asks students to represent what they know in terms of essential relationships. By looking at prevalent errors within a class or the pattern of errors for one student, a teacher can identify gaps in knowledge and failures of comprehension. The list of terms in Figure 5.3 was used in a self-administered diagnostic test of thinking for college freshmen (Clarke & Wittes, 1977). Students saw two words in the list as possible category labels, the word *light* and the word *sun.* Students who chose *light* as the category could list the remaining three words as sources of light. Students who chose the word *sun* as the category label probably used size as the dominant idea. The choice of *sun* as a label, however, forces the remaining words into equivalence, a choice hard to defend. Students who used *sun* as the category label also tended to have systematic problems in learning (Clarke, 1983).

When students are asked to create their own lists in a topic area and then create categories, circle diagrams can also reflect the degree of

FIGURE 5.3   Circle Diagrams Reflecting Knowledge Structure

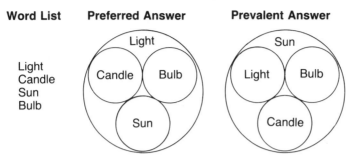

Reprinted with the permission of Academic Therapy Publications, Novato, CA.

elaboration students have achieved within that content area. If a class of students were asked to brainstorm a list of words describing the word *book*, for example, and then to create a circle diagram expressing relationships among the words, the products would reflect the conceptual sophistication the group had achieved for the idea of book (see Figure 5.4).

FIGURE 5.4   From Simple to Complex Category Systems

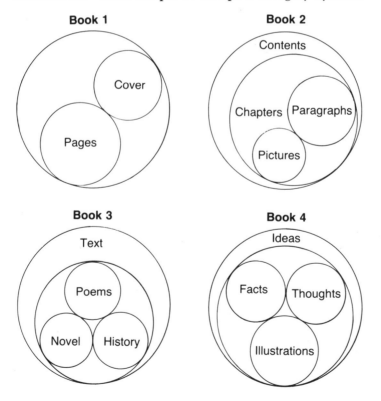

Book 1 and Book 2 in Figure 5.4 both result from a brainstormed list of physical attributes, but the second diagram reflects some understanding of the underlying structure of a book. Book 3, at again a higher level of abstraction, creates a typology for kinds of books with different purposes. Book 4 treats books as a vehicle for communication, with little reference to surface characteristics. These four circle diagrams reflect the continuum from grouping by surface attributes to grouping by deeper attributes related to purpose. As we gain knowledge in a subject area, we also use increasingly refined grouping strategies to break it into different kinds of "pieces." If all four diagrams were to come out of one seventh-grade class, the teacher might have reason to individualize her or his reading program.

When assessing student knowledge, it can be useful to give students a list of core concepts in random order and ask them to reorganize the list so it makes sense. There are several kinds of order represented in Figure 5.5, all of which are "right" within some system of categories. One kindergarten class decided that the best order for the random-order list in Figure 5.5 was alphabetical, a surface attribute of the words. They were practicing the alphabet at the time and had no better frame to use in rearranging the words. Students who can manage the concept of pollution in the environment, however, may well choose one of the three "right orders" shown in the diagram. Some will move from smallest to largest category (group #1), an inductive ordering. Some may choose to work from the largest to the smallest (group #2). Some may assume that an "hour glass" shape is the best order, beginning with the word *pollution* and ending with the word *environment*, with the transportation and industry categories sandwiched between. Others may choose a causal order based on their own beliefs about cause and effect.

In fact, all three lists in Figure 5.5 reflect the classification scheme shown in Figure 5.6. If asked to draw a circle diagram from their list, the students might indicate the pollution is a concern within the larger environment. They would have to invent two classes not explicitly

FIGURE 5.5   Lists as a Basis for Category Exercises and Diagrams: From Lists to Categories and Concepts

From Lists to Categories and Concepts

	#1	#2	#3
Random Order cars, refineries, pollution, trucks, factories, buses, environment	cars trucks buses factories refineries pollution environment	environment pollution factories refineries buses trucks cars	environment cars trucks buses factories refineries pollution

FIGURE 5.6   From List to Circle Diagram

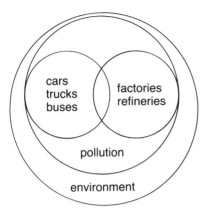

shown in the list, a category for transportation and another for industry. Some students might insert these organizing labels in their circle diagram. Some might lap the transportation and industry categories, to suggest some unspecified relationship. Helping students organize lists can prepare them to discover categories and concepts that they can use to read, write, and think more effectively.

Final Tests   If grouping, classification, and categorization have played a part in the teaching of a unit, the final test for that unit can take the form of a circle diagram. Jori Dean, a seventh-grade teacher of language arts, developed a literature unit on myths, legends, and fairy tales as forms of fantasy in literature. She wanted her seventh-grade students to understand the distinctions between the three kinds of fantasy. As part of her final test, she included the circle diagram in Figure 5.7. Because

FIGURE 5.7   Circle Diagram Testing Comprehension of Relationships

Use the words on the right to lable the following circle diagram.

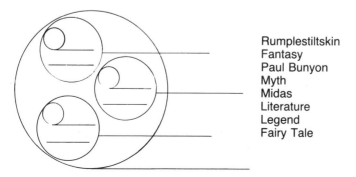

the item list includes two categories that could describe the largest circle, the students were forced to work inductively. That is, they needed to start with particular stories and work toward general categories to succeed with the question.

CIRCLE DIAGRAMS IN TEACHING

Circle diagrams can serve two purposes in teaching content. They can give teachers a way to represent the relationships within the content, as the teacher sees them, and they can provide the teacher with a medium for the discussion of categorization as a thinking skill.

Ruth Roy, a high-school English teacher, faced the problem of teaching her students how to debate. She and her students saw the idea of debate from different perspectives. She viewed debate as a set of procedures in argumentation based on a clear set of terms, whereas they saw debate as a "free for all." To convey her vision of debate to the students who wanted to fight more than listen, she created a set of circle diagrams that she taped to the wall. Her circle diagrams gave students a language to use in making or analyzing a logical argument. Figure 5.8 presents aspects of debate as a system of embedded categories. With these and similar wall-hangings in view, Roy had a means of leading students to see fallacies and flaws in their arguments during the process of debate. With the conceptual organization of the process visible on the wall, students

FIGURE 5.8   Circle Diagram Defining Concept Relationships

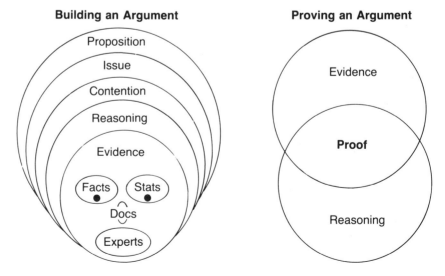

became more discriminating in devising their arguments and more rigorous in analyzing the arguments of their friends. Used by teachers—in handouts, overhead projections, or blackboard illustrations—circle diagrams help organize student perception of a concept or category.

CIRCLE DIAGRAMS IN LEARNING

Circle diagrams can play a role in supporting concept development. When students describe similar objects with two lapped circle diagrams, the organizing concept for both emerges in the overlapped area. The overlap asks students to seek out similarities. Those similarities can describe a shared class or concept.

Diane Quebec wanted her second-grade class to develop a concept for fruit during a pre-Halloween unit on apples. She made a lapped circle diagram representing a pumpkin and an apple. As a whole class, the students worked out the similarities and differences in Figure 5.9. Her students found it easy to see differences. The apple was red; the pumpkin was orange. You could peel an apple; you could carve a pumpkin. Slowly, however, the second-grade students began to see shared characteristics of these dissimilar objects. Both apples and pumpkins were round, with a stem on top and seeds in the middle. You could eat them. To the extent they could see similarities, the students were discovering a definition for the technical concept of "fruit." They were constructing a new category.

Teachers can help students develop categories and concepts in the subject areas simply by helping them make lists and create circle dia-

FIGURE 5.9   Circle Diagram Guiding Concept Acquisition

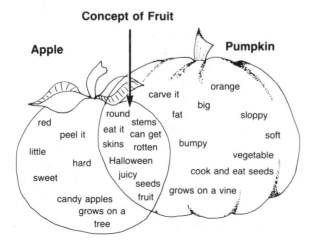

grams. Teachers should allow flexibility in categorization. After all, the language we use to create categories is largely a convenience; locked up in its boney house, our minds have nothing else with which to play. Working with categories allows our minds to work with larger chunks of information than our senses can handle by themselves. The type of category we use depends on the purpose we bring to the exercise. For any list of related words there are many categories, perhaps unstated, that would give order to the list.

To show students the flexibility of some categories in science, John Rouleau asked his twelfth-grade biology students to create five different categorization schemes for one list of 10 animals.

cow	lamprey
crawfish	perch
eagle	snail
earthworm	sponge
hookworm	tapeworm

The students created five lists: (1) least familiar to most familiar; (2) smallest to biggest; (3) simplest to most complex (whatever that means); (4) the animals with least economic importance to most; and (5) oldest (evolutionarily) to youngest. As students struggled with making the lists, they also began to ask questions about relationship. What does complexity have to do with age? Or economic importance? As Rouleau watched his students work with different lists, he began to understand the level of sophistication they were bringing to the unit on ecological biology.

In the hands of students, circle diagrams can guide the process of discovery. Developed by students individually or in collaborative groups, circle diagrams can guide inquiry in the form of individual projects or group discussion. Gregory Wright, a biology teacher, wanted his students to distinguish between viruses and bacteria as they read their homework assignment. He gave them a blank Venn diagram as they left the room and asked them to fill in the blanks (see Figure 5.10). The student in this example accomplished a number of things as he read the assigned chapter. He was able to read with a clear purpose—to distinguish between viruses and bacteria. He built parts of a classification scheme for both organisms. More important, perhaps, he employed a simple schema for a complex intellectual task—the comparison/contrast analysis. Wright could tell at a glance how much each student understood before plowing on with viruses and bacteria of different types. If all the students in the class checked homework with each other, Wright could be fairly well assured of a common basis of understanding among them.

The two lapped circles that can guide comparison and contrast can also guide metaphoric thinking (McTighe & Lyman, 1988). Metaphor uses language to weigh dissimilarity between ideas and emphasize a few

FIGURE 5.10   Circle Diagram Guiding Analytic Reading

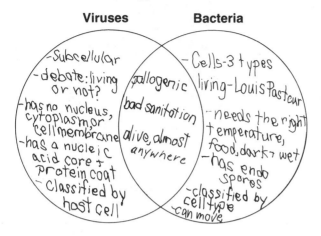

Biology Homework

Viruses   **Bacteria**

similarities. Teachers can use a two-celled circle diagram to analyze poetic metaphor, such as "My love is like a red, red rose." They can also use a circle diagram to encourage metaphoric thinking among their students (see Figure 5.11).

In more complex constructions, circle diagrams can guide complex thinking and problem solving, even among younger children. As a fourth-grade teacher, Sandy Williams struggled to lend interest to the task of learning the multiplication tables. Using attribute blocks, she showed her class how to make a three-celled circle diagram. Combining a color (red) with a size (large) and a shape (square) gave them a figure with common attributes, a large red square. Shortly, they were ready to wrangle

FIGURE 5.11   Circle Diagram Guiding Metaphoric Thinking

Making Metaphors
Choosing a word from the first list and a word from the second,
create a circle diagram of shared and distinguishing characteristics.

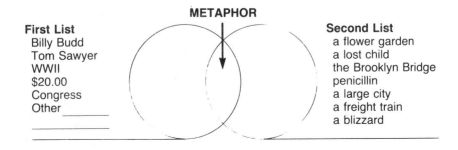

METAPHOR

First List
Billy Budd
Tom Sawyer
WWII
$20.00
Congress
Other _____
_____

Second List
a flower garden
a lost child
the Brooklyn Bridge
penicillin
a large city
a freight train
a blizzard

with multiples and shared number values in arithmetic. Using the diagram in Figure 5.12, Williams asked her students to group numbers that share a common factor.

Working in collaborative groups allowed the faster students to bring others along. With three odd numbers in the cells, the common attributes were many. With mixed odd and even numbers, the shared values were fewer. With two odds and an even (3, 4, 5), there was no common number in the central space. Most of the class was excited by these discoveries and the challenge of making them. Some found it hard but still persevered. Apart from perception of pattern in the multiplication table, circle diagrams added some excitement to a difficult memorization task. Although they did not hear the word *factoring*, their work with shared values in mathematics may better prepare them for algebra.

Apparently, the number of circles that can overlap in a two-dimensional diagram reaches its limit between 20 and 30. Carol Hickey, a second-grade teacher, used five overlapping circles to guide her class in an investigation of ecology. Very large circle diagrams hung on Hickey's wall. As the class watched films, read books, heard from visitors, or simply watched nature and though about what they had seen, they added information to the diagram, gradually assembling an image of how their own lives intersected with the world around them. On a large bulletin board, drawings, photos stories, and things found at home could all find a way to represent some aspect of interdependency among aspects of the environment. The circle diagram in Figure 5.13 organizes analysis of sharing among living and nonliving things, with us in the center of it all.

Sometimes, however, the simplest circle diagram can have the most powerful effect on discovery and discussion. The Venn in Figure 5.14 was used to drive six weeks of inquiry in a home economics class. What are

FIGURE 5.12   Circle Diagrams for Math Concepts

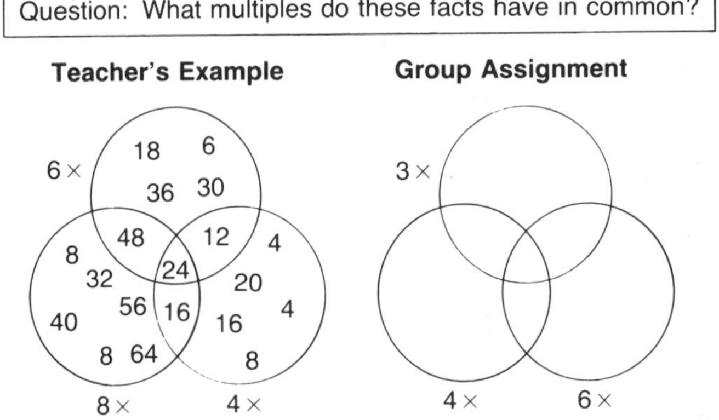

FIGURE 5.13   Circle Diagram as a Unit Plan

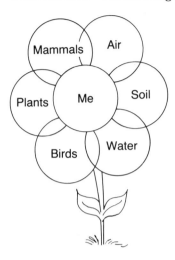

FIGURE 5.14   Circle Diagram Driving Group Inquiry

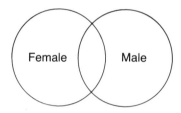

the shared attributes of the sexes? What are the differences? With personal bias to defend, a group of students may invest considerable energy in filling boxes. In this instance, they had to seek out information in the library. By introducing new information, a skilled teacher can help guide inquiry, slowly changing the character of categories and concepts. A student who has experimented with lapped circle diagrams may be preparing the base for more intricate patterns of thinking with the same basic structure, such as dialectical reasoning, pro-con argumentation, and debate (see Chapter 8).

A CASE STUDY: AMERICAN INDIANS

Elaine Pinckney, a fourth-grade teacher at Stowe Elementary School in northern Vermont, decided to integrate thinking skills with her existing unit on American Indians. Her purpose in the unit was to let students explore similarities and differences in Indian culture when the European settlers arrived. She wanted to impart some basic information about Indian culture, showing similarities and differences among representative tribes, but she also wanted students to see how the culture of a group may relate to its geographic region. Pinckney wanted the fourth-graders to recognize that cultural attributes, like food, shelter, and clothing, are determined in part by climate, economy, and natural resources. In short, she wanted to make information on Indians a vehicle for the development of higher-level thinking skills including causal analysis. Consequently, she developed a pre- and posttest that reflected both content knowledge and classification skill. The test in Figure 5.15 reflects what one student (Maggie) knew, and how she organized what she knew. This kind of test gave Pinckney a reference point, both for Maggie and for the

FIGURE 5.15   Pretest on Unit Concepts in Social Studies

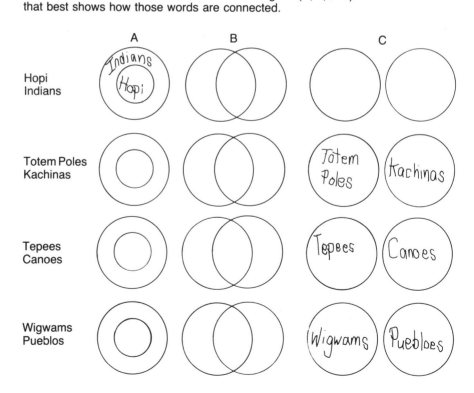

class as a whole. Maggie, like most others, knew that the Hopi are a subgroup of American Indians. She knew that canoes and tepees probably fell in different categories, but she also saw no relationship between kachinas and totem poles. She did not know enough about either wigwams or pueblos to think they shared a purpose.

Pinckney began teaching the unit by asking the whole class to brainstorm a list of all the words they knew about American Indians. On the blackboard, their list was extensive, but garbled. Her class spent the first day simply looking at their list and linking related items to form general categories. Working from some basic categories in the brainstormed list, she began to create exercises that would focus student inquiry and prepare the way for analytic thinking. Her early circle diagrams included the categories she would use later to encourage comparison and contrast of particular cultural attributes.

In Figure 5.16, the students had to create basic categories for comparison among Indian groups from different regions. Later exercises with circle diagrams gave students specific examples of culture in a format that encouraged comparison and contrast. Rather than lead the whole class in examining two or more tribes, she provided smaller groups with library resources and let them work cooperatively on two tribes of their choice (see Figure 5.17). The groups reported their findings to the whole class periodically.

Because related exercises contained identical items, students could use what they learned one day to learn more the next day. Also, by creating categories within categories, for example, the word *peaceful* next to the word *fishermen*, and the word *warriors* near the word *hunters*, Pinckney was making room both for specific examples from student reading and for hypothetical thinking. Does a source of livelihood relate to the extent of peace with one's neighbors? Is that true today in other cultures?

FIGURE 5.16 Circle Diagrams Guiding Cooperative Research Groups

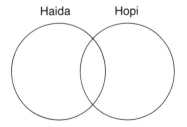

Haida   Hopi

myths, fishermen, farmers, carvers, skin and bark clothing, cotton clothing, weavers, plankhouse, pueblo, ceremonies, sign language, peaceful

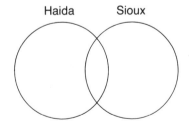

Haida   Sioux

fishermen, hunters, skin and bark clothing, carvers, tepee, warriors, plankhouse, ceremonies, myths, peaceful

FIGURE 5.17   Circle Diagrams Guiding Group Discussion

North American Indians

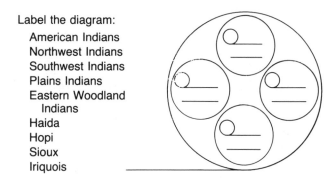

Label the diagram:
  American Indians
  Northwest Indians
  Southwest Indians
  Plains Indians
  Eastern Woodland
    Indians
  Haida
  Hopi
  Sioux
  Iriquois

By using simple circle diagrams as basis for one-dimensional comparison and contrast, Pinckney was also getting her fourth-graders ready for matrix analysis, a much more challenging visual and intellectual medium requiring well-developed skills with categories (McTighe & Lyman, 1988). To develop a matrix from her organizing categories, she simply extended the circles for regions over the circles for cultural attributes. Hanging on the wall, the lapped circles of the matrix in Figure 5.18 allowed her students to summarize their research on cultural differences among Indian groups. The matrix on newsprint became a wall-hanging for the classroom, an ever present reminder of what the class had already done—and what they were aiming to do. The matrix was based on their previous circle diagrams, but it opened the door to causal analysis and higher-level questioning.

FIGURE 5.18   Circle Diagrams Unified in Matrix for Summaries

North American Indians

	Shelter	Clothing	Food	Economy
Northwest				
Southwest				
Plains				
Eastern				

From the information in the matrix and the evidence attached to circle diagrams hanging around the room, Pinckney began to ask questions that depended on the information students had gathered, but extended beyond the limits of their research:

1. Questions requiring logical inference:
   a. What kind of shelter might you build if you lived in the Northwest? (or Plains? or Northeast?)
   b. What would you eat if you lived in the Northwest?

2. Questions requiring causal analysis:
   a. Why were the Northwest Indians particularly skilled in art?
   b. Why was art in the Plains and in the Northeast usually found on things the people used to make a living?

3. Questions of judgment:
   a. Which tribe was kindest to its neighbors?
   b. Which tribe was more peaceful?
   c. Which tribe made the best use of its natural resources?
   d. Which tribe was most likely to develop sign language?

4. Questions of value:
   a. Which tribe would you like to belong to if you were old?
   b. Which tribe would you want to belong to if you were poor?
   c. To which tribe would you want to belong?

Maps, circle diagrams, and matrices remained on the wall throughout the unit, changing as students gathered new information or recognized the potential of a hidden category. Each time the class finished a section, Pinckney asked the students if there was anything they would want to change on existing diagrams. Soon, the students recognized that they were working with broad geographic regions rather than narrowly defined tribal groups, a paradigm shift that would allow them to analyze the relationship between culture and environment. As they extended their investigation from the tribe to the region, one girl said, "Look how much more information we have now!" After other students challenged her observation, she said, "Well, we really don't have more, but it seems like a lot more because it's more organized and it makes so much more sense."

AN EXPANDING MARGIN OF ERROR

Working with categories opens the door to discovery—and to error. In a limited number of fields, a limited number of categories (linked to proven laws) can be assumed to be immutable. Biological taxonomies, for example, which put all living things in a hierarchical system of groups, are exceptionally stable because they are relatively free of anomalies. (Still, scientists argue whether a dendrite is vegetable or mineral [Gould, 1987].) Circle diagrams in those areas can have "right answers." In other areas of inquiry, the creation of categories is an exercise in concept development. Circle diagrams in those areas provide a medium for inquiry and even speculation. In inquiry, error is part of the learning process.

Surely, our minds and hearts yearn for categorical accuracy in all of our concept making. But our hearts and minds want more as well. We want to know what facts "mean." We want a sense of what is true in the broader scheme of things. We want to predict the future based on what we know now. We want to control the future based on trends we perceive in the present. Categories provide the mind with a way to escape from its dependency on the senses. Categories bring order to the disarray of the mind's daily work. Order gives us power. It also give us wrong answers a good part of the time.

In working with circle diagrams, teachers should recognize potential tension between accuracy and utility as categories expand from the particular to the general. The senses have a wonderful corrective influence on the mind's play with categories. They bring us new information that destroys old categories and moves us toward more powerful concepts. Teachers should support students in seeking reliable information to assemble reliable categories. They should also support students in working from reliable categories toward concepts that may be less reliable but potentially more powerful. Causal speculation, hypothesis generation, prediction activities, and planning are high-level conceptual skills. All depend on categories that are a bit loose, questionable, and risky.

SUGGESTIONS FOR TEACHERS

1. Consider any of the following as sources of categories defining a subject area or unit:
   a. Table of contents in a text
   b. Topic headings within a chapter
   c. List of subjects in a curriculum guide
   Create a circle diagram that would allow you to introduce the course or unit to your students on the first day of class.

2. For any general topic in your subject area, brainstorm a list of words that represents essential concepts for a unit in that area. Using those words, create a pre- or posttest for the unit, using circle diagrams as a medium for answers.

3. Line the front of your room with shoe boxes. Over a week's period, ask students to drop in the boxes things they have found

that may be interesting to others in the class. On the final day, ask the class to begin reducing the number of boxes and developing labels that will let them quickly locate objects they have found. Go for the fewest boxes and the greatest efficiency.

4. Create metaphor exercises with two-celled diagrams in which one cell is a set of terms requiring memorization. When students have labeled the second cell, ask them to fill in the circles with shared attributes and distinguishing attributes.

5. For a homework assignment with reading, develop a simple circle diagram that asks the students to use categories or concepts to collect examples. Use student diagrams to start the next class.

6. For any assignment using circle diagrams, ask students to write a paragraph explaining why they would use a simple circle diagram or why they would use a lapped circle or Venn diagram. Record what the students say about categories and about language on the blackboard or overhead.

Helping Students Reflect on Their Thinking

Even when your students experience success in using a graphic organizer for understanding the subject area, they will not automatically see wider usage for the technique they employed. They will need your help in finding other situations where the same technique would work as well. When your students are using a graphic to think about some part of content, make some effort to let them: (1) review the process they used to think and (2) look for other situations in or out of school where the same process might work. We can call the transfer of a thinking process a "Bridge."

A Bridge for Thinking

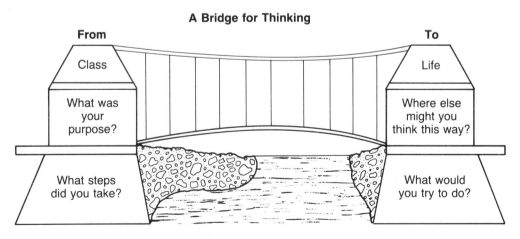

- What other subjects use categories to organize information?
- What careers or jobs depend on clear categories or groups?
- What are the risks in making a mistake?
- When you are in a situation requiring grouping for a distinct purpose, what tricks have you learned?

REFERENCES

Chomsky, N. (1973). *Language and Mind.* New York: Harcourt Brace Jovanovitch.

Clarke, J. H. (1983). The effectiveness of remediation among high risk students of different ages. ERIC HE 015–832, ED227–723

Clarke, J. H., & Wittes, S. (1977). *The Clarke Reading Self Assessment Survey.* San Rafael, CA: Academic Therapy Publications.

Feuerstein, R.; Rand, R.; Hoffman, M.; & Miller, R. (1980). *Instrumental Enrichment: An Intervention Program for Cognitive Modifiability.* Baltimore: University Park Press.

Gardner, H. (1983). *Frames of Mind: The Theory of Multiple Intelligences.* New York: Basic Books.

Gould, S. J. (1987). Animal, vegetable or mineral? *Harvard Magazine.* November/December, 73–74.

Halpern, D. (1984). *Thought and Knowledge: An Introduction to Critical Thinking.* Hillsdale, NJ: Lawrence Erlbaum.

Hill, J. M. (1986). Geometry for grades K–6. *Readings from the Arithmetic Teacher.* Reston, VA: National Council of Teachers of Mathematics. ED280699

Husaim, J. S., & Cohen, L. B. (1981). Infant learning of ill defined categories. *Merrill-Palmer Quarterly,* 27(4), 443–456.

Jones, B. F.; Palincsar, A. S.; Ogle, D. S.; & Carr, E. G. (1987). *Strategic Teaching and Learning: Cognitive Instruction in the Content Areas.* Alexandria, VA: ASCD Publications.

Justice, E. M. (1985). Categorization as a preferred memory strategy: Developmental changes during elementary school. *Developmental Psychology,* 21(6), 1105–1110.

Kinnison, L. R., & Pickens (1984). Teaching vocabulary to the learning disabled student from an interactive view of reading comprehension. ED276222

Kuhn, T. S. (1970). *The Structure of Scientific Revolutions.* 2nd ed. Chicago: University of Chicago Press.

Letteri, C. A. (1982). Teaching students how to learn, *Theory into Practice,* 35.

Lingle, J. H.; Altom, M. W.; & Medin, D. L. (1984). Of cabbages and kings: Assessing the extendability of natural object concept models to social things. In R. S. Wyer & T. K. Krull (Eds.), *Handbook of Social Cognition,* Vol 1. Hillsdale, NJ: Lawrence Erlbaum.

Marzano, R. J.; Brandt, R.; Hughes, C.; Jones, B. F.; Presseisen, B.; Rankin, S.; & Suhor, C. (1987). *Dimensions of Thinking: A Framework for Curriculum and Instruction.* Alexandria, VA: ASCD Publications.

McTighe, J., & Lyman, Jr., F. T. (1988). Cueing thinking in the classroom: The promise of theory embedded tools. *Educational Leadership,* 45(7), 18–25.

Nickerson, R. S.; Perkins, D. N.; & Smith, E. E. (1985). *The Teaching of Thinking* (Chap 5). Hillsdale, NJ: Lawrence Erlbaum.

Neimark, E. D. (1987). *Adventures in Thinking.* New York: Harcourt Brace Jovanovich.

Piaget, J. (1964). *Judgment and Reasoning in the Child.* Patterson, NJ: Littlefield.

Postman, N., & Weingartner, C. (1969). *Teaching as a Subversive Activity.* New York: Dell.

Sternberg, R. J. (1985). *Beyond IQ. A Triarchal Theory of Intelligence.* Cambridge/New York: Cambridge University Press.

Travers, R. M. (1982). *Essentials of Learning.* New York: MacMillan.

Vygotsky, L. (1986) *Thought and Language* (trans by A. Kuzulin). Cambridge, MA: MIT Press.

Wilson, J. (1963). *Thinking with Concepts.* Cambridge: Cambridge University Press.

Winocur, S. L. (1987). Developing lesson plans with cognitive objectives. In A. Costa (Ed.), *Growing Minds: A Resource Book for Teaching Thinking.* Alexandria, VA: ASCD Publications.

6

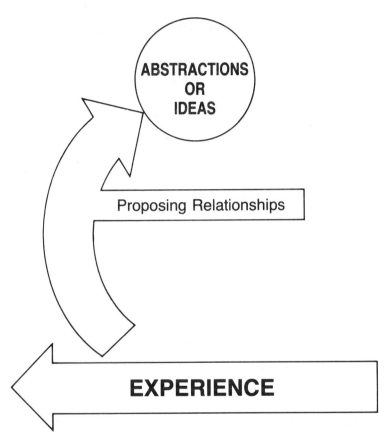

To say that intellectual structures are built by the learner rather than taught
by a teacher does not mean they are built from nothing.
—SEYMOUR PAPERT, *Mindstorms*

Organizing Propositions

IN THIS CHAPTER, WE WILL USE THE PROPOSITION AS THE basic building block for thinking, much as categories and concepts were the building blocks in the preceding chapters. A proposition is a statement of relationship among concepts. A proposition can be almost any declaration, including statements of fact or far-reaching abstractions such as hypotheses, rules, principles, or laws. Various subject areas use many different symbol systems to create propositions: math can use numbers, letters, and relational signs; chemistry can use element symbols and other relational signs; films juxtapose images to assert relationships. Any of these languages can create propositions, but verbal language in the form of sentences provides the basis for most propositions in school, as well as in this chapter.

INDUCTIVE BREAKDOWN: ELEVENTH GRADE

My oldest daughter, Cindy, returned from high school one day last year to face the usual battery of questions: "What happened in school today?" I asked. Her habitual reply, "Nothing," was meant to signal me away to other subjects, but this time I held the course.

"Come on, just tell me something," I asked again.

"Wet hair in math," she said.

I sat down with pencil in hand to indicate my resolve. "Just start at the beginning and take me through," I said. "Start with first period." As she spoke, I wrote out a synopsis of her day:

	Period	Activity
8:00	Gym	Volleyball
8:43	Math	A^2 plus B^2 equals C^2
9:28	French	Irregular verbs
10:17	Study Hall	Brian broke up with Heather; he was devastated.
11:00	Music/Lunch	"Adeste Fidelis," five times; macaroni and cheese; more "Adeste Fidelis"
12:32	American Studies (English & Social Studies)	*The Open Boat*; U.S. Grant and Reconstruction
2:14	Study Hall	Did half the math problems; Heather wants me to call Tim for her.

Bus ride: 45 minutes

"That's quite a lot," I said, somewhat at loose ends. "What do you make of all of that?"

"Wet hair in math," she said. "I hate having wet hair in math."

With considerable effort, I was able to extract an "episodic" record of my daughter's day, represented by the time line in Figure 6.1. Was my daughter's day a meaningless series of unrelated events? The day at school seemed to wash around her, leaving scant residue, like "wet hair in math" and her friend Heather's need to get a signal to Tim. I was not able to overcome the obstacles to obtaining a "semantic" record of meaning derived from that day. Perhaps my status as father made that unlikely. Perhaps the press of her need to call Tim intervened. Still, I was troubled by the possibility that all the activity at school arranged for the purpose of meaningful learning should leave no meaningful trace.

The task of preparing the mind to make meaningful connections among events in experience cannot be taken lightly. After all, the episodic memory and all the buffers in the perceptual system are there to protect the delicate machinery of reasoning from overloading. The days and minutes pass. If mere survival is the goal of our days, we can succeed simply by getting one minute to blur into the next. Unless we make a special effort to find meaning among the events in our experience—and have the tools to locate relationships—we may not find much meaning at all.

We are asking too much of any day if we ask that events line up nicely to support the development of meaning. Meaning is not embedded in experience the way diamonds are embedded in the mother stone. Our minds create meaning by juxtaposing related events and defining their

FIGURE 6.1   A Day at School as a Series of Episodes

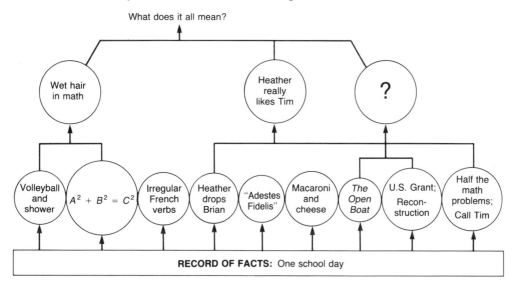

relationship. To find a relationship, we have to seek it out. We are able to draw inference automatically, but the ordinary flow of events does not necessarily trigger our ability to infer and make meaning. My daughter's teachers had gone to the trouble of lining up social studies and English in a thematic block called American Studies. Still, she treated Stephen Crane's *The Open Boat* and Grant's reconstruction as unrelated episodes. If we want students at any grade level to seek out relationships in the content of our classes, we have to tell them about that purpose and give them some tools for making connections. An inductive tower is a graphic organizer for making meaning from potentially related propositions.

MAPPING INDUCTION WITH PROPOSITIONS

To a large extent, success in the subject areas depends on using an established symbol system to organize propositions that describe some general truth about experience. Students need practice to learn any symbol system. They also have to practice to gain control of the process by which they organize propositions and construct abstract propositions with explanatory power. The purpose of this chapter is to introduce a graphic organizer for this kind of induction. An *inductive tower* is a graphic organizer that represents the process of gathering factual propositions at the concrete level into more abstract propositions at the conceptual level.

Inductive thinking such as that represented in a "tower" is one way the mind can construct a model for thinking in the subject areas. The term *abduction* has been used to describe this kind of inductive thinking—the process of generating hypothetical propositions from a set of inconclusive facts (Holland et al., 1986). Inductive towers represent a special way of thinking:

1. Small bits of perceived experience are linked to form larger ideas, stated as propositions.
2. One proposition becomes meaningful through its relation to other propositions.

Teachers can help students develop reliable propositions in the subject areas and then organize related propositions into hierarchical structures. As they do, they will also encourage awareness of inductive skill, with a rough language to use in managing its structure. Figure 6.2 represents the basic structure of an inductive tower, a structure of propositions with facts on the bottom and theory at the top (Clarke, Gilbert, & Raths, 1989).

The graphic form of an inductive tower lets teachers and students manage the process of deriving meaning from experience. It assumes that the teaching of content may rely on a vast and often amorphous array of

FIGURE 6.2   Graphic Structure of an Inductive Tower

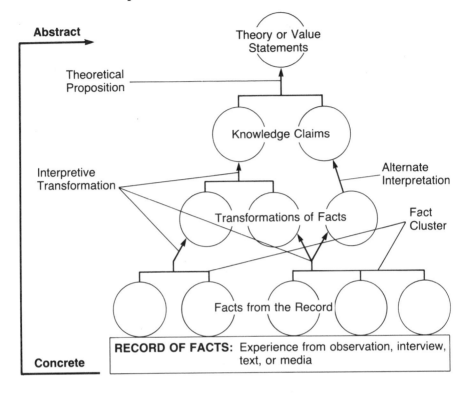

"factual" information. In making a tower from any source, students *search and scan* their experience of the material to find a *record of facts* that seem to imply some meaning. They make connections or *links among facts,* drawn as arrows in the diagram, to express *interpretive transformations,* propositions that can stand in place of the facts that generated them. Two or more transformations can also be linked to form *knowledge claims,* assertions of generalized truth at a more abstract level. Two or more knowledge claims can generate *theoretical propositions,* which propose cause/effect relationships, *or value propositions,* which use general knowledge to assert something about the way things ought to be. The lines (links) and circles (nodes) become a map of inductive thinking.

Inductive towers give teachers and students a way to "map" the process of abstracting meaningful inferences from concrete information in the subject areas. Whether the concrete, factual information comes from books, films, lectures, library research, or physical experience, an inductive tower shows all the facts that contribute to meaning as well as steps in the path toward generalization. An inductive tower gives students and their teacher a medium for reducing observations, which may be numerous, to a lesser number of meaningful, useful, and durable ideas—theories, laws, value statements, and related predictions.

Since we can neither monitor all the observations a young person makes from the classroom nor trace the connections among those observations, we find it hard to spot the errors in perception or induction that inhibit further learning. An inductive tower lets us see the concepts a student is using to construct some small part of a world view. It also lets us see the inductive links among concepts. Making both the material and the process visible helps students and teachers to build intellectual structures from content in the subjects areas. Inductive towers use some of the conventions of concept mapping: lines for expressing relationships (links) and circles or boxes for expressing concepts (nodes). Teachers use inductive towers to teach their students how to organize an array of concrete facts so the facts support the emergence of theories or value positions.

Gowin (Novak & Gowin, 1984) provided a theoretical basis for towers by proposing a model of learning and thinking with two wings (see Figure 6.3). On the left wing of Gowin's "vee," an individual's prior knowledge (in the form of theories, principles, and concepts) directs and controls the acquisition of new knowledge from experience. On the right wing, the mind transforms a record of perceived facts into more abstract propositions which then transform the structure of prior knowledge. The left side of Gowin's "vee" represents the mind's work with prior knowledge, the theories, principles, and concepts we use to organize our understanding, to create or modify existing value positions. On the left side of the "vee," prior knowledge directs how we perceive the world of experience. The right wing of Gowin's "vee" gives teachers guidelines for creating a map of induction from any "record" of experience, as in an inductive tower. In Gowin's conception of learning, both sides of the "vee"

FIGURE 6.3 Inductive Thinking as the Right Side of Gowin's "Vee"

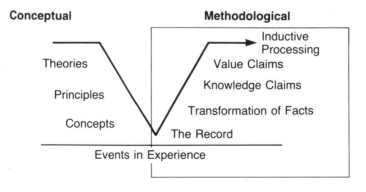

interact continuously, with perceptions changing what is known and the known influencing what is seen. In constructing a tower, students link and interpret propositions from content, adding in pieces of their prior knowledge as it affects their thinking.

In classroom teaching, the purpose of the tower format is to allow students to visualize their own processing and to compare their inductive thinking with the thinking of others. In using a tower, students can see themselves changing their minds as they confront new facts or alternative interpretations. The structure of an inductive tower also lets students think together in cooperative groups working on any array of facts from a record. Towers can provide the basis for independent research papers in which students work to develop a theoretical position grounded in "facts."

BUILDING AN INDUCTIVE TOWER

In constructing an inductive tower, students work from a base of facts they have collected or the teacher has collected for them. If the students arrange their facts at the bottom of a large piece of paper, they can make connections between related facts with circles and linking lines. If the students have collected their facts separately on 3 × 5 cards, they can simply use a paper clip to tie the cards together. Every time students link two or more propositions, they must write out a new proposition that interprets the linked facts (on a new 3 × 5 card or above their line of facts). They treat their inferred propositions as true, because the facts on which they are based is true. When they have linked and interpreted the facts, they can link their interpretations in a similar manner and propose a "knowledge claim" or generalization. Their knowledge claims can be linked to support a theory, prediction, or value position. Figures 6.4, 6.5, and 6.6 constitute examples of how a teacher might introduce inductive thinking using node-link connectors.

To learn to manage inductive mapping, students should start with simple exercises and work toward more complex problems. In teaching inductive processing using the visual medium of a tower, a teacher should consider beginning with simple transformations from a few facts on a handout or overhead transparency. Most subject areas are replete with facts that can be used to create practice exercises. The U.S. Census, newspaper and magazine articles, and films can provide a steady source of potentially meaningful facts. The first step for a teacher is simply to define the factual base. When students are just practicing, it is usually best for the teacher to hand out some facts, arranged along the base of the paper. Several transformations are possible from the record of the facts in Figure 6.4. Different students will draw different inferences from these

FIGURE 6.4   Using Induction to Transform Two Facts

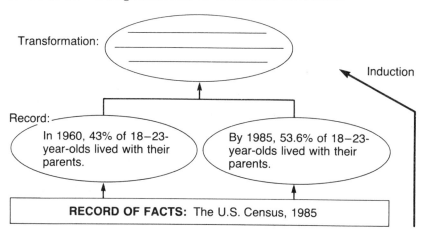

two facts. Some students will make low-risk transformations, logical inferences based directly on the facts. Other students will generalize more wildly, based on the facts and their own prior knowledge. Any of the following propositions could be asserted from the two facts in Figure 6.4:

> *Logical Inference:*   More young people today stay home longer
> (Low Risk)   than did young people a generation ago.
>
> More young people prefer to stay home now.
>
> It's getting easier to stay at home longer.
>
> Parents are getting easier to live with.
>
> (High Risk)   Parents have greatly improved their perform-
> *Generalization:*   ance.

A large class might quickly generate these transformations—and many more. It might take a class period to arrive at resolution.

The closer the students stay to logical inference, the safer their propositions would be. The further they move toward generalization, the more vulnerable their propositions would be—to countervailing facts, alternative interpretations of fact, and counterarguments. Students who leap toward generalizations based on the facts are usually asked by others for more facts. They may respond with more facts, or with further generalizations and related knowledge claims. Through discussion, students can be led to see that many transformations may be consistent with the facts, but that logical inference is easier to defend. The task of the teacher is to show students how inferential leaps carry greater risk and call for further facts and further induction. Several rounds of exercises might be necessary before students adopt a critical perspective on their own reasoning, or the reasoning of others.

With more facts in the record, students have to make choices in finding inductive links and generating new propositions. Figure 6.5 contains four additional facts about young people. Mathematically, there are 24 possible interpretive clusters in a set of four facts (4 × 3 × 2 × 1 = 24). Different students will make different links and draw different inferences. Some students might draw an inference from a single fact, such as the suicide rate, based on their assumptions about suicide. "Young people often feel despair," they might assert. They might draw one inference from three facts, as in Figure 6.5, which together can suggest one interpretation. "Divorce rates, marriage rates, and unemployment rates all point to a lack of positive choices for the young," they could assert. Under most circumstances, the teacher can put all the student interpretations into the tower. If an interpretation is ill founded or risky, it may not get any attention when students try to link interpretations to make knowledge claims. On an inductive tower, faulty lines of reasoning come to a natural end.

As students move up the tower, their language becomes more abstract. Their need for qualifying words becomes greater. Potentially, they can be led to see the increasingly hypothetical nature of their thinking. As they move higher toward abstraction, they may also be led to recognize their increasing need for more facts. As they establish generalizations or knowledge claims with which they are satisfied, they are reach-

FIGURE 6.5   Using Induction to Transform Generalizations to Theory

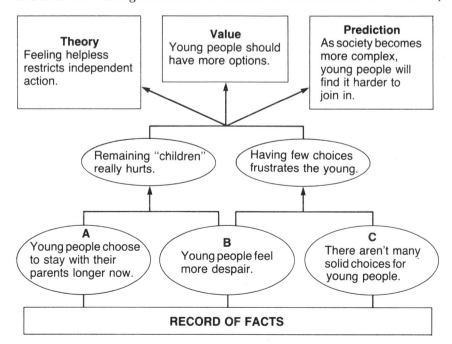

ing the top of the tower. At the teacher's direction, they can use their knowledge claims to generate an explanatory theory, a value position, or a prediction. Figure 6.6 contains examples of three varieties of abstraction from two illustrative knowledge claims at the top of a tower.

By linking propositions A and B (see Figure 6.6), students could generalize on the pain of remaining childlike. By linking B and C, they could generate a related proposition about frustration. Other links and propositions are possible. With those two generalizations established, a teacher could ask students to develop an explanatory theory, a prediction based on current facts or a value statement about what should be true. To avoid a confusing mix of propositions at the top of the tower, a teacher should be specific about the type of propositions he or she wants, perhaps by specifying the type of question he or she wants answered:

> A *theory* proposes a cause/effect relationship, answering the question "WHY?"
>
> A *value statement* proposes a standard or course of action, answering the question "HOW SHOULD IT BE?"
>
> A *prediction* describes a likely future, answering the question "WHAT WILL HAPPEN NOW AS A RESULT?"

All three types of propositions depend on causal reasoning. All are hypothetical and all develop power through reasoning based on current facts. Figure 6.7 is an inductive tower based on the six propositions from the preceding examples, arranged to support a prediction: What will happen

FIGURE 6.6   Linking Several Facts to Make Several Transformations

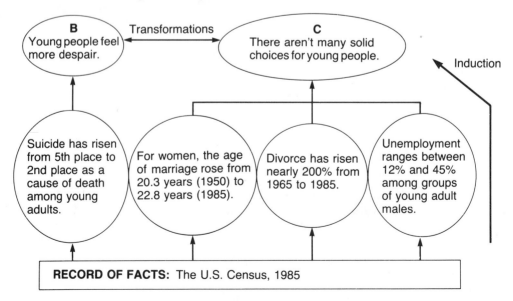

FIGURE 6.7 An Inductive Tower Supporting a Prediction

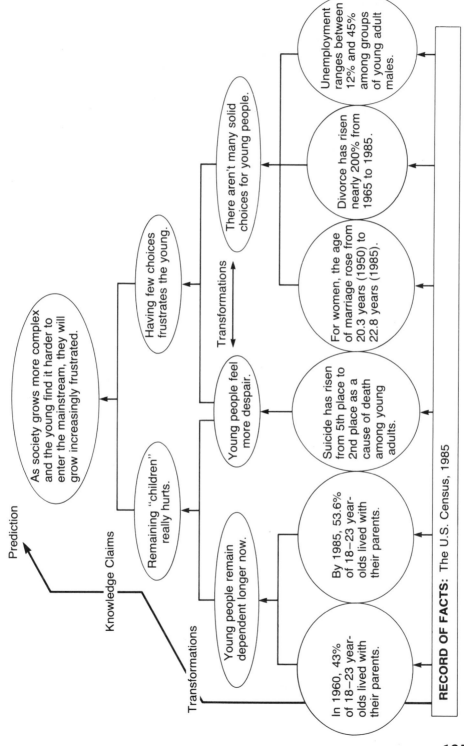

to the young during the next decade? The tower in Figure 6.7 supports the proposition that the young will experience increasing frustration as society becomes increasingly complex and difficult to enter. Is this proposition supportable, given the facts? Probably. Is this the only prediction the facts would support? Clearly not. Is the prediction accurate? Further facts and further interpretation are necessary to answer this question.

The purpose of a tower is to let students think through the facts and generate theories, value positions, or predictions consistent with the facts. From a fully constructed tower, students can write conventional research papers, with the facts as documentation in separate paragraphs. They could also present speeches and answer questions from their classmates on the quality of their reasoning. Differences in value positions can become the basis of debates within a class. Different predictions can generate independent projects on "The Future of Youth" or field investigations of military service, college education, entry-level work requirements, or the psychology of suicide. Inductive thinking allows great latitude and usually opens more questions than it closes. The purpose of inductive towers is to raise further questions and to support the development of hypothetical thinking.

MAPPING PROPOSITIONS IN CONTENT TEACHING

As sap began to flow in March, Terri Sturgeon wanted to begin a unit on Making Maple Syrup with her kindergarten class. This unit had been popular with the students in previous years. It involved lots of activity—a trip to the maple orchard and the chance to taste some fresh maple candy on snow. To see whether her students could think inductively, Sturgeon devised an experiment in which the children would go to a sugar house and test the quality of the syrup. Figure 6.8 shows the experiment with induction for kindergarten students: three glasses of syrup that the students would have to judge—a subject in which they already had developed some expertise.

The sugar maker filled three glasses with syrup of different grades. Sturgeon gave each student three round pieces of paper labeled *dark*, *darker*, and *darkest*. She gave them three more circles labeled *sweet*, *sweeter*, and *sweetest*. As they looked and tasted, they put their labels next to the glasses they thought darkest and sweetest. When they counted the labels for each glass, they could see that the lightest syrup was also thought to be sweetest—a transformation of facts. Asked to draw a conclusion from the way they had labeled the glasses, two students soon stated in unison that the sweeter the syrup, the lighter the color (a knowledge claim). At the level of causation, they had more trou-

FIGURE 6.8   An Inductive Tower from Experience

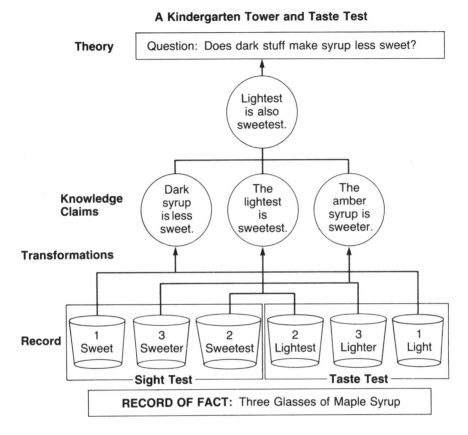

A Kindergarten Tower and Taste Test

ble. Was something in the darker syrup to make it less sweet? (They could not know that nitrates darken syrup.) Value questions were also troublesome. Several students preferred dark syrup with its stronger taste to lighter syrup. The class could see that lighter syrup was always sweeter, but it was not always best.

In the early grades, the inductive tower technique can help students look carefully at stories they read and make personal interpretations. The frame of the tower helps students develop a purpose for their reading and a way to focus on that purpose. With success in simpler focusing techniques such as time lines and story frames, Sally Kaufman found that she could teach her third-grade students to build inductive towers from the fables they were studying. The fables were quite popular among the students. What did they "mean"? After reading a fable and reacting to it in small groups, her students went back to the story to select critical events from the story line. They put their critical events on 3 × 5 cards, which they could move around on their desks, physically linking related "facts."

Figure 6.9 is an inductive tower based on the time line of events students selected as the meaningful record.

The third-grade team in this example was highly eclectic in gathering a record. Four "facts" from the story generated three transformations showing who was happy and who was not. Because the cheater was not happy, the team decided it was usually not worth it to cheat. Using three levels in a tower can reduce frustration among younger students, who may not need to discriminate between knowledge, value, theory, and prediction.

This third-grade tower is quite simple, but it represents some of the characteristics of inductive thinking. One fact, such as "the wolf stole some sheep," can have more than one meaning (one for the shepherd who becomes "unhappy" and one for the wolf who does the stealing and becomes a cheat). The facts available may not always justify a firm conclusion. This group was able to generate only a tentative knowledge claim, "It is usually not worth it to cheat," they wrote. The group chose to avoid absolute statements because they could not tell from the story whether the wolf had succeeded at cheating before. They could not tell whether the shepherd might also be a cheat. In the small group discussion, they had become a bit suspicious of the "facts" in their record. Were they look-

FIGURE 6.9 Third-Grade Inductive Tower from Reading

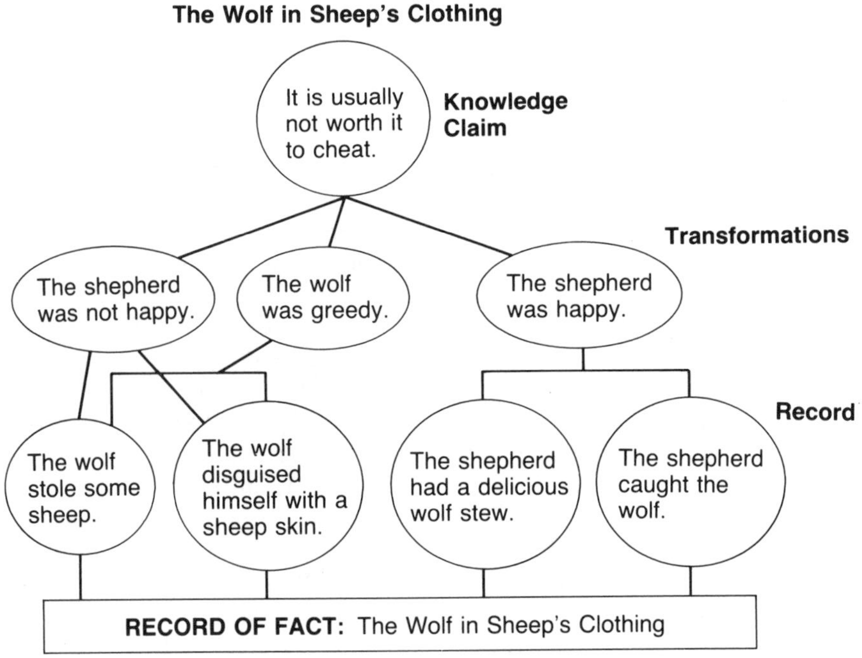

The Wolf in Sheep's Clothing

ing at the whole story? Inductive thinking very seldom leads to final statements of the truth, in third grade or in scientific research.

As Sally Kaufman's third-grade class became increasingly skillful in building towers, they began to include more facts and make more inferential links. Even in the third grade, inductive towers can help students manage complex forms of thinking, as the tower on "The Country Mouse" shows (see Figure 6.10).

This third-grade team selected six "facts" from the record. Six facts could generate mathematically about 700 possible transformations of fact. Facing that number of possibilities, the country mouse team settled on three strong themes: being frightened, being lonely, and being happy. They could gather several facts for each knowledge claim. In choosing their road toward a value statement, they left other themes behind, such as the possible relationship between leaving home and being frightened. It is quite possible that this group (with prior knowledge) simply could

FIGURE 6.10 Third-Grade Tower from "The Country Mouse"

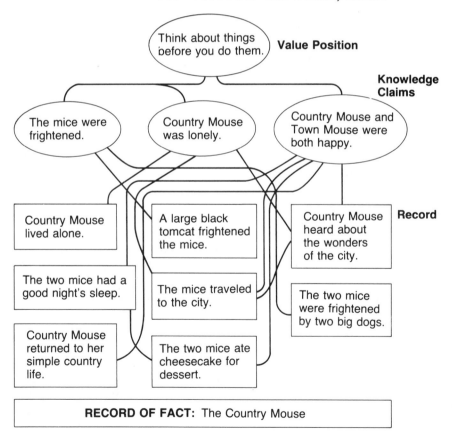

not accept the value position implied by that construction of facts. In their tower, the idea that both mice were originally happy is based on the largest number of facts. It is central to the reasoning that led them toward a fairly soft value position—that we should think before we act. Within the limits of their team structure and a class period, that is the position they close to develop.

A teacher does not have to let students search and scan to locate a suitable record of facts. To focus student attention on a certain construction of facts, a teacher can simply define the base and then let students work inductively from there. Peter Huber wanted his eleventh-grade American history class to review the causes of the American Revolution and to make connections between economic, political, and philosophical forces in history. Using the textbook as a base, he created a record from all three realms, including ideas as well as facts. The base of facts in Figure 6.11 could become a small group or individual homework assignment. Because the groups tended to link different "facts" to make transformations and different transformations to make knowledge claims, they could arrive at different theoretical explanations or value positions:

- England should have known that the Enlightenment would breed in the Colonies.
- In the end, having the resources is the key to independence.
- Ideas have to wait until time is right.

Each of these statements has explanatory power. Each is "grounded in the facts" and each is quite different. The differences provoke discussion, including returning to the base of facts and to the text for more support. In creating a base for a tower, a teacher can provide facts consistent with one idea, present facts that point in two directions, or offer facts that suggest ambiguities and conflict in the record. Some teachers have presented a few facts that point in one clear direction, and then added in further facts that complicate the issue and force rethinking.

The role of the teacher in showing students inductive towers is not to guide the students toward preordained answers or to insist on a certain set of transformations. Inductive thinking can only generate probable right answers. When students are working with towers, they are working with probabilities. In using an inductive tower to help students manage facts, the teacher's job is to keep the goal in view and to help students recognize the problems they face and the decisions they make. The teacher's role is to help students recognize the limits as well as the power of their inductive thinking. A teacher can help by showing students the influence of prior knowledge on making new knowledge. If a student believes that additional facts are necessary, these too can become special "cards" in the "record." If students have overlooked a transformation, a teacher can ask about it—or not. Even in the early grades, collaborative

FIGURE 6.11   Homework Assignment as a Tower, Grade 11

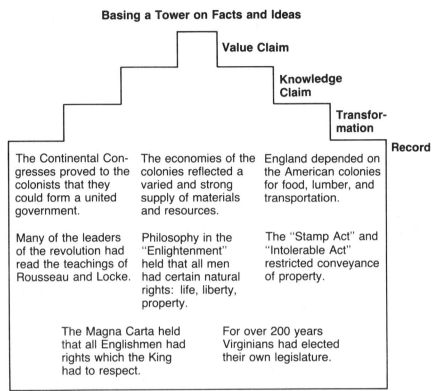

Basing a Tower on Facts and Ideas

Value Claim

Knowledge Claim

Transformation

Record

The Continental Congresses proved to the colonists that they could form a united government.	The economies of the colonies reflected a varied and strong supply of materials and resources.	England depended on the American colonies for food, lumber, and transportation.
Many of the leaders of the revolution had read the teachings of Rousseau and Locke.	Philosophy in the "Enlightenment" held that all men had certain natural rights: life, liberty, property.	The "Stamp Act" and "Intolerable Act" restricted conveyance of property.
The Magna Carta held that all Englishmen had rights which the King had to respect.	For over 200 years Virginians had elected their own legislature.	

thinking in the towers format is political. Discussion can easily become heated. The value of the tower format is its visibility. It can provide a path to answers; it can also raise further questions.

GRADUAL DISCLOSURE OF THE RECORD

One way to reduce impulsive leaps past links in the evidence is to reduce the speed at which evidence is presented. Gradual disclosure of the record can force students to look more closely at each "fact" they see (Ducharme, 1970). It can also allow them time to feed in prior knowledge and make the basis of their interpretive transformations explicit. Gradual disclosure of the facts has application in any subject where students must interpret carefully to find meaning. Teachers can use several techniques to slow the flow of facts and encourage students to make new interpretive links as new information appears, such as the following.

Overheads With a poem, statistical evidence, quotations, or even photographs on a transparency, teachers can cover parts of the evidence with a paper and then reveal it frame by frame, asking students to make interpretive transformations as each new frame is revealed.

Data Cards Teachers can create collaborative groups of 3 to 5 members and hand to each member a different part of the record. With a different card in every hand, students have to work through the record one piece at a time. Poem pieces, story parts, facts in word problems, or newspapers clippings all can work.

Independent Research On a question of general concern, teachers can assign all students to collect a record of facts on 3 × 5 cards. Library resources, interviews with peers or parents, films, and personal observation can all provide part of the record. Then, working in groups or as a class, students can begin constructing a tower.

Rather than hand out the poem "The Red Wheelbarrow" by William Carlos Williams, I once chose to present the poem in four sequential frames, using a free write between frames as a medium for capturing student interpretations (see Figure 6.12). I used the short free writes as a base for discussion, then represented a general interpretation on the blackboard.

At first, each frame became the subject of interpretation. Then links between frames were also transformed. The first frame, "so much depends upon" generated only questions. With the second frame, "a red wheelbarrow," some students became suspicious. Others became derisive. The word *manure* captures their reaction. With the third frame, one student saw and tasted candy. Her response cast the wheelbarrow in a new light. It became "tasty." When the "white chickens" appeared in the fourth frame, she tasted feathers. "Yuck," she wrote. But another student imagined green grass sparkling. In linking knowledge claims, the students soon rejected the inferential path represented by "manure" and saw only a pretty picture, almost tasting good. As I slowly revealed new frames, the students' interpretations became more positive. The positive path in their interpretations and knowledge claims eventually allowed them to assert a final value position—that a great deal does depend on seeing well and remembering. They had begun to understand William Carlos Williams. Slow disclosure helped them see the poem as a mystery they could unravel. It may have prevented instantaneous (impulsive) rejection of the text.

Teachers can also use gradual disclosure to help students manage word problems in mathematics. Students may have difficulty with word problems not because they cannot do the computation, but because they cannot reason their way to seeing how computation applies to a particular problem. Slow disclosure and a tower format can help them think

FIGURE 6.12   Gradual Disclosure as a Tower Foundation

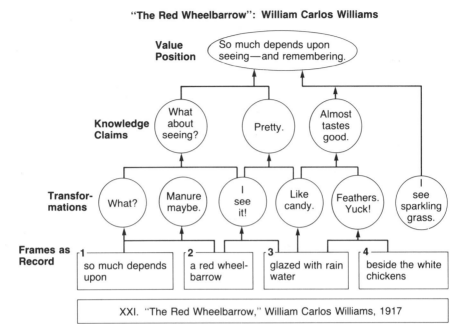

"The Red Wheelbarrow": William Carlos Williams

XXI. "The Red Wheelbarrow," William Carlos Williams, 1917

William Carlos Williams, *Collected Poems, Vol. I, 1909–1939.* Copyright 1938 by New Directions Publishing Corporation. Reprinted by permission of New Directions Publishing Corporation. U.S. and Canadian rights. For British rights, please refer to Carcanet Press.

through relationships before they impulsively start to plug in numbers. If elements of the problem are disclosed slowly, students have a chance to make some early connections, assessing what they have in terms of what they need. The word problem map in Figure 6.13 shows how certain facts, like river speed and boat speed, can be transformed to make a "real" speed for the boat. It also provides the base for intuitive guessing: Chicago is not that far. It shows the students a clear goal, time of arrival, which may prevent them from stopping at the moment they have calculated 1 2/3 hours as elapsed time. It can also show them when prior knowledge is needed: How many minutes are in 2/3 of an hour? By making the steps visible, a tower may also help students troubleshoot their thinking and find errors.

Inductive and deductive thinking both play a role in problem solving. (Deductive problem solving is treated in Chapter 10.) Most teachers would agree that having the facts straight is a critical first step in problem solving, surely as important as having a clear goal. Teachers can use a tower format to emphasize the importance of data collection to problem solving.

High-school teacher Scott Link used the inductive tower as a frame

FIGURE 6.13   Tower Map of a Word Problem

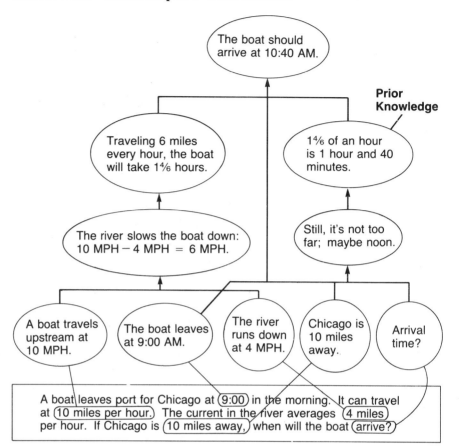

for teaching data collection in his automobile mechanics course. After he had introduced parts of the ignition system, the fuel system, and the basic mechanics of a car engine to his class, he shifted focus to the collection of facts as the key to success in engine repair. He did not try to tell the facts to the class. Instead, each morning he sabotaged a working engine to eliminate a critical link—one important fact about why engines work each day. Using an inductive tower, the class then had to locate the missing "fact" and start the engine (see Figure 6.14). Using an inductive process of fact gathering, rather than a series of preordained procedural checks, Link was able to prove to his students that they could discover problems and solve them. Their knowledge of procedures grew as they succeeded each morning in starting the sabotaged engine. Inductively, through gradual exposure to an engine that would not start, the students developed more abstract models of the systems that make cars work.

FIGURE 6.14   A Tower as a Aid in Problem Solving

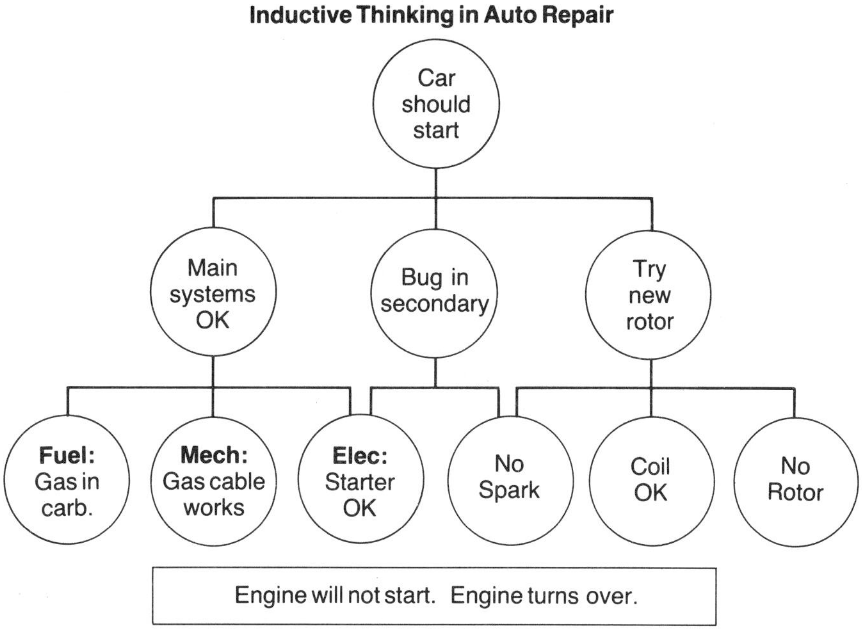

Inductive Thinking in Auto Repair

STREET LAW: A CASE STUDY

Larry Trombley teaches an elective course called Street Law in Social Studies for students who are about to finish high school. For many of his students, Street Law will be among the last formal courses they ever take. His purpose in the course is to introduce legal issues, procedures, and problems that his students may confront as adults in the community. The text proves difficult for many of his students, who often are not skillful readers, because it treats aspects of law in large conceptual clumps. One chapter, entitled "The Criminal Justice System," had proven particularly difficult for his students. Trombley did not believe that most of his students would understand the criminal justice system simply by reading the text and discussing it in class. He decided to make "The Criminal Justice System" an inquiry project for the whole class and to use an inductive tower as a medium for the investigation. He designed the unit on Street Law as an inductive process from fact gathering to theoretical analysis (see Figure 6.15).

An inductive tower would frame the unit and give the class a visual medium for their investigation. As shown in Figure 6.15, Larry Trombley assigned each class member to a collaborative group and each group to

FIGURE 6.15   A Tower as a Format for a Unit Plan

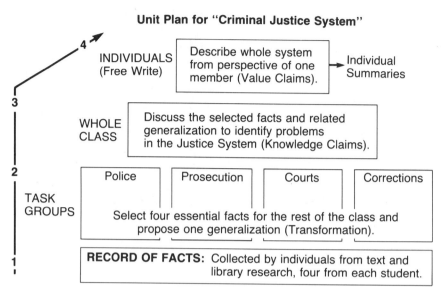

Unit Plan for "Criminal Justice System"

an aspect of the criminal justice system: police, courts, prosecution, and corrections. The first job of all students was to collect "facts" on their part of the justice system and to explain the facts to their group. Trombley gave each group a stack of 3 × 5 cards. On the first day, each team sent "runners" to the library to find relevant books and articles. Remaining team members began to scan the text for facts for the record. Most teams had amassed approximately 20 facts on 3 × 5 cards by the end of the second day.

On the third day, Trombley showed the whole class how to make inferences from facts by linking related ideas (cards) and making a transforming proposition on a new card. He also explained how some facts would become more important than others because of their support for a new inference. He asked each team to select four cards the whole class should understand and to generate a single transformation for those four facts. Sifting through the collection of facts and generating an acceptable transformation from four facts took each group an additional 40-minute period of argument and negotiation.

On the fourth day of the unit, the teams prepared to explain their four facts and transformations to the whole class. Trombley took his class to the auditorium and rolled out 30 feet of brown wrapping paper. Using magic markers, each team wrote out the facts they had selected from the "record" and the "transformations" they had generated from them. One group, the "police team," selected the four facts and interpretive transformation in Figure 6.16.

FIGURE 6.16   Selection of Facts with Interpretation from One Cooperative Group

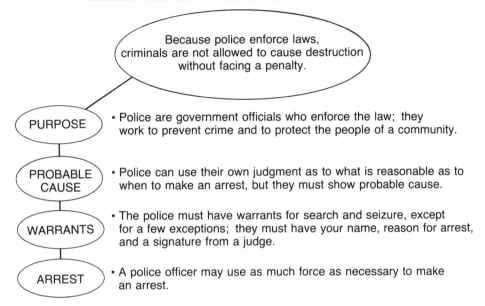

Selected Facts and a Transformation from Police Team

Because police enforce laws, criminals are not allowed to cause destruction without facing a penalty.

PURPOSE
• Police are government officials who enforce the law; they work to prevent crime and to protect the people of a community.

PROBABLE CAUSE
• Police can use their own judgment as to what is reasonable as to when to make an arrest, but they must show probable cause.

WARRANTS
• The police must have warrants for search and seizure, except for a few exceptions; they must have your name, reason for arrest, and a signature from a judge.

ARREST
• A police officer may use as much force as necessary to make an arrest.

The police group selected facts (from more than 20 possibilities) from their research—which defined the role of police, and then narrowed in on probable cause, the need for a warrant and the use of force—as most important for the whole class to understand. As the example from the police group shows, the groups also provided a label reflecting their reasoning in selecting the four facts. By the end of the period, the brown paper contained more than 16 factual statements, four interpretive statements, and a variety of cartoons and graffiti. The tower had a foundation.

On the fifth day, Larry Trombley again rolled out the wrapping paper covered with facts and transformations developed by the four collaborative groups and asked the entire class to peruse the whole thing, taking notes for their final paper and also looking for "claims" they could make about the entire criminal justice system. "What can you say about the criminal justice system?" he asked. "What general statements do you think you can defend on the basis of what you see here?" For 15 minutes, individuals walked up and down the tower, laid out in a hallway to allow access, with paper and pen in hand. They took notes and argued quietly with each other about different ways of looking at the facts. All the students wrote out at least one "claim" from the notes they had gathered.

When Trombley called the class back together to discuss their knowledge claims about the criminal justice system, discussion was vigorous. Using different links and different bases in fact, the class had generated a long list of possible knowledge claims, some of which were antithetical. Discussion grew hot. Some students thought the system oppressive and unfair; others thought it ineffectual and needlessly weak. Protagonists of one claim or another resorted to their bank of selected "facts," then to facts from their original research, then to facts picked up elsewhere, from the *Reader's Digest* and the daily paper, for example. Trombley tried to note important knowledge claims on the third layer of the huge brown paper tower. The bell cut short an active discussion.

Aiming to use the heated debate to propel the students into individual summaries, Trombley hung the now massive tower on the wall of his classroom. Each student would have to assert a single "conclusion" from the evidence in the tower and then define a clear line of reasoning. When the sixth class began, he pointed out lines of contention and debate resumed. Twenty minutes of argumentation followed, involving virtually every member of the class. Students could not agree on the purpose, the facts, or the primary problems in the justice system. Because discussion had led to no resolution, he used a focused "journal entry" to let each student stabilize a value position (see Chapter 3). "Assume that you are a working member of the system—a police officer, a prosecutor, a judge, or a corrections officer. In a seven-minute journal entry, describe the criminal justice system." The class ended with each student writing a concentrated version of criminal justice from one perspective.

Student journals were energized by the sense of conflict students had developed in working with the text and library research in the criminal justice system. The journals tended to crystalize the issues at the heart of earlier debate.

> **JOURNAL ENTRY: PROSECUTOR'S PERSPECTIVE**
> *My God, I can't believe this week. I've had 20 cases and I worked 80 hours and on weekends. The criminals just keep popping up everywhere. I haven't seen my wife in days. Why doesn't this system give me a break? Why doesn't the city hire more prosecuting attorneys so I don't have to take on 200 cases a year? As if my job isn't hard enough, I have to put up with all the red tape that comes between a degenerate and a cell.*

Using the free writes as a starting point for the next class, Trombley was able to move the students as individuals toward an explanatory statement of theory. Then he set about seeking one theoretical statement for all the individual theories. Collapsing antithetical knowledge claims into one involved considerable negotiating skill and editorial care. Still, on the basis of their own research and their collaborative work, the Street Law class could finally agree "The extent to which the criminal justice

His students did as well or better on the factual portion of the test as had students in prior years who had not constructed an inductive tower. On the essay portion of the test, however, they did considerably better than students from earlier years. The unit consumed as much time as it had in prior years, but it generated additional effects. His students were prepared to understand the procedures of the criminal justice system and adopt an evaluative stance. They could use the information they acquired in class to analyze problems in the criminal justice system and in the daily paper. They could also describe the process of induction that led them to their conclusion.

In describing induction, one student wrote:

> *The inductive tower, a huge visual aid, serves one purpose and serves it well. The purpose is to make a very specific response to a very large amount of information. As each group made a concluding statement, the vast broadness of the information was becoming much more narrowed. . . . As the class pondered on each concluding statement, (it) could make a final statement on the criminal justice system. The group that I was in (Five Starring Intellects) played a large role, as did the rest, in coming up with this statement. . . . With all of the information in hand, we put together our incredible brain power. Without the format of the inductive tower, I believe that the final statement would be very hard to come by and if reached it would be very painstaking and tedious. . . .*

In addition to seeing how the criminal justice system works, this member of "Five Starring Intellects" had gained a vision of the mind making sense of experience.

WHAT TOWERS CAN SHOW

In practicing with inductive towers in any content area, students begin to see a number of limitations in the inductive process:

1. Two people scanning experience for meaningful facts select different facts to make up a record. *None of us see experience through the same lens.*
2. There are many ways to make transformations from any record of facts, some of which emerge from the prior knowledge of different individuals. *In a group, prior knowledge expands the base of "facts."*

3. In moving toward knowledge claims, students usually experience some conflict and disagreement. *Prior knowledge contributes to interpretation, but it makes agreement difficult.*
4. In making value propositions or theoretical propositions explaining cause and effect, students begin to feel the insecurity that accompanies abstraction. *Students begin to see that theory making is often tentative, conditional, and fraught with perplexity.*

The visual convention of the tower lets students see the process of their own inductive thinking. If students work in small groups to build a tower, they learn to accommodate the perceptions, prior knowledge, and value positions of others. In a class-sized group, they can be led to see an "expert" teacher work through the process of reasoning which generates kowledge in most fields. Over time, students develop a language for describing their own inductive processes. Practice with propositions and induction, verbal and visual, can give them greater control over their own thinking (see Figure 6.18).

In creating an inductive tower, a student must represent the factual base and the process of arriving at conclusions. Because it is visible and public, a tower can help teachers reduce impulsive leaps toward value positions or global responses to limited facts. It can encourage focused scanning of the record, recognition of complex relationships, and the habit of testing and retesting abstract ideas against a continually emerging record of facts.

The purpose of inductive towers is not to represent truth as a given, but to show students how to work their way from any record of experience toward conclusions that are defensible in light of the facts available. When those facts reflect complexity, students have to use what they see in the facts, and what they know from prior experience, to reason well. They may have to introduce new facts at the base to arrive at a defensible theory. They have to balance the evidence and qualify categorical assertions. They may have to imagine a research process that would create new facts to test their theory. The tower lets them see their reasoning, in comparison to the reasoning of others. Applied with creativity, inductive towers can promote questioning and considerable controversy in academic subjects.

SUGGESTIONS FOR TEACHERS

1. To give students experience in identifying factual propositions, assign them the task of collecting five to ten facts from newspapers and magazines. For each fact, they should be able to identify a method they could use to verify the proposition as fact. If they

Helping Students Reflect on Their Thinking

Even when your students experience success in using a graphic organizer for understanding the subject area, they will not automatically see wider usage for the technique they employed. They will need your help in finding other situations where the same technique would work as well. When your students are using a graphic to think about some part of content, make some effort to let them: (1) review the process they used to think and (2) look for other situations in or out of school where the same process might work. We can call the transfer of a thinking process a "Bridge."

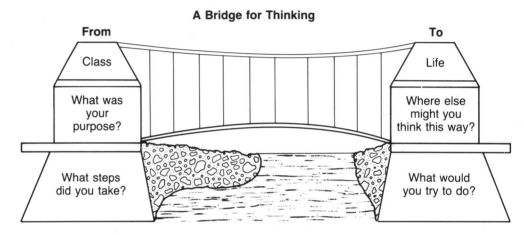

A Bridge for Thinking

- In what kind of school assignments does inductive thinking play a role?
- What jobs or careers depend on gathering facts and drawing conclusions?
- What are the biggest problems in this kind of thinking?
- Try to think of specific instances in which someone drew a wrong conclusion from the facts available. What caused the mistake in judgment?
- What guidelines would you offer to someone just starting to gather facts for an Inductive Tower?

REFERENCES

Clarke, J. H.; Gilbert, G.; & Raths, J. (1989). Inductive towers: Helping students see how they think. *Journal of Reading,* 33(2), 86–95.

Ducharme, E. (1970). Close reading through gradual disclosure. *English Journal,* Fall.

Holland, J. H.; Holyoake, K. J.; Nisbett, R. E.; & Thagard, P. R. (1986). *Induction: Processes of Inference, Learning and Discovery.* Cambridge, MA: MIT Press.

Novak, J., & Gowin, D. B. (1984). *Learning How to Learn.* Cambridge: Cambridge University Press.

SECTION III

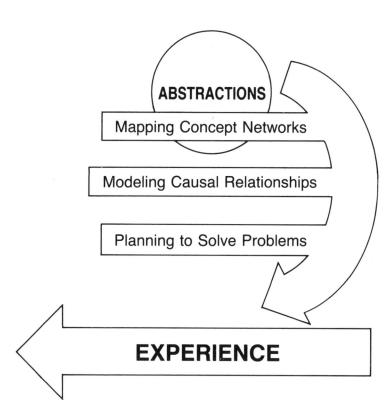

ABSTRACTIONS

Mapping Concept Networks

Modeling Causal Relationships

Planning to Solve Problems

EXPERIENCE

Frames for Deductive Thinking

LET US IMAGINE AGAIN THAT THE HUMAN MIND IS A HOUSE with many rooms. At the moment of birth, the doors are opened and load upon load of new information is trucked to the front porch. Mathematicians have estimated that the adult mind has the capacity to store somewhere between 100 trillion and 280 quintillion bits of information (Hunt, 1982a). Cognitive science has not yet figured out what a "bit" might be in the physiology of the brain, but if "bits" looked like ping-pong balls and the brain were an ordinary house, the human mind would have a space shortage within a few weeks after birth. Even if information in the mind consists of transactions among synapses, perhaps coded chemically and transmitted electronically as a frequency signal, the number of separate processes making up one memory creates a huge problem of access. The problem of access to stored information is formidable. Imagine recognizing a sudden need and then having to ransack an ordinary house full of ping-pong balls to find ball number 45,237,890,459. Bits of information dumped in random order on the porch of the mind are useless. Teaching should have the purpose of helping students organize what they know so it is both useful and accessible.

What do we do with information to make it meaningful, useful, and accessible when needed? The linear order of experience is perhaps the least useful structure for managing large volumes of information. The normal school day may be little more than a line of unrelated events. As in most of human affairs, the answer to the question of efficiency lies in organization. In previous chapters, you have already encountered some of the patterns that create efficiency in different kinds of mental processing. Episodic memory, the record of our perceived experience, may be organized in long "strings" of images linked in time-series order by association (Tulving, 1983). We use labels, categories, and concepts to group different "bits" in units, which we can then treat as larger clumps. Our minds are continually linking new and old information to make it more compact and more powerful. Most important, our minds are built to transform meaningless raw material into meaning-related, semantic structures.

The following three chapters describe three kinds of graphic organizers for teaching and learning in the content areas. These three organizers support deductive thinking processes and are symbolic representations of the organizing structures that some psychologists believe help the mind manage information. Thinking deductively, the mind uses a general model it has created, along with more specific factual information, to "deduce" new ideas or solutions to new problems. We rely on deductive thinking to create ideas, plan out the future, and solve the problems we face in daily experience. In classroom teaching, we can help students organize information so they can use it in creative thinking, planning, and problem solving. Following this introduction of deductive thinking and schematization, the balance of Section III includes:

Teachers can help their students further develop the knowledge that they already have by showing them how to map concepts, causes, or procedural steps (Mayer, 1989). As the graphics in Section II were designed to help students see how they can organize new information, the graphics in Section III have been developed to help students organize and reorganize what they already know in preparation for learning new information, predicting the future, planning the future, or solving problems.

THINKING DEDUCTIVELY

We are thinking deductively whenever we use general propositions to understand, evaluate, or manage specific events. In other words, we think deductively a great part of the time. Deductive thinking is highly efficient, requiring much less processing space and time than induction. Airline flight provides a good example of deductive thinking in daily affairs. All flights start with the same basic routine. As the plane taxies toward the runway in preparation for takeoff, a flight attendant stands in the aisle and holds a card above his or her head. The card shows a picture of the airplane with all of the emergency exits marked in red.

"The plastic card in the seat pocket in front of you contains a diagram of emergency exits on the DC3," the flight attendant recites, usually without great inflection. "The exits to the DC3 are located over the wings and at the rear of the aircraft." The attendant then walks the length of the plane pointing out the actual exits in the wall of the fuselage. "In the event of an emergency. . . ."

With the word *emergency*, most passengers begin thinking deductively:

1. They struggle to understand the *general model* of the aircraft printed out on the plastic card.
2. They watch the flight attendant point out *specific exits* in the aircraft fuselage.

may be better able to manage new information or invent new ideas. The most potent influence on student learning is what students have already learned (Ausubel, 1968). Deductive forms of graphic representation give teachers a way to activate prior knowledge and then make room for new ideas. To think deductively about content, we need to arrange general ideas with more specific information in ways that allow us to create new information—ideas, predictions, plans, or procedures for solving problems. If we show students how to think deductively, we will be showing them how to take control of events in their own experience.

SCHEMA THEORY: PATTERNS OF ORGANIZATION FOR KNOWLEDGE

Schemata are mental structures that let us access and use what we know (Gentner & Stevens, 1983; Chase, 1973; Simon, 1979). It is our schemata that allow us to find what we know efficiently and then use the information to think things through. Schemata are unconscious mental structures assembled from past experience that we reapply as general frames in trying to make sense of new experiences (Rumelhart & Ortony, 1977; Brewer & Nakamura, 1984). Concept networks, abstract causal models, and procedural scripts are three kinds of schemata used to organize different kinds of information. Schema theory helps explain how old knowledge, developed through inductive processes like those described in Section II, becomes the basis for acquiring new knowledge, for reasoning, and for solving problems.

Schemata appear to be organized as networks; that is, large concept networks connect more narrow concept structures; larger process schemas have embedded subroutines and scripts. Schemata can represent knowledge at many levels of abstraction. They can link information in several different ways. The concept schema for dog includes a general list of abstract attributes, like *tails, fur,* and *bite* as well as an extensive list of specific dog experiences: Fido, Bowser, and the brute that lives down the street. Our schemata *are* our knowledge. Schemata are active processes; they allow us to manage information or to dream of new inventions. They are infused with the feelings that accompanied their development (Glasser, 1984). In the life of the human mind, abstract schemas are continually growing and changing, not only in response to new information but in response to new ways of organizing old information.

Figure 7.2 represents one kind of schema, a semantic network, for the idea of "animal" (from Hunt, 1982b). The structure of this semantic network is hierarchical. For example, the mind uses a prototypic idea for "animal" to index many kinds of living creatures, including birds, mammals, and fish. This capability in semantic networks extends from the

FIGURE 7.2 Representation of a Semantic Network for the Concept of "Animal"

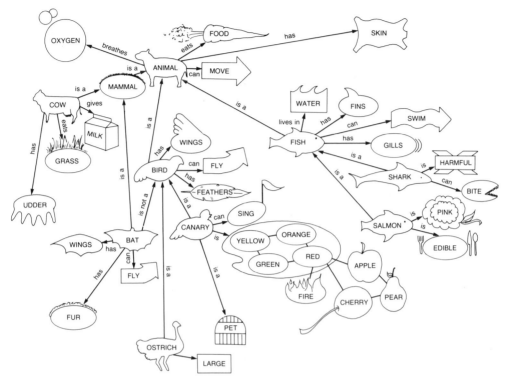

THE SEMANTIC NETWORK: Unlike a computer, which retrieves data according to a fixed program, the mind—as this diagram illustrates —can creatively summon up words, images or memories by proceeding along one or several interlacing networks of association.

M. Hunt, "How the Mind Works," *The New York Times,* January 24, 1982. Copyright © 1982 by The New York Times Company. Reprinted with permission.

idea of categories (described in Chapter 4) to include the attributes, actions, and relationships typical of some kinds of creature. Schemata are not neutral; they are energized by the feelings that accompanied their construction. They can include visual, auditory, and feeling dimensions. The semantic network also includes expectancy for the relationships among different creatures, expressed as verbs in the diagram. Beyond hierarchical semantic networks, there are other schematic structures for linking cause and effect as well as different kinds of automatic "scripts" for common actions and activities.

What are the characteristics of these mental constructs called schemata? According to Rumelhart and Ortony (1977), schemata have variables. They are general models for which we expect a considerable range of variation. Most of us, for example, have "scripted" knowledge of

TEACHING DEDUCTIVE THINKING: CONCEPT MAPS, CAUSAL CHAINS, AND FLOWCHARTS

Teaching can aim to help students construct schemata and to practice deductive thinking. Each of the content areas offers students a new way to create and test a model of the world. As we develop and test models of the world, we will be practicing deductive thinking. The subject areas may be the ideal medium for learning to think deductively because each of the subject areas is already an organized body of concepts and factual material. Learning to think deductively through involvement in academic content is perhaps most visible in the example of graduate school. Some disciplines, like medicine and psychology, require students to think deductively using statistical rules. Other areas, like chemistry, require a more inductive approach to learning by experience. Do graduate students in medicine and psychology become better deductive thinkers than chemists? Apparently so. Nisbett and colleagues (1987) described a 30% gain in deductive reasoning skills for graduate students taught to apply rules of statistical reasoning in disciplines like medicine and psychology. No comparable gain was made by students in inductively based disciplines. Nisbett and his coworkers concluded that the disciplines that use deductive logic can teach deductive logic—if they make a purpose of it.

The same patterns of thinking that lend structure to the content areas can support experimentation with deductive forms of thinking. Developed inductively, a child's concepts are not connected systematically. The value of school-based subjects and their embedding language is the presence of a system (Vygotsky, 1986, p. 205). There are two ways students can learn to think deductively in content areas:

1. Teachers can show students the abstract concepts (rules, theories, principles, etc.) and the factual base that lets experts in the subject think deductively.
2. Students can experiment with abstract concepts and factual material in the subject areas and thereby discover the power of deductive thinking.

Most classroom teaching includes both approaches, and both teacher-developed graphics and student-designed experiments are covered in this section. Because learning to think in any pattern requires a lifetime of recursive trials, I favor an approach that leans heavily on student experimentation. Small group investigations and student projects may be less efficient than teacher-led demonstrations and lectures, but in learning to think there is no effective substitute for active involvement under helpful guidance. The process of changing the structure of schemata is probably a dialectical one (Anderson, 1977). Schemata are developed, not imposed.

The simple pattern of the syllogism often suggests that learning "the rules" and then applying those rules to a specific circumstance should also be simple. A number of factors make learning to think deductively about content much more complex than we might expect. First, the more one learns about a subject, the more one recognizes the degree of relativism embedded among the ideas and facts. Experts in a field are even more likely than novices to see things differently. Among experts in a field, there may be considerable variation in schema structure and content (Donald, 1983). On the other hand, just because we are teaching "novices" in the subject does not mean they have no ideas on the subject. Teachers must remember that schemata, even among young children, may be deeply entrenched. All new learning depends on prior learning, whether we happen to know a lot or a little.

MAPPING WHAT THEY KNOW

In contrast to the patterns in the previous section, all data-driven or "bottom-up" processes, the techniques of mapping in this section are concept-driven or "top-down" processes. That is, they begin with general concepts either in the content or in the active schema of the mind, and then test those concepts in the world of experience. Figure 7.3 includes schematic representations of three types of graphic organizers for deductive thinking. Concept mapping, and related graphics, can help students organize concepts with related evidence in ways that help them either link or contrast concepts, develop new hypotheses, or generate questions. Chain mapping can help students visualize abstract processes that depend on the idea of cause and effect—and support prediction, planning, conditional if/then logic, and experiment design. Flowcharting and PERT diagrams can help students plan the steps of decision making or problem solving.

These general frames allow a great deal of flexibility. Teachers can create a specific graphic organizer to represent the pattern and the process they are trying to teach. In other words, by shaping the "map," we can shape the process students use to think about the content. Concept maps can be structured by the teacher to support comparison and contrast, pro and con evaluation of positions, or the thesis-antithesis-synthesis structure of dialectical reasoning. Causal chains can be structured to explain how something happened or to plan for a desired result. Flowcharts can be written out with mathematical or scientific symbols, or in English sentences.

"How do I want my students to think about the subject?" is the first

students and teachers think about it. On a large sheet of paper, overhead transparency, or handout, the schematization can help an individual or class manage the process of thinking. "Reasoning, and particularly abstract syllogistic reasoning . . . implies stepwise combining of small sets of concepts, whereby new arrangements of these concepts develop in working memory. In reasoning, previous steps have to be remembered; dead ends occur so that one must be able to retrace. Therefore one can easily run out of memory space" (Breuker, 1984). The graphic organizers described in this chapter have the purpose of helping students and teachers organize and reorganize their understanding of relationships within the content areas.

REFERENCES

Anderson, R. C. (1977). The notion of schemata and the educational enterprise: General discussion of the conference. In R. C. Anderson, R. J. Spiro, & W. E. Montague (Eds.), *Schooling and the Acquisition of Knowledge.* Hillsdale, NJ: Lawrence Erlbaum.

Ausubel, D. (1968). *Educational Psychology: A Cognitive View.* New York: Holt, Reinhart and Winston.

Breuker, J. A. (1984). A theoretical framework for spacial learning strategies. In *Spacial Learning Strategies; Techniques, Applications and Related Issues.* Orlando, FL: Academic Press, pp. 21–46.

Brewer, W. F., & Nakamura, G. V. (1984). The nature and functions of schemas. In R. S. Weir & T. K. Krull (Eds.), *Handbook of Social Cognition.* Hillsdale, NJ: Lawrence Erlbaum.

Bruner, J. (1986). *Actual Minds, Possible Worlds.* Cambridge, MA: Harvard University Press.

Chase, W. G. (1973). *Visual Information Processing.* New York: Academic Press.

Dansereau, D. F., & Holley, C. (1984). *Spacial Learning Strategies: Techniques, Applications and Related Issues.* Orlando, FL: Academic Press.

Donald, J. G. (1983). Knowledge structures: Methods for exploring course content. *Journal of Higher Education,* 54(1), 31–41.

Flavell, J. H. (1985). *Cognitive Development.* Englewood Cliffs, NJ: Prentice-Hall.

French, L. A. (1985). Real world knowledge as the basis for social and cognitive development. In J. Pryor & J. Day (Eds.), *The Development of Social Cognition.* New York: Springer-Verlag.

Gentner, D., & Stevens, A. L. (1983). *Mental Models.* Hillsdale, NJ: Lawrence Erlbaum.

Glasser, W. (1984). *Control Theory: A New Explanation of How We Control Our Lives.* New York: Harper & Row.

Halpern, D. F. (1984). *Thought and Knowledge: An Introduction to Critical Thinking* (chapter 3). Hillsdale, NJ: Lawrence Erlbaum.

Holland, J. H.; Holyoak, J. K.; Nisbett, R. E.; & Thagard, P. R. (1986). *Induction*. Cambridge, MA: MIT Press.

Hunt, M. (1982a). *The Universe Within*. New York: Simon and Schuster.

Hunt, M. (1982b). "How the mind works." *The New York Times Magazine*, January 24, 1982.

Larkin, J.; McDermott, J.; Simon, D. P.; & Simon, H. A. (1980). Expert and novice performance in solving physics problems. *Science*, 208 (20 June), 1335–1342.

Letteri, C. A. (1983). An introduction to information processing, cognitive controls and cognitive profiles. Unpublished manuscript.

Letteri, C. A. (1988). The NASSP learning style profile and cognitive processing. In J. W. Keefe (Ed.), *Profiling and Using Learning Style* (chapter 2). Reston, VA: NASSP Publications.

Lipson, M. Y. (1982). Learning new information from text: The role of prior knowledge and reading ability. *Journal of Reading Behavior*, 14(3), 243–261.

Mayer, R. (1989). Models for understanding. *Review of Educational Research*, 59(1), 43–64.

Mirande, M. J. A. (1984). Schematizing: Technique and application. In D. F. Dansereau & C. D. Holley (Eds.), *Spacial Learning Strategies: Techniques, Applications and Related Issues*. New York: Academic Press.

Neimark, E. (1987). *Adventures in Thinking*. New York: Harcourt Brace Jovanovich.

Nisbett, R. E.; Fong, G. T.; Lehman, D. R.; & Cheng, P. W. (1987). Teaching reasoning. *Science*, 238, 30 October, 625–631.

Norman, D. A. (1983). Some observations on mental models. In A. L. Stevens and D Gentner (Eds.), *Mental Models*. Hillsdale, NJ: Lawrence Erlbaum.

Novak, J. D., & Gowin, D. B. (1984). *Learning How to Learn*. Cambridge: Cambridge University Press.

Rumelhart, D. E. (1975). Notes on a schema for stories. In D. G. Bobrow & A. Collins (Eds.), *Representation and Understanding*. New York: Academic Press.

Rumelhart, D. E. (1984). Schemata and the cognitive system. In R. S. Weir & T. K. Krull (Eds.), *Handbook of Social Cognition*. Hillsdale, NJ: Lawrence Erlbaum.

Rumelhart, D. E., & Ortony (1977). The representation of knowledge in memory. In R. C. Anderson, R. J. Spiro, & W. E. Montague (Eds.), *Schooling and the Acquisition of Knowledge*. Hillsdale, NJ: Lawrence Erlbaum.

Simon, H. A. (1979). *Models of Thought*. New Haven, CT: Yale University Press.

AS TEACHERS, WE TEND TO FOCUS OUR ATTENTION ON new skills, facts, and ideas that we want to introduce to our students. From the standpoint of some cognitive theory and research, we could more effectively teach if instead we designed our teaching to augment what the students already know. The idea that we should create conditions in the classroom that help students revise their understanding of the content would imply changes in the way we teach. To help students revise what they know in light of new information, we must spend more time looking at what they already know, and help them recognize what they already know as the platform for learning more. We must represent new information clearly and explicate conceptual relationships in the material. We then should help the students engage the new information, as in a dialogue, and slowly reconcile their prior knowledge with new facts and ideas. Finally, we must help them represent the new structure of what they know in a way that integrates facts, skills, and ideas.

MEATEATERS FROM SPACE: A STRUGGLE WITH CONCEPTS

My son, Ethan, suddenly stopped sleeping when he was five years old. Darkness would fall. We would tuck him into bed and leave a night-light shining dimly on the wall. In the half dark, we could still see his eyes staring wide at the ceiling. He would not sleep.

"Ethan," my wife asked one summer night from the chair by his bed, "what are you thinking about?" She waited.

"The meateaters," he said at last.

She looked around at the posters of dinosaurs taped to his walls. Every one featured tyrannosaurus rex, standing five meters tall and ten meters long, with knife-like claws extended and two full racks of teeth displayed along the jaws. Pterodons, displaying similar dental equipment, swooped among the spooky trees.

"Meateaters," she sighed, thankful that she had happened upon the simple answer. "We can just take them down."

"No," he said quickly, "I like those dinosaurs." She looked around the room again at the plastic models of dinosaurs and the model set of "dinosaur land," with volcanoes included.

"Well, which dinosaurs bother you the most?" she asked.

"The meateaters," he said again.

"That tyrannosaurus and the pterodactyls and maybe that megalosaurus are the only meateaters in the room, right now," she said.

"Not them," he replied, "The ones that fall from the sky." She glanced at the ceiling, looked around the room again, and thought a while.

"Can you point one out?" she asked.

"You can't see them, not after they fall." She sat quietly, trying to think of invisible dinosaurs, now fallen. How to banish them from the room?

"You know," he went on, "when we were lying out back at night, looking at the stars, you said meateaters were falling. I saw them glow a line down the sky. Then they disappeared. You said some of them landed. I asked you, remember?"

"Oh, those are meteors," she laughed.

"Right," he said. "Meateaters from space."

"Those were meteors from space, Ethan." She went back to explain it again. And again. It took a long time that night, and the nights thereafter, to disentangle meteors from their close relatives, meateaters. When they were separate, Ethan started to sleep better.

A concept map can let us "see" how Ethan was thinking. If we try to imagine how Ethan saw meateaters in meteors, we will be constructing a concept map with two confused concepts. Figure 8.1 represents Ethan's understanding of dinosaurs, with one area of confusion between meteors and meateaters.

FIGURE 8.1 A Diagnostic Concept Map

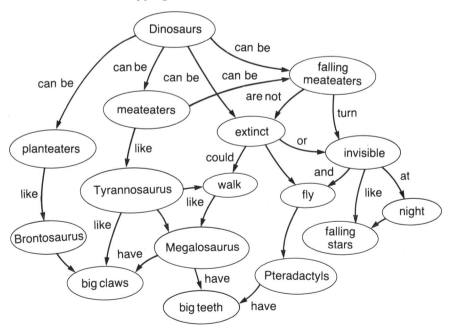

Mapping Meateaters from Space

mapping can be used to support dialogue between learners about what is known, while giving teachers a way to work with their students on making sense of the content.

Research on the effects of concept mapping as a study technique is mixed. Used as a study skill, concept mapping has been shown to increase knowledge acquisition (Ault, 1985; Arnaudin et al., 1984). However, the technique is not equally effective among all students. Low-achieving and midrange students appear to benefit most from mapping content, whereas high-achieving students may see it as a diversion from techniques that already work for them (Holley & Dansereau, 1984, chapter 4). Using "free form" mapping may fail to clarify the nature of relationships included, leaving vagueness in both concepts and their relationships (Van Patten, Chao, & Reigeluth, 1986). Concept mapping can also be time consuming, first in learning the technique and then in putting it to use. With limited prior knowledge, students may find concept mapping of little value (McKeachie, 1984).

As soon as concept mapping became a fad, it also began to generate dissatisfaction when it failed to solve all the learning problems to which it was applied. Clearly, the success of concept mapping depends on a close fit between the technique and the purpose for which it is used. A well-drawn concept map can serve the same purpose as any well-designed advance organizer or postorganizer: it can hold the whole topic in view while the student explores each part. It can also serve as a diagnostic tool.

The procedures for concept mapping vary somewhat depending on the intended purpose. When mapping is taught as a study technique, refinement of the process to ensure accuracy and inclusiveness can take several weeks (Dansereau & Holley, 1984; Arnaudin et al., 1984). Still, the basics of mapping can be mastered in less than an hour by individuals who complete a few mapping exercises and get feedback on them from teachers or peers. Whether taught in depth or developed briefly as an illustration, mapping aims for the same representational form—a hierarchical graphic arrangement of conceptual terms and supporting evidence from most abstract to most concrete. In a concept map, one dominant concept is defined in terms of subordinate concepts, then clarified and illustrated with concrete evidence or instances. Finally, a complete concept map is woven together with explanatory crosslinks. Figure 8.2 describes a general approach to concept mapping that can be adapted as a guide to conducting interviews, developing study sheets, outlining text from reading, or creating explanatory graphics for lectures.

Both teachers and students can create concept maps. Teachers can use concept maps to convey ideas in a structured manner, guide planning, help assess the structure of what their students know, and add information to what is already there. With information left out of the structure, concept maps can even be used as achievement tests at the end of a unit. Students can use concept maps to organize their learning—individually, in collaborative groups, or in larger class-sized groups. Concept maps can

FIGURE 8.2   Basic Steps in Concept Mapping

Step 1:   Identify the major concepts.
In a text, the dominant concepts often appear in the titles, subtitles, and lead sentences in paragraphs. In an interview, dominant concepts can be identified by asking: "What do you mean by this word?" or "What can you tell me about this concept?" Look for major subcategories in the concept, definitions, causes, or effects.

Step 2:   Place the concepts on paper from most inclusive (abstract) to most specific (concrete).
Dominant concepts are most often placed at the top of a page, with subordinate concepts further down the page and with explanatory or illustrative concepts at the bottom, toward the margins or linking more inclusive concepts. Mapping may have to go through several drafts to achieve a hierarchial (or other) shape. Concepts are usually noun forms.

Step 3:   Link the concepts and label each link.
Linking lines between concepts explain their relationship. In English, the linking words are most often verbs. Active and passive verbs usually indicate cause/effect relationships. Variations of "to be" verbs usually indicate membership in a category. Conjunctions (e.g., *and* or *but*), subordinating conjunctions (e.g., *since* or *although*), and prepositions (e.g., *by, from, in,* or *to*) can all serve as useful linking words.

Step 4:   Branch out from each concept to include definitions, illustrations, and factual evidence.
Generally speaking, the more specific information that can be included in a concept map the more useful the map will be as a study guide and writing guide. Names, dates, statistics, and specific instances prove more memorable when linked to an organizing concept. Maps as guides to lectures or presentations usually contain less information.

Step 5:   Use cross-links to analyze additional relationships.
Working "top down" usually explicates the main relationships. Other relationships (links) appear when one looks at any two concepts on an evolving map and asks, "Is there a connection between these concepts?" Often there is. Significant cross-links can be labeled.

be free form or have different kinds of organizing structures. (Examples in this chapter include free form, parts/whole relationship, cause/effect relationship, comparison and contrast, and logic/problem solving.) When concept mapping is used for several purposes in teaching, the resulting maps may be large enough to cover a major portion of a classroom wall— or even two walls. A large class map may include pictures, artifacts, and student essays as well as words linked with lines or colored string.

PRE- AND POSTMAPPING:
ASSESSING THE STRUCTURE OF KNOWLEDGE

Except through rote memorization, it may not be possible to learn material that is totally "new." In learning most material, we actually restructure what we already know to accommodate a new instance, a variation

An Adult's Conception: John's Parent, Age 38

exposure increases and broadens interests

effective

role model teacher

environment is positive

then

Students and teachers pool knowledge and work together

one statement/day might be what gets a kid going

not necessary for

phonetic rules

becomes meaningful learning

Spelling

common patterns

group

Mandatory (School)

brings about

human relationships

and

facts

cognitive

put into schema assimilation and retention

the teacher is in a rut (same for 15 years)

because it is

takes place

good learning doesn't take place

Learning

through

Interest

end results

have goals

psychological

home-environment—personality—personal relationships

teacher-assigned project

is contingent on

ex

Presentation

learning takes place even in adverse conditions

able to relate to kids (not)

is

meaningful

Individual

Example

brings about

increased self motivation

Trial & Error

Discovery

Increased likelihood of long-term memory

developmental

are they ready? developmentally unique?

teachers goals & objectives

which

supply

horses

read about horses

got a horse

read technical book on horses

171

by interview from an 11-year-old boy named John and the other obtained in the same way from his 38-year-old mother. Basically, the child's map represents what Tulving (1983) might see as an "episodic" memory structure, characterized by "strings" of loosely associated words, whereas the mother's map represents a "semantic" or hierarchical structure characterized by several "layers" of organizing concepts.

Even without reading the words on these two maps, some differences between young and older learners are evident. The child's map is simple; the adult's is complex. The child's map includes two or possibly three levels; the adult's has several hierarchical layers. The child's map has no crosslinks; the adult's has many. The child uses no categories to organize his concept list; the adult creates many categories that carry different implications for the central concept.

A closer look at the words themselves reveals more differences. Essentially, young John's map of learning is just a list of related words. His mother's map is a hierarchy of differentiated concepts, principles, examples, and explanatory links. The child's map amounts to a single proposition: "Learning comes from many sources." The adult's map could produce many different propositions. Eleven-year-old John surrounds the concept of learning with a list of information sources—one category with several illustrations. The adult's map includes several alternative ways of seeing one idea; the adult can see learning as "developmental, cognitive, or psychological" or alternately as "individual versus group." For the adult, different views of cause produce different views of effect. The child's map contains no references to cause and effect. (In fact, John recognized through the mapping interview that he "can't explain" learning.) The adult's map contains several cause/effect statements which constitute "principles": "interest increases the likelihood of long-term memory," for example. In the difference between an adult's map and a child's map of the concept of learning, we can begin to see the relationship between knowledge and power. Young John sees learning as a string of events over which he has little control. His mother sees learning as a set of processes she can observe and control. Knowing about learning implies control over learning.

In looking at the developmental differences reflected in these two maps, we can begin to infer instructional purposes or goals for John aimed at helping him build a conceptual structure with greater explanatory power. There are many gaps apparent in his map; for example, the absence of any reference to learning from experience. John's list of sources for learning is not grounded in examples. John's map does not link related sources of learning, even those that share common characteristics. What activity might let him see how much he has learned from experience? How could we get him to look carefully at some examples of learning to see how learning occurs? How could we introduce the concept of self-directed learning? Would that concept alone change the structure of John's map? The opportunities are numerous. In comparing a simple and complex structure for a central concept, teachers can develop instructional goals from the existing knowledge of their students.

Research has most often treated concept mapping as an individual enterprise. In teaching, concept mapping can also be useful in focusing small group and whole class activity. Mapping what an entire class knows about a subject can be a good way to introduce a new unit. Interviewing a class is like interviewing an individual, but a bit messier, of course. To develop a class map, it may be useful to start with small groups of 2 to 4 students and ask them to brainstorm a list of all the things they know about the topic. Then, when the teacher is developing a concept map for the whole class on the board or on wrapping paper, the students can contribute appropriately from the brainstormed lists they have developed. By premapping student understanding of the new topic, a teacher can avoid leaping past misunderstandings or repeating what students already know.

Grace Sweet had that purpose when she began her second-grade Colonial Times unit with a concept mapping interview of her whole class. "What do we already know about Colonial Times?" she asked. Figure 8.4 represents the class's understanding of Colonial Times before Sweet did any teaching. Her class's premap suggests how the students organized the bits of colonial history they had accumulated. Basically, the class organized its knowledge by contrast. They understood Colonial Times by "things that weren't," like refrigerators and ballpoint pens, or aspects of life that were "different," like guns and money. The class knew very little except by contrast. That colonials "dug gold out West" is a misconception. That George Washington was a colonial figure misconstrues his significance in history. Sweet's students had no organizing conception of time. She would have to create a simple concept structure so they could add in the essential features of that period and then focus on historical time.

To give her class an organizing structure to use in understanding colonial times, Grace Sweet chose to develop two concepts, Pilgrims and Indians. Pilgrims and Indians represent two dominant forces during that period. The contrast between the two groups might be used to accentuate puritan life. Figure 8.5 is a postmap of her students' understanding of colonial times taken by interview after one month of study.

In a few weeks, the class had assembled the beginnings of a semantic or hierarchical structure for the concept of Colonial Times. One can read interlaced propositions from the map, "The pilgrims kept animals like pigs for meat and fat," for example. Each category in the postmap, like clothing, reading, and hunting, is carried down to the concrete level and explained. The class postmap is more than a set of lists; its components represent propositions that include cause/effect statements. By hanging both the premap and the postmap on the classroom wall, Sweet was able to show her students how much they had changed their view of Colonial Times through the course of the unit.

FIGURE 8.4 Second-Grade Premap of Colonial Times

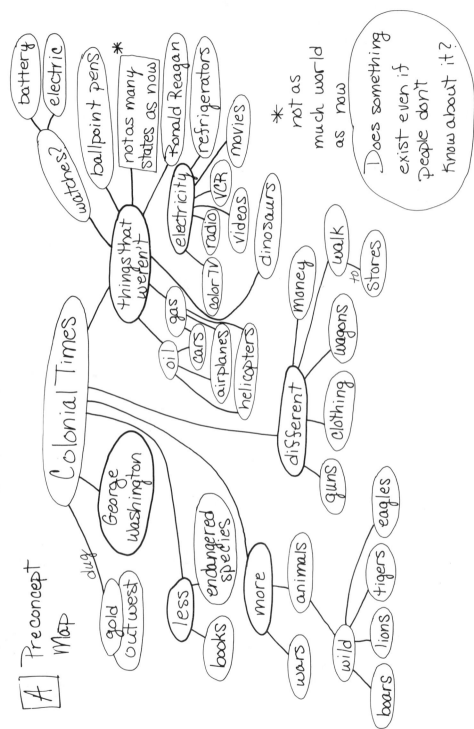

FIGURE 8.5 Second-Grade Postmap of Colonial Times After One Month of Study

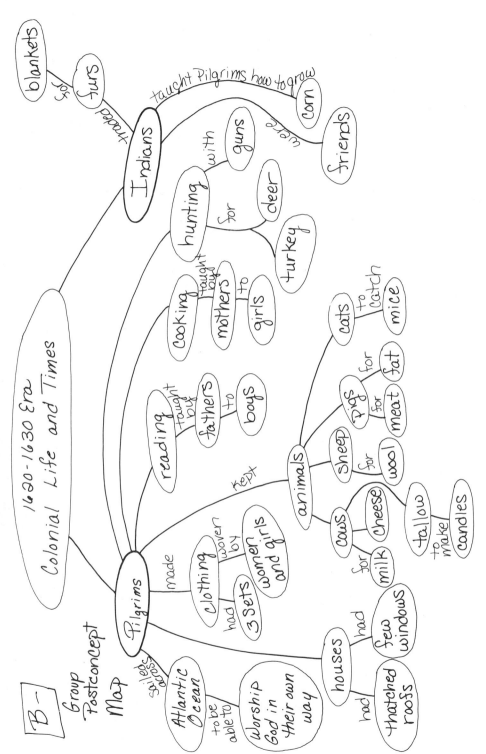

In using concept maps diagnostically, teachers can gain a two-dimensional sense of what is happening in the multidimensional minds of their students. A two-dimensional map can give the teacher a place to start correcting misconceptions, introducing new ideas or changing interpretations. Asking students to map what they know before they begin a new unit also has a felicitous effect on the way they see the task ahead. Mapping what they know establishes their strength before they have to confront weakness. A premap lets students gather and organize what they have already acquired; a postmap lets them see what they have learned. Used as an advance organizer or as a summary, mapping can increase comprehension (Ausubel, 1978; Barron & Schwartz, 1984). For teachers who use maps as an assessment device, I believe it is best to use them both before and after instruction. In the students' own notebooks or hanging on the classroom wall, a concept map serves as a continual reminder of where a unit began and where it is heading. As new information comes to view, it can be used to revise the "old" map to make it better. In a specific class period, a visible map reminds students that the particular information they are confronting is part of a larger frame, some of which they already understand and some of which they are adding in.

CONCEPT MAPPING IN TEACHING: CREATING STRUCTURE FOR KNOWLEDGE

Most of the research on concept mapping has focused on its use as a study device. That is, students are taught to use a concept map for reading or preparing for examinations. They use the technique for a period of time, then their scores are compared with scores of students who do not map. In supporting learning, concept mapping can serve this purpose, and others as well. In support of teaching and learning, concept maps convey a sense of the whole subject in relation to its parts.

- Teachers can develop maps to convey their expectations of what students should understand, in general and in particular.
- Students can develop maps that help them understand the meaning of the concepts they are trying to learn.

By controlling the structure of student mapping, teachers can influence the way students think about the content.

By nature, a concept map represents a general view of a subject that can be examined in greater depth. Concept mapping can be used to establish a base line for student exploration of a subject area. Suzanne LaRocque used concept mapping to organize her third-grade writing program.

Among younger students, the physical challenge of putting letters on a page may temporarily obscure the purpose of using writing to create meaning. Concept mapping is quicker. It creates a snapshot of a whole subject area. By concept mapping before writing, LaRocque's young students could get a view of the whole subject, with its meaning embedded, before they had to labor through the process of sentence generation.

For a unit lasting for one quarter, LaRocque focused student writing on "ME." All of her students wrote a book about themselves, complete with illustrations. Figure 8.6 represents the organizing maps developed by one student writer for the book called "ME, Amy." Essentially, Amy's book and map consisted of all the things she really liked, to be developed in detail as she wrote.

Books, music, TV, food, toys, sports, hobbies, and her family find a place in the map. Working from theme to theme around the map, Amy could generate chapters, not simply by converting aspects of the map to sentences, but by using the map as a source of inspiration and working toward particular instances. For example, Amy wrote a chapter called "Eat," based on further mapping of the cell called "Food."

FIGURE 8.6   Amy with the Concept Map Organizing Her Book

FIGURE 8.6   (continued)

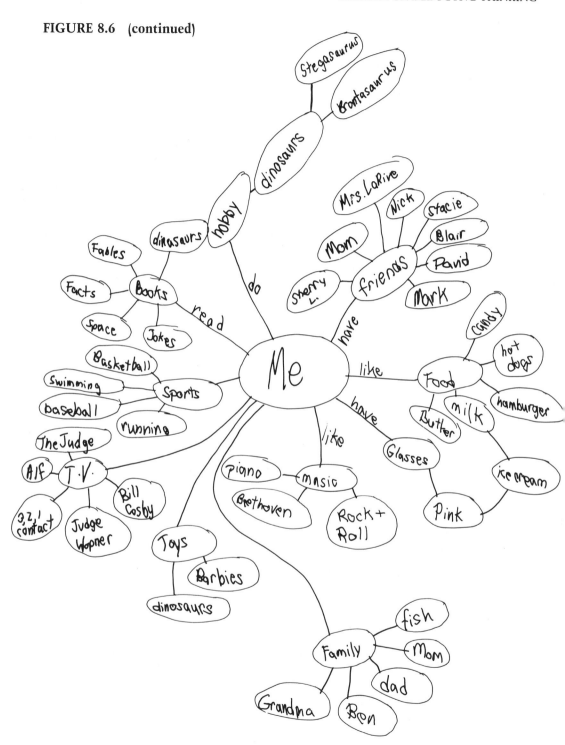

EAT

I love to eat it is fun I can do it with Will it is fun
to eat a apple or a little pare. My friends can to.
It is very fun. It fills my stumick.

The overview map allowed Suzanne LaRocque to lead her students to describe themselves and celebrate their lives, one chapter at a time.

The overview map also gave the second-grade class a starting point for further exploration. "People are different in different places," LaRocque said. "We will use your book to look at what you do in different places where you spend time." She then led the students to look at themselves "At Home," "At School," and "At Play" by creating submaps for each context. In the submaps, LaRocque showed the students how to develop examples for each general topic, as shown in Figure 8.7.

In this submap, the hierarchical arrangement of concepts is easy to see, moving from most abstract to most concrete, from "home" to cookies and cake. "Me at home" becomes the general organizer for three activities, "Bakeing," "Reading," and "T.V.," each of which Amy can take down to the concrete level, apple crisp, Bugs Bunny, and Nancy Drew.

FIGURE 8.7 Amy's Submap for the Chapter of ME Called "Eat"

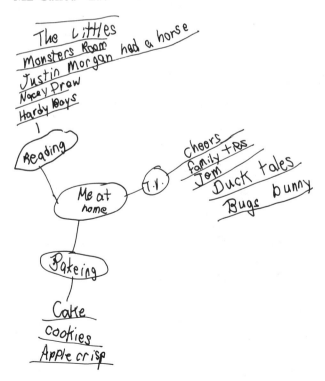

By writing from general topic toward illustration, LaRocque's students followed the most common pattern of the expository paragraph (Clarke, 1980). As they worked words onto paper, they also practiced patterns of expository writing within a meaningful topic area.

When each person in the class had finished the body of a book, Suzanne LaRocque gave a final assignment. "Read your book," she said, "and try to figure out how you feel about yourself." The vast majority of the students felt very positive. The book called "ME" did not give them a reason to feel good; it just gave them a way to express what they felt. Amy's final chapter says as much.

> AMY
>
> **HOW I FEEL ABOWT MYSELF**
> *is happy because I do not have a reson at all*
> *I just feel the enjoy reading about myself.*

Perhaps that will do.

In many areas of content, the sheer volume of detail may overwhelm the ideas they are meant to exemplify. Also, when a unit of study takes place over several weeks or even months, students are apt to forget the beginning by the time they reach the end. If a teacher's purpose includes having students compare several instances reflecting one concept, trace the evolution of an idea through stages, or distinguish between two or more concepts, a concept map can serve to hold a general focus against a storm of details. Hanging on the wall or copied and placed in student notebooks, a teacher-made map can remind students that their work with specifics is meant to help them understand a meaningful idea. Teacher-made maps have the purpose of guiding students toward general understandings that are grounded in concrete facts.

Jori Dean used a concept map to frame a literature unit for her eighth-grade language arts students. In planning the unit, Dean knew that student interest would fix itself on the stories the class read and not on the purpose they had in reading those stories. Her goals for the unit included having students distinguish between fiction and nonfiction. In her fiction unit, she wanted the students to be able to distinguish between fantasy, myth, legend, and fable, and relate each form to the central value of all fiction—its ability to reflect the durable qualities of the human spirit. Dean had selected fiction with strong evocative power, including several filmed versions of written works. Because she recognized that the emotional power of "stories" could obscure the purpose of the unit, she created for the first class a concept map that briefly outlined differences and similarities for the forms of literature (see Figure 8.8).

Jori Dean's concept map hung on the wall and slowly made its way into student notebooks as the unit progressed. As the students analyzed the stories and films, she added new information to the map. Simply by

FIGURE 8.8 Using Mapping to Structure a Brainstorm

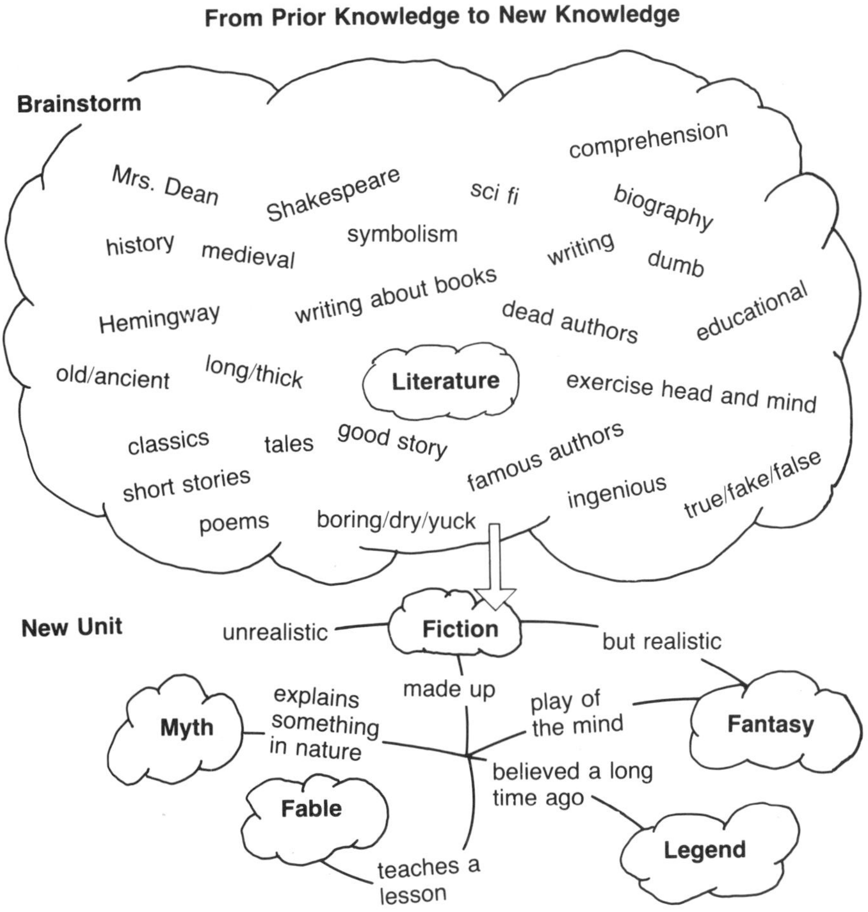

From Prior Knowledge to New Knowledge

Brainstorm

Mrs. Dean   Shakespeare   sci fi   comprehension   biography

history   medieval   symbolism   writing   dumb

Hemingway   writing about books   dead authors   educational

old/ancient   long/thick   **Literature**   exercise head and mind

classics   tales   good story   famous authors

short stories   ingenious   true/fake/false

poems   boring/dry/yuck

New Unit

unrealistic — **Fiction** — but realistic

Myth — explains something in nature   made up   play of the mind — **Fantasy**

Fable   believed a long time ago — **Legend**

teaches a lesson

walking to the concept map and pointing, she could make conceptual transitions, help students make comparisons, and remind students of what they had already seen or read.

USING CONCEPT MAPS TO GUIDE THINKING

By designing the structure of a concept map to reflect a specific kind of thinking, teachers can begin to shape the processes students use to think about the content. Teacher-made maps can be used to guide student research projects. In developing a unit on endangered animals for his fifth-grade students, Guy Viens wanted them to see how different factors threaten different species. He also wanted to give his students experience in library research and public speaking. Working in groups of four, his students began to discuss all the factors threatening animals in the world today. With the whole class, Viens then compiled the concept map shown in Figure 8.9, "Animals Are Endangered Because. . . ." The map is "shaped" to capture all the causes for one effect—endangerment. The whole class created the categories of threat. Individual students added specific animals, using the library to conduct research on the nature of the threat and the chances for survival.

With the organizing concept map on the wall behind them, the students presented information they had gathered from the library. Looking at the concept map, the whole class then tried to decide which category of threat applied to the animal being described. When all the students had reported and attached their own animal to the map, the class could count the number of animals facing a particular kind of threat. It appeared that man-made changes in the environment were most threatening, particularly those that changed the nature of a habitat.

By imposing some form on the map that students make, as Guy Viens did with endangered species, the teacher can begin to influence the way students think about the subject. By adjusting different parts of a map, a teacher can guide students toward different kinds of thinking. If a teacher eliminates cells in a concept map which could contain an example, students have to conduct research to locate specific instances. If a teacher creates a basic structure for a map, emphasizing comparison and contrast, cause and effect, or problem and solutions, the students can be guided to think about the subject using that specific frame and that clear purpose. By managing the structure of the map, a teacher can direct student attention toward the relationships that the teacher wants students to examine.

Concept mapping often provokes some reference to causes and effects for a topic. By creating a "core map" with a cell for causes and another for effects, a teacher can guide students toward explaining some events as having causal force and other events as being effects. (Causal chain maps are described more extensively in Chapter 9.) Then students begin to filter the information they have, seeking those facts that have explanatory power for a cause/effect relationship. In the concept map included as Figure 8.10, the teacher wanted her eighth-grade class to focus their test preparation on three aspects of militarism that contributed to World War I and its immediate results. She created a core map containing seven concepts, organized from causes, through the War period, to effects following the War.

Thus for each student, the resulting map is built around an abstract causal model, or hypothesis, asserting a linear relationship between nationalism and the costs of war. Working in groups of two, the students then went through their notes and added details from the unit they were

FIGURE 8.9 Map of Causes for Extinction, with Examples

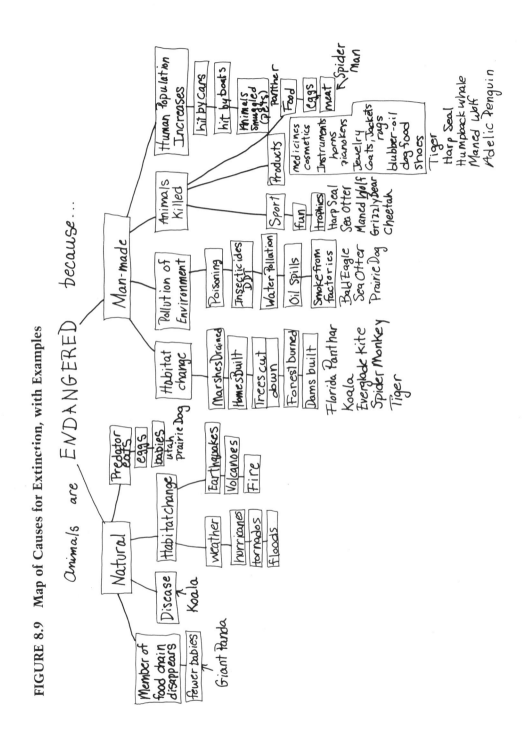

FIGURE 8.10   Teacher-Developed Guide (in Grey) for Student Notes (in White)

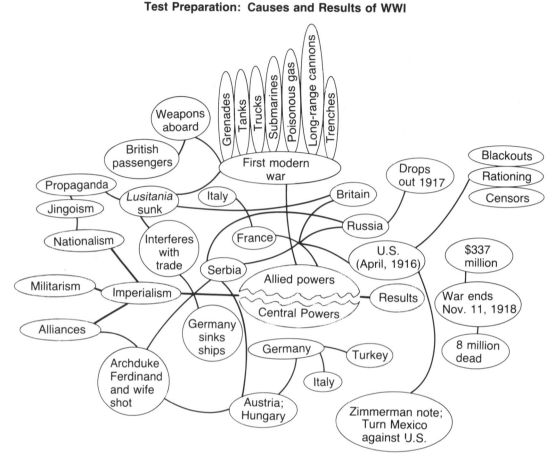

completing that would let them write short-answer and essay questions. After they completed their map, the eighth-grade class was able to discuss the causes of war and assess the contribution of different forces in their essays.

The same principle organizes the structured concept map on pollution in Figure 8.11. In this map Judy Boucher wanted her composition students to think about causes of pollution and write an essay recommending a solution to the problem. She handed out a concept map organized to emphasize causes and solutions that can be deduced from each. Her handout, however, was largely blank. Using the blank map, she was able to explain how problem solving depends on our ability to identify main causes and then reduce or eliminate those causes in order to reduce or eliminate their effects. As they filled in the blanks in small groups,

FIGURE 8.11   Concept Map Organized to Support Problem Solving

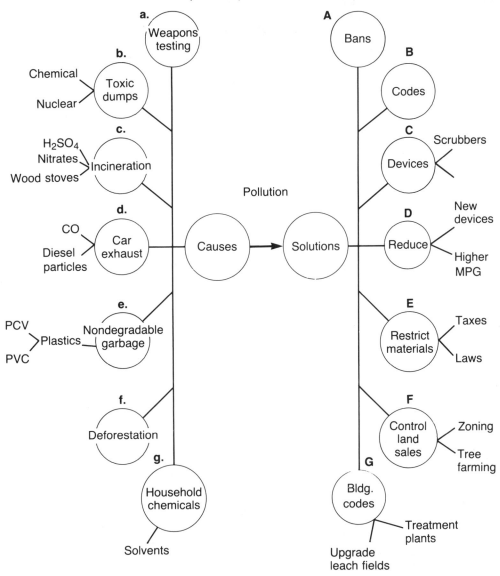

Problem-Solving Concept Map

For each cause of pollution you can identify, outline several solutions

FIGURE 8.12   Blank Map as a Guide for a Writing Assignment

Setting Up Your Book Review

You can use this concept map as a guide for the analysis of the nonfiction book you have chosen to review. In each blank, put the concept word that represents your focus and the page numbers that will let you find specific quotations to analyze or interpret. Remember, this is only a guide. The number of explanatory concepts and references to factual support is up to you.

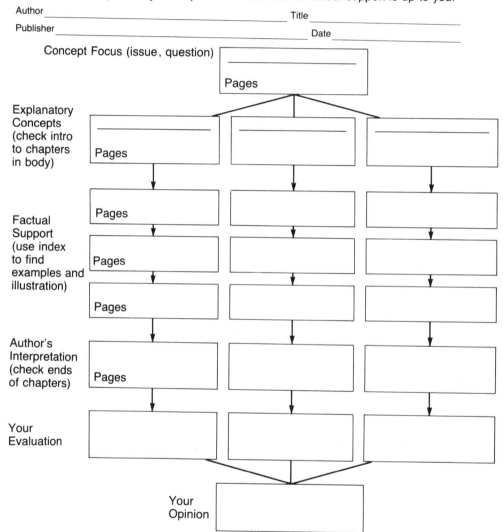

her students produced more "solutions" than any student—or society—could handle. Which solution should they recommend? Individually, the students had to wrestle with the question of feasibility to generate a clear recommendation in writing.

Concept maps can also represent "pure pattern," without reference to any subject area. The blank map included as Figure 8.12 has been used to guide students through the process of writing a book review. Rather than containing information itself, the blank concept map was built to organize topic words and simple page numbers for supporting material. In the assignment, the instructor explains where students might find information of different kinds in a nonfiction book. They could locate the conceptual focus of the book in the first and last chapters. Explanatory concepts (the teacher and the guide suggested three) would probably appear in the first paragraphs of chapters in the "body" of the book. Once the students had identified explanatory concepts and selected three, they could locate those concepts in the index of the book. The index would lead them back into the book and help them locate specific facts or evidence used as illustration. As they examined each of three or more conceptual themes, working backward and forward in the book, they would also develop a point of view of their own.

SHAKESPEARE FOR EVERYONE: A CASE STUDY

Sara McKenny teaches *Taming of the Shrew* to ninth-grade students in Swanton, Vermont, one of the poorest corners of the state. Her college-prep students usually take the play in stride, treating it as some long-ordained part of their future, at last coming to be. Her noncollege students, however, recoil in dread from the idea of reading Shakespeare. How can they be expected to understand Shakespeare when virtually all of them have already failed ninth grade once? In teaching Shakespeare to students who have little confidence in their own ability, McKenny aims to change how her students think—not so much about Shakespeare but about themselves.

For one noncollege-prep class she began *Taming of the Shrew* with a song from the radio. Her students listened, if only to anchor themselves in the familiar. "Good lovin'," the song implored, "good lovin'." The ninth grade lip-synced along, happy humming their own era. "What is this song trying to say?" Sara McKenny asked when the song was done. Each student had a response to that question. They started to talk, forgetting Shakespeare for a moment. In talking about the song, about the power of love and about struggle between the sexes, the class formed the base for its study of Shakespeare. *Taming of the Shrew* is about love and struggle, they discovered, the same then as now. This ninth-grade class consisted of students 17 or 18 years old; they knew a bit about love and struggle.

Before they began to read Charles Lamb's version of the story, Sara McKenny wanted them to have some background about Shakespeare's time, 350 years ago. McKenny showed them a filmstrip on the Globe Theater at the end of the sixteenth century. Perhaps washed forward on the wave of "Good Lovin'," the ninth grade watched carefully. Each of them took notes, as they were told. "You are going to work up a concept map, with a partner, of what you learn from the tape," McKenny warned. "So get some facts or ideas to add in." The class remained highly focused as the filmstrip ran.

As class began the next day, McKenny grouped the students in twos to map the filmstrip. To prepare them to map, she asked them about the purpose of concept mapping. "Why map a filmstrip?" she questioned, "Why not just write some stuff down?"

"Concept maps are looser, like brainstorming," one young man observed. His friends jostled him for the good answer.

"They are easier to look at," a jostler continued, getting jostled in turn.

"They are easier to study," a quiet young woman said from the front of the room. After a year off from school, she has been studying harder this year.

"They are easier to add to as you go along," her friend said in support, "as you get new ideas."

"And that is what we will do," Sara McKenny said. "We will hang these maps on the wall; then as we read the play, we can look back, see where we started, and add in new ideas." As the groups got to work, McKenny asked them to set up their maps in complete sentences this time, so that others would be able to read them. Figure 8.13 is a concept map in complete sentences developed by two ninth-grade Shakespeare students, quiet young women who spoke from the front seats.

The map developed by the two women in the class reflects some of their thinking about the Globe. Several of the items they chose to include are interesting but unintegrated facts, like "People came from miles around." Most of the map, however, is organized around themes they identified as important. One theme related to social class or privilege, and another related to sex inequality in Elizabethan London. Both themes, made explicit in student maps, represented teaching opportunities for Sara McKenny. She could exploit student interest in the actors, who built their own theater but didn't let women take dramatic roles. She could also choose to look at the conflict between rich and poor, who apparently heaved garbage at each other in the theater. Both themes find some expression in *Taming of the Shrew* and can become a purpose for close reading. Because Kate and Petrucchio so clearly represent a battle between the sexes, McKenny chose to focus her teaching on the sexes.

FIGURE 8.13   Concept Map in Sentences Summarizing a Filmstrip

From reading about Shakespeare, the ninth grade extended its mapping activity first to the historical person of Shakespeare and then to the play itself. In Shakespeare's life, the mapping focused on events that could clarify the theme of sex equity, like the early death of his sisters and his marriage to Anne Hatheway, who was a decade older than he. On the walls, the student maps incorporated information from many sources and grew each day. To keep her students focused and moving, McKenny developed short quizzes on parts of the play. Some quizzes were time lines in which students arranged dates, events, or speeches in a logical order (see Chapter 3). Other quizzes took the form of concept mapping activities. By leaving some empty nodes in a concept map, McKenny tested for specific details. By not specifying links between nodes, she asked her students to define conceptual relationships in the play. She told her students they would get full credit for filling in the blanks on a test map. They would also earn extra credit, much to their delight, if they added more nodes and defined the linking relationships for the information they added.

Figure 8.14 includes the blank pop quiz Sara McKenny developed to test her students on Act I, with a sample student response. This student earned extra credit by adding supporting details about each of the characters and about several linking relationships. Virtually all of McKenny's students earned extra credit by adding extra nodes to the test map.

As they finished the play, McKenny began turning back toward the original themes from "Good Lovin'." How can we characterize the struggle between the sexes? What were the issues in Shakespeare's time? What are the issues now? Could *Taming of the Shrew* take place today? To force the question, McKenny showed her ninth-grade students an episode from the TV series "Moonlighting" that was adapted from Shakespeare's play. "As your final project in Shakespeare, you will have to compare and contrast these two plays, one from our time and one 350 years old," Sara told her students. "Are the conflicts the same today as they were then? The solutions? To succeed in writing an essay on this topic, you will have to use specific information from both plays."

To help her students prepare to write, a task for which they felt little confidence, she created a blank concept map arranged to support comparison and contrast as a way of thinking. Figure 8.15 is the blank map and circle diagram that McKenny used to guide students to think in the pattern required by comparison and contrast essays. She suggested that the students design blank maps of their own choosing; several did, using squares instead of circles or conventional concept map form instead of Venn form. To prepare for writing, they worked together, again in teams of two, to locate information that would show clear similarities and differences between the two plays. McKenny said she would give them only one period to write out the answers they discovered. As the noncollege-bound ninth grade packed up to leave for the day, some were still nervous.

"How can we do this?" a male voice asked from the back of the room. "I mean, we don't *know* the differences between the plays. I mean, you haven't *told us* the answer, so how can we *know* it?"

The class dropped into silence. He was right. She hadn't told them the right answer. So how were they supposed to write the right answer? The question shattered their confidence again. McKenny leaned over her desk at the front of the room. All eyes turned in her direction. She waited.

"Sometimes, you can tell the intelligence of a person," McKenny said slowly, "by how they deal with what they don't know." It took a few seconds for the group to understand that their teacher was not questioning their intelligence. She was affirming it. "As you go along," she continued, "learning becomes more difficult. You have to use what you do know to figure out what you don't understand. That is called deductive thinking."

"How we deal with Shakespeare is a sign of our intelligence?" a quiet girl asked from the front of the room.

FIGURE 8.14 Blank Concept Map as a Quiz (a) with One Student's Answers (b)

(a) Quiz on *Taming of the Shrew*

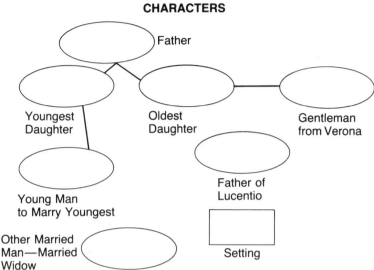

CHARACTERS

Father

Youngest
Daughter

Oldest
Daughter

Gentleman
from Verona

Father of
Lucentio

Young Man
to Marry Youngest

Other Married
Man—Married
Widow

Setting

(b) Quiz on *Taming of the Shrew*: One Student's Answer

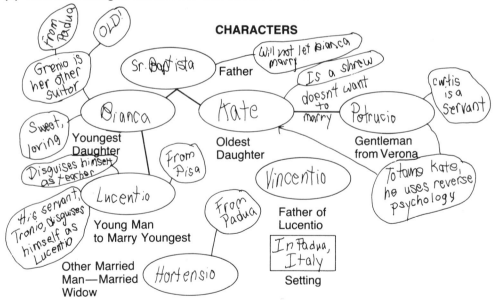

FIGURE 8.15 Concept Map for Comparison and Contrast (Partly Completed)

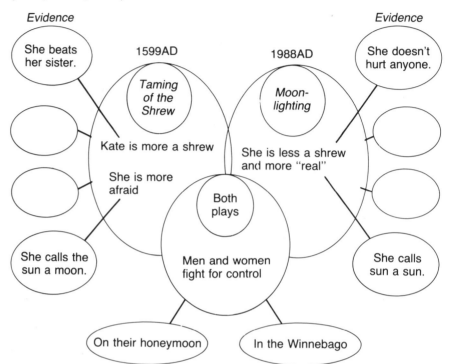

"How you have dealt with Shakespeare has already shown your intelligence," Sara smiled. Relaxation returned to the room. The boys started to swagger and jostle again. The girls cracked their gum.

"Yeah," a very large young man asserted. "We know the plot—two ways, two times!"

"And we know the characters in both plays," his sidekick added.

"So we handle the rest with our brains," the very large student said as the bell rang. "We're pretty deductive."

SUGGESTIONS FOR TEACHERS

1. The best way to learn concept mapping is to try to make a few. A pleasant way to try is to interview a friend or relative on a topic in which you both share an interest. The questions in Figure 8.16, from top to bottom, can help you develop a fairly complete map of the concept structure of your interviewee. As an interviewer, you should see your role as maintaining the focus

FIGURE 8.16   Concept Mapping from an Interview

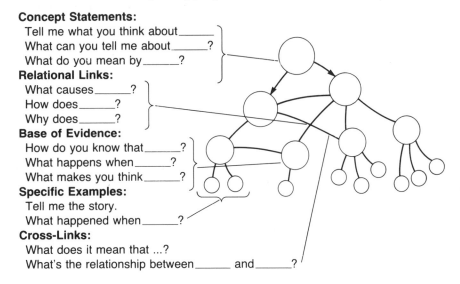

Concept Statements:
 Tell me what you think about_____
 What can you tell me about_____?
 What do you mean by_____?
Relational Links:
 What causes_____?
 How does_____?
 Why does_____?
Base of Evidence:
 How do you know that_____?
 What happens when_____?
 What makes you think_____?
Specific Examples:
 Tell me the story.
 What happened when_____?
Cross-Links:
 What does it mean that ...?
 What's the relationship between_____ and_____?

on the concept and pursuing it to the level of instances. Follow the leads you are given, unless you sense a shift to another concept. As your map begins to fill out, use what is written to probe for linking statements. In teaching your students to develop maps, you should show them an example. After they have seen an example, an interview might teach them aspects of the technique.

2. Assign your students a concept map with one of the reading assignments you require. With their maps in hand, your students may be asked to:
   a. Summarize the reading for the whole class, with the map as a guide.
   b. Work in collaborative groups to create a summary map.
   c. Write a short summarization paragraph.
   d. Generate questions to start the next class.

3. For a unit you plan to teach in the future, create a concept map that you could hand out on the first day to all your students. To create the map:
   a. Develop a complete list of all concepts in the unit, using reading, texts, films, and problem sets as a base.
   b. Group the concept words logically.
   c. Draw a basic concept map including all the words.
   d. Label the linking lines for all relationships between concepts.
   e. Add factual references to all concepts that need illustration.

4. After developing a concept map for a unit of study, try to develop a test for your students by erasing information from the cells or from linking lines. Can you write objectives for this test?

5. As an exercise in test preparation for your students, show them how to concept map an entire unit of study. In collaborative groups ask them to use their maps to generate essay and short-answer questions that you can use on the test.

6. For a content area in which you teach, which of the following learning skills is most essential?
   a. Illustration, facts to concepts
   b. Comparison and contrast
   c. Cause/effect analysis
   d. Developing solutions to problems
   e. Defining a value position
   Design a blank map that asks students to use specific information within the general frame you have designed.

Helping Students Reflect on Their Thinking

Even when your students experience success in using a graphic organizer for understanding the subject area, they will not automatically see wider usage for the technique they employed. They will need your help in finding other situations where the same technique would work as well. When your students are using a graphic to think about some part of content, make some effort to let them: (1) review the process they used to think and (2) look for other situations in or out of school where the same process might work. We can call the transfer of a thinking process a "Bridge."

A Bridge for Thinking

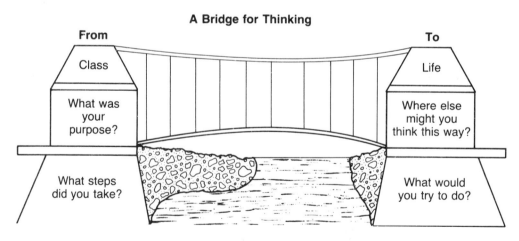

- In what areas do you know a great deal? How much room would it take to map what you know?
- What careers require a well-organized body of concepts and facts?
- How do people in those careers develop their mental "maps"?
- In what school tasks might mapping be useful?

REFERENCES

Arnaudin, M. W.; Mintzes, J. J.; Dunn, C. S.; & Shafer, T. S. (1984). Concept mapping in college science teaching. *Journal of College Science Teaching*, November.

Ault, C. R. (1985). Concept mapping as a study strategy in earth science. *Journal of College Science Teaching*, September/October, 38–44.

Ausubel, C. (1968). *Educational Psychology: A Cognitive View*. New York: Holt, Rinehart and Winston.

Ausubel, D. (1978). A defense of advance organizers. *Review of Educational Research*, 48(2), 259–272.

Barron, R. F., & Schwartz, R. M. (1984). Graphic postorganizers: A spacial learning strategy. In D. Dansereau and C. Holley (Eds.), *Spacial Learning Strategies: Techniques, Applications and Related Issues*. Orlando, FL: Academic Press.

Brooks, M. (1987). Curriculum design from a constructivist perspective. *Educational Leadership*, January, 63–67.

Clarke, J. (1980). The learning cycle: Frame of discourse for paragraph development. *New England Association of Teachers of English Leaflet*, 79(3).

Dansereau, D., & Holley, C. (1984). *Spacial Learning Strategies: Techniques, Applications and Related Issues*. Orlando, FL: Academic Press.

Donald, J. G. (1983). Knowledge structures: Methods for exploring course content. *Journal of Higher Education*, 54(1), 31–41.

Flower, L., & Hayes, J. R. (1984). Images, plans and prose. *Written Communication*, 1(1), 120–160.

Holley, C. F., & Dansereau, D. F. (1984). Networking: The technique and the empirical evidence. In C. F. Holley & D. F. Dansereau (Eds.), *Spacial Learning Strategies: Techniques, Applications and Related Issues*. Orlando, FL: Academic Press.

Jones, B. F.; Pierce, J.; & Hunter, B. (1989). Teaching students to construct graphic representations. *Educational Leadership* 46(4), 20–24.

McKeachie, W. (1984). Spacial strategies: Critique and educational implications. In C. F. Holley & D. F. Dansereau (Eds.), *Spacial Learning Strategies: Techniques, Applications and Related Issues*. Orlando, FL: Academic Press.

Novak, J. D. (1977). *A Theory of Education*. Ithaca, NY: Cornell University Press.

Novak, J. D., & Gowin, D. B. (1984). *Learning How to Learn*. Cambridge: Cambridge University Press.

Perkins, D. N., & Simmons, R. (1988). Patterns of misunderstanding: An integrative model for science, mathematics and programming. *Review of Educational Research*, 58(3), 303–326.

Surber, J. R. (1984). Mapping as a testing and diagnostic device. In C. F.

Holley & D. F. Dansereau (Eds.), *Spacial Learning Strategies: Techniques, Applications and Related Issues.* Orlando, FL: Academic Press.

Tulving, E. (1983). *Elements of Episodic Memory.* Oxford: Oxford University Press.

Van Patten, J. V.; Chao, C.; & Reigeluth, C. M. (1986). Strategies for sequencing and synthesizing information. *Review of Educational Research,* 56(4), 437–472.

9

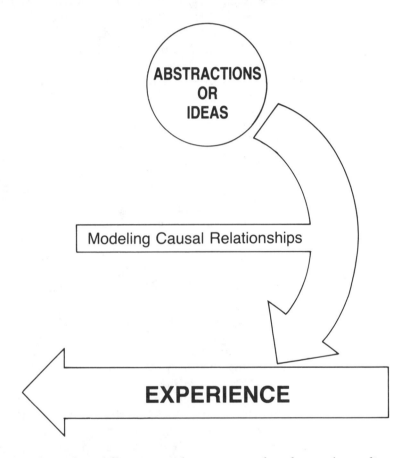

ABSTRACTIONS
OR
IDEAS

Modeling Causal Relationships

EXPERIENCE

The idea of one thing following another in time is the schema of causality.
—IMMANUEL KANT, 1781

Modeling Causal Relationships

A S ADULTS WHO ARE EDUCATED TO SPEAK AND WRITE EN-
glish, we can talk quite glibly about causes and effects. Our talk is pep-
pered with causal assumptions, which many younger people find unsup-
portable.

"That Barney will *cause* you no good," we insist.

Or we might assert, "*If* you keep putting on that red lipstick you
will end up in jail." How do we know so much about lipstick and jail?

Or we make rules based on arbitrary judgments. "You can't go out
tonight *because* you will just get in trouble."

Our causal assumptions lead us to expect things that just may not
happen. "I don't care how hard you studied. I want *results!*"

Some of our causal statements are disguised in subtle verb-adjective
forms.

"That Mrs. Blinn *is* just too *permissive.* How could she *let it
happen?*"

We really mean, "Mrs. Blinn's attitudes *cause* chaos. Chaos causes
us pain."

Our causal assertions may startle the young. They can't understand
where we get our information. On the basis of no verifiable facts whatso-
ever, we put forth our sure vision of the future. To them, Barney is not a
"cause"; he is just a fat guy who knows some good jokes. Red lipstick
may smear easily, but it isn't a felony. Trouble is not necessarily their
fate if they go out tonight, or if they make any similar choice. How can
we always trace steps in studying to the same effect? As Figure 9.1 suggests, young people tend to see experience, in school and out, as a series
of events that are largely unpredictable. Adults, in contrast, may see too
much predictability.

In this kind of dispute I tend to favor the young. They see the world
as it really is. In contrast, we are seeing the world through filters provided
by our past experience—our "models" of how things happen. They see
events; we see causal models that explain events. For young people, the
world is a place where almost anything can happen. For us, the events of
the world follow repeating patterns. For the young, every minute can
bring a surprise. For us, every cause is likely to bring on a predictable
effect. The young respond to concrete stimulae: sights, smells, tastes, and
touches. We respond to abstract models rather than events. Any sensory
stimulus suggests to us the probability of effects we should either seek
out or avoid. Cause/effect thinking makes us very careful (the young
might call it "boring.")

Adults have learned that thinking about causes gives them a way to
control effects. Causal thinking is a source of adult power. We don't want
our children or our students to become the victims of uncontrollable conditions—their friends, their lipstick color, or the time of night. In our
abstract model showing how pain comes to be, abstract words like

198

FIGURE 9.1   Two Views of Experience: Adult versus Child

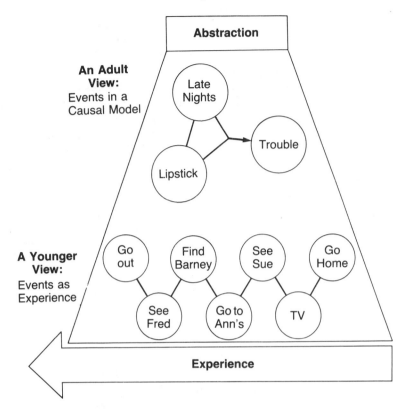

friends, dress, and time of night all play causal roles. Still, we can't expect young people to put aside red lipstick in favor of our obscure cause/effect models. They need to learn to use models to get what they want. Part of our purpose in teaching is to help young people gain control of their own lives. In teaching cause/effect thinking in the content areas, we are teaching our students to manage abstract models that give them access to greater personal control.

Cause/effect thinking is essential to effective personal control. It is also the basic thought process in the sciences and social sciences. In teaching causal thinking in any subject area, we are helping young people see events as partially predictable. We are helping them create a causal model of a world in which they too have causal power. The purpose of this chapter is to introduce techniques for helping students develop causal perceptions in the content areas.

BOILING EVENTS DOWN TO CAUSES: AN EPISODE

Chattering and jostling, the kindergarten class tumbled through the sugarhouse door. From sugar maple tree to market, the class was going to construct a model of how maple syrup is made and sold. Each kindergarten student carried a drawing pad and pencil. At each step of the way they would draw a picture of the sugar-making process—tapping trees, boiling sap, and selling syrup. Back in their classroom, they would draw a large model of how sap is collected from a hillside sugarbush, boiled down to sugar, and sold in the city. Their teacher thought she might be able to use the sugaring process to teach some kinds of cause/effect thinking.

Rushing in from the hillside, however, the kindergarten was simply happy to be out of class on the first beautiful day of spring. With luck, the sugar maker would throw some syrup on the snow and let them taste it.

Up on the hillside, the children had watched the sugar maker drill holes in each maple tree and hammer a tap carefully into each hole. Even before the tap was set, sap had come dripping from the holes. They tasted drops, each child in turn, to make sure. Yes, a taste of sugar in each drop. They had followed drops of sap through the pipeline running from tree to tree downhill through the sugar bush. From the bottom of the hill, they had looked up at the vast web of plastic tubes bringing the flow of sap toward the big tank by the sugarhouse. They had watched the clear stream of maple sap flowing from the main pipe into the gathering tank. Taps, tubes, and tank all made sense to their eyes. Collecting sap was just plain sense.

In the sugarhouse, they were anticipating magic—clear sap becoming amber syrup in the long steel evaporator. Once inside, however, they hit a wall of heat. The air was thick with steam. Moisture wrapped around their faces and made them squint. In the haze, the iron door of the evaporator glowed a menacing red. Once inside the sugarhouse, heat and steam backed them to the walls. This was something not quite expected and not understood. Quietly, they watched.

"Where's the syrup?" a small voice inquired at last. The steam had deepened his voice. Other children giggled.

The syrup maker smiled and pointed to a faucet at one end of the long evaporator. He opened the valve near them and drew off a quart of amber liquid in a tin container. The sight of golden syrup reassured them. Many smiled. The smell was intoxicating.

"What happened to the clear stuff, the sap?" the small voice continued. The sugar maker walked to the other end of the evaporator and dipped a cup into the boiling froth. When he poured liquid from the far end of the evaporator on the ground, it was as clear as water.

"Ah," escaped from the crowd of children. Something was happening in that tank that turned clear sap to amber sugar.

The sugar maker began to explain his evaporator. He showed the class where a pipe ran through the wall, bringing in sap from the big collecting tank. He showed them the valve that let more sap in when the sap level in the evaporator went down. He showed them the tin channels in the evaporator pan, running back and forth, slowly bringing sap across the fire from the back to the front. At each stage, he dipped his tin cup in the boiling froth and poured the liquid back. At each stage, the sap was getting darker and thicker. The children relaxed. They could see the change in the sap, even if they could not explain it.

"But where did the clear sap go?" the inquisitive voice continued. "Why is the syrup getting darker?" The children looked up expectantly, but the sugar maker couldn't answer. Then the teacher brushed her finger against a wooden beam where clear drops were forming. The children watched her taste the drop on her finger. Her face showed no response. Soon all the children were tasting clear drops hanging from the beams. They wanted sugar. They tasted water. Then they knew. Water was in the air.

"Where is the sap?" the teacher asked. One small girl waved her arms in the air, as if to part the steam. Soon all the children were waving their arms and laughing. The water was in the air. It was steam.

"Evaporation," the sugar maker said. Evaporation was the trick. "The fire drives the water out and leaves the sugar in the pan." To demonstrate, he opened the arch door and heat from the fire again drove the children back to the wall. The fire was driving water away and leaving syrup. To reassure them, the sugar maker took his tin cup full of syrup out the door into the cold and threw it on a bank of snow. Even before the syrup congealed, the children were running their fingers from the sweet goo to their mouths. Maple syrup, the sweet surprise.

"This must be worth a lot of money," a voice said from the snowbank, as a way to say thanks.

"Well, this is a good year for sap," the sugar maker said. "There is plenty of sap so the syrup is very good but it is not worth as much as last year."

The children looked up, waiting. They were confused. "When you have a lot of sugar, the price goes down," he said by way of explanation. Children fidgeted. Some scraped deeper in the snow for lost drops. The sugar maker looked to the teacher for a cue. She stood helpless. "Sometimes it's better to have less sap so you can get a better price." Another failure. How can you explain that less brings more? He dove in. "When the nights are cold and the days are warm, the sap runs up the tree and comes out the pipe. If the days are cold or the nights are warm, the sap won't run. With more sap you get more sugar but less money for it." The children had turned back to scavenging a few remaining drops of sugar from the snow bank. As the drops decreased in number, their value increased, but that was something none of them could see.

LEVELS OF CAUSAL THINKING

Although causal thinking probably develops on an ungraded continuum for specific knowledge in any domain, it is useful to think of it as having three levels. Figure 9.2 represents three levels of cause/effect thinking required of the kindergarten class by their exposure to the sugar-making process.

At the most concrete level, the class had no trouble understanding cause and effect. At the most abstract level, none of the children found

FIGURE 9.2   Three Levels of Causal Thinking

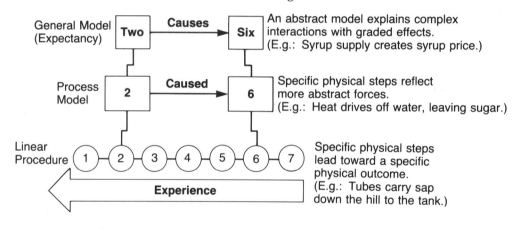

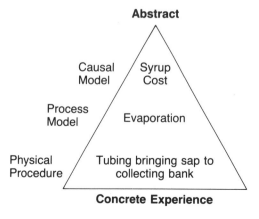

it comprehensible. At the midlevel, the class was ready to make some tentative discoveries about some aspects of a fairly complex physical process. Causal thinking at different levels requires different kinds of reasoning. All three kinds of causal thinking can be mapped or schematized graphically.

The Sugarbush: A Procedure

Up among the trees on the hillside, the children had a chance to map a procedure. The procedure for bringing sap down to the sugarhouse was represented physically by the taps, tubes, and tanks they saw there. Each of the children could draw a diagram of sap-gathering procedures (see Figure 9.3). The sequence of flow from trees to tank was just a bit different from other familiar processes for which they had developed some internal schematic, like watering the lawn or running a tub of water for a bath. There were more abstract causal forces afoot in the sugar bush, like the difficult idea of capillary action pulling sap up a tree and the idea of gravity. Gravity and capillary action are more truly "causes." The children did not see them or seek them out. They were well prepared to see liquid flowing down a hose; later they might begin to think of causal forces operating against other forces like gravity. From what their eyes had seen, all the children could draw a picture of the sugar-gathering procedure. All were content with their representation.

FIGURE 9.3   Graphic of a Procedure in Sugar Making

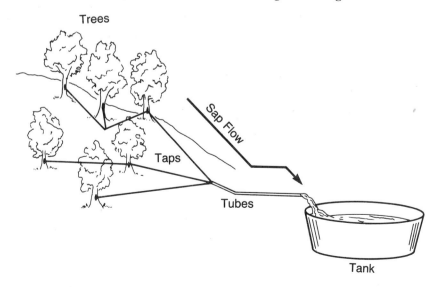

The Sugar House: A Process

The children faced a greater intellectual challenge in the sugarhouse. Initially, they found the heat, steam, and changing sap confusing. They had no hinge in prior knowledge for what they were seeing. Part of the challenge lay in trying to distinguish physical procedures for boiling sap from the process of evaporation that actually produces the syrup. As shown in Figure 9.4, a boiling procedure and an evaporation process may not be the same. The process is an abstraction from the procedure.

   With help from the sugar maker and their teacher, the children could begin to see and feel the steam resulting from the heat. This physical experience let them infer the existence of a process—the syrup making in the pan as a result of water evaporating. All the children could draw the physical layout of the evaporator and include all the causal agents. Very few, if any, could represent those causal agents as parts of a causal process. The task of understanding evaporation was harder because, suddenly, the idea of cause and effect was no longer a matter of one event following another.

FIGURE 9.4   A Process and a Related Procedure in Syrup Making

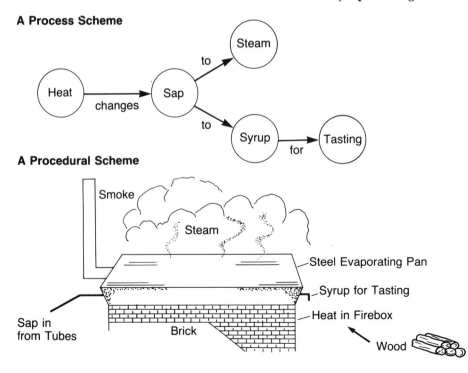

1. *Some parts of the boiling process were counterintuitive:* The reason you boil sap is to drive off what you don't want, rather than change what you want. Boiling sap looks like the process of cooking. Despite appearances, making syrup is not exactly like boiling carrots for dinner. The children expected to see something cooked; instead, they saw a hidden material revealed.

2. *In the sugarhouse, causes and their effects appear to be simultaneous, rather than sequential:* That is, fire is blazing, sap is boiling, steam is rising, sap is flowing, and syrup is coming off—all at the same time. To perceive cause and effect in boiling sap, the students would have to abstract an idea of sequence first, then postulate a cause and effect relationship. When causal models do not follow clear procedural steps, thinking about them is much more difficult.

Sugar on Snow: An Abstract Model

When the kindergarten class tried to figure out why syrup prices would fluctuate with the weather, they were no longer looking at a process with a precise physical base. To understand the phenomenon of price change, they would need to envision an abstract economic model more broadly explanatory than anything visible in a sugar bush—or indeed, anywhere on this price-tormented globe. All the causal processes in a market system are abstract. Words like *market, scarcity, demand,* and *price* do not stand for objects. They stand for abstract ideas—forces. Discovering that an idea has causal force and great explanatory power (whether or not it has physical form) requires years of observation and practiced reasoning. Developing abstract causal models brings great benefit to the mind, but takes extensive education.

This kindergarten class was just beginning to learn about causes, and the children were interested in the maple industry. They were thankful for a chance to taste syrup. They all seemed worried that the sugar maker would not make enough money by selling syrup. They all seemed troubled by the idea that syrup would bring less return in a good year than in a bad one. None of them, however, was ready to create a causal model of price change that would explain the words they were hearing. To do so, they would need to access an abstract schematic model based on the law of supply and demand and linked inversely to a schematic for weather and sap flow, something like that in Figure 9.5. None of the children could sketch a schema that would explain the complex causal sequence that dictates prices in the sugar market.

Understanding price fluctuations in the syrup market takes a more highly developed causal schema than kindergarten children—or many sugar makers—can construct. In the causal schematic for sugar prices,

FIGURE 9.5   Abstract Causal Model for Syrup Supply and Price (by Terri Sturgeon)

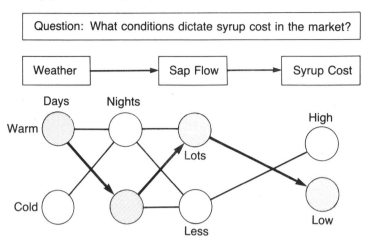

Arrows indicate critical path.

some causal links are counterintuitive: More gets you less. Some causes are interdependent: Cold is only useful if it happens at night; warmth is only useful in daylight. All the causes and effects are graded. As sap flow increases, you theoretically get a proportionate price reduction. In this schematic for causation, the idea of optimal path is visible. Across a matrix of interacting causes in the sugar season, one seeks a path toward optimal effects. In comparing the procedure in Figure 9.3 to the abstract model in Figure 9 .5, we can see the difference between expert and novice perceptions of cause/effect relationships within a narrow domain—maple sugar production (Clement, 1979). The focus of this chapter is on the development of higher-level, abstract, causal schemata for subject area knowledge. Chapter 10 will focus on scripts and procedural knowledge as a basis for problem solving.

THE DEVELOPMENT OF ABSTRACT CAUSAL THINKING

From our exposure to events unfolding in serial order, we slowly develop more abstract models of the way the world works. Our mental model of "how things work" includes events we learn to label "causes" and others we label "effects." We do not develop a causal sense for all of experience together; we build causal schemas one domain at a time. Like concept networks (Chapter 8), causal schemata become deeply embedded scaffolding for the development of both character and intellect. Once we have induced from repeated patterns in serial order some general models of how things work, those models exert a powerful influence on how we see experience from then on.

> *Causal schemata reflect the individual's basic notions of reality, and his assumptions about the existence of a stable external world—a world comprised of permanent, though moving and apparently variant objects; a world separate from and independent of himself; and a world seen by other persons in the same way as by himself. (Kelley, 1972, p. 152)*

Causal schemata give us a way to explain the past, predict the future, and manage events in a comprehensible present. Without causal schemata, we would fall helpless before an endless flood of unforeseeable circumstances.

Causal thinking develops slowly over time, first through exposure to events that recur in serial order and then through the development of language which is capable of describing the causal relationships we have inferred from observation. Once we have developed a causal sense, we can learn causal sequences without going through a long inductive learning process. When someone says, "Sugar causes tooth decay," we do not need 100 fillings to know what that means. At some point in the development of the individual, perception of causes in experience and conceptualization of causes in language become simultaneous and mutually supportive (Vygotsky, 1986). Among most adults, thinking in terms of causes and effects has become a mental habit based on many overlapping causal schemata.

Piaget studied causal thinking by watching the emergence of the words *because* and *since* in a child's vocabulary (Piaget, 1964). Piaget believed that children achieved skill with the word *because* and its relatives through a process of successive approximation. At first, events simply happen in juxtaposition to each other. With support, the child will begin to experiment with *because*, first using it as an exclamation and slowly using it to test for recurring patterns. In Piaget's early studies, children did not begin to use causal conjunctions reliably to describe physical events until the beginning of adolescence. In focusing only on conjunctions, Piaget may not have achieved a full view of causal thinking. *Because, since, therefore,* and *although* are only a small part of the linguistic equipment we bring to causal analysis. A more flexible system for describing cause and effect is embedded in all the English verbs that describe supporting or restricting conditions (see Figure 9.6).

The idea of causation embedded in the mind and in language confers to us the power of higher-level reasoning. The assumption that some events have causal force lets us *analyze* a series of episodes and isolate critical events in a path toward some "effect" (see Trend Analysis, Chap-

**FIGURE 9.6   Some Verbs Used to Designate
Different Cause/Effect Relationships**

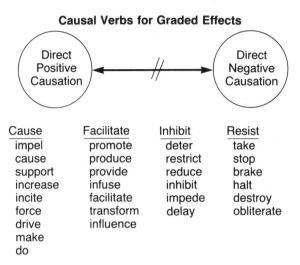

Causal Verbs for Graded Effects

Cause	Facilitate	Inhibit	Resist
impel	promote	deter	take
cause	produce	restrict	stop
support	provide	reduce	brake
increase	infuse	inhibit	halt
incite	facilitate	impede	destroy
force	transform	delay	obliterate
drive	influence		
make			
do			

ter 4). With a generalized model of cause and effect working in our minds, we are able to *predict* the future. Whenever we see a "cause" pop up in our experience, we prepare for the expected "effect." Causal models let us *solve problems* in experience. If we see a problem as an effect in a chain of causes, we can try to eliminate the problem by eliminating some causes. Cause/effect thinking is essential to *planning*. In planning, we imagine the effect we want to achieve (call it a goal) and then try to line up a series of events that will cause the goal to be achieved.

By refining the causal models students carry in their minds, we are aiming to increase the extent to which they can analyze, predict, solve problems, and plan. In other words, we are looking for ways to increase the control they are able to exert over their own lives. Children need to recognize their own causal powers in the cause/effect chain of their own experience, if only to balance the influence of others (Glasser, 1984; Holloway, 1988; Weiner, 1974; Clarke, MacPherson, & Holmes, 1982).

TEACHING CAUSAL CHAIN MAPPING

Causal mapping is a technique for representing causal relationships between concepts. A causal map is organized to fulfill a specific purpose: to represent stages, forces, or causes in a sequential process in which early events give rise to later events. Causal mapping has also been called schematization and chain mapping (Holley & Dansereau, 1984). The following are ways to use causal chain mapping in teaching:

- *Causal analysis* (backmapping): the process of tracing causal sequences backward from some effect through a sequence of generating causes
- *Prediction and hypothesis generation* (forward mapping): the process of identifying causal trends and then projecting effects of those trends toward the future.
- *Planning and decision making:* (hypothetical chaining): the process of identifying a goal or outcome in the future and then mapping the steps (causes) necessary to achieving that goal

Although procedural maps are also "causal" to some extent, I have saved them for Chapter 10, where they can better support problem solving.

Figure 9.7 is a causal map or schematization for acid rain. The map combines two different processes, coal burning and weather patterns, which make up parallel "chains" in the map. It tries to show how weather and coal burning might interact to form clouds with high acid content. Students might develop this kind of causal map from library research, from class presentations, from reading, or from teacher-designed exercises. One way to get students to create such a map is to give small

FIGURE 9.7   A Causal Map Supporting Analysis, Prediction, or Planning

Question: How do weather patterns and coal burning contribute to acid rain?

Use the following terms to construct a causal flow map: convection currents, clouds, low pressure, weather changes, acid rain, CO_2SO_4, coal burning, H_2O, condensation, prevailing winds.

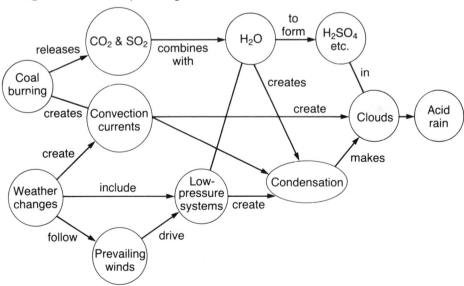

groups a list of words and a governing question, as Figure 9.7 shows. Once students have developed such a map, it can become the basis for several kinds of follow-up activity, such as:

Assignments from Acid Rain Map

Analysis: The rain on Lincoln Mountain this morning had a pH of 4.2, close to the acidity of vinegar. Using weather maps for the last week, trace the acid from its origin to the mountain.

Prediction: Using today's weather map and a map of coal-burning facilities, predict the pH level of water in three areas where rain is expected.

Planning: Using the model of acid rain formation you have developed, design three ways to reduce acid rain.

Design: Design a method for locating the source of acid in rain molecules and tracing their path from their geographic point of origin.

A causal flow map provides students and teachers with a medium in which they can struggle with questions of cause and effect. In that struggle, greater understanding of causes can lead toward greater understanding of effects. This chapter explores schematization as a technique for general use in teaching, where understanding cause/effect processes is the purpose of instruction.

Most of the research on schematics has focused on schematic or causal mapping as a reading or study technique. Using schematics can increase comprehension and retention of concept relationships in prose (Camstra & van Bruggen, 1984; Vaughan, 1984). In this chapter, methods of causal mapping can serve this purpose and several others as well. Causal mapping can support small group discussion, class projects, and individual research. Students can use a causal map or schematization to represent any sequence in which causes may be lining up to create effects. By linking causes in a causal map, students can practice causal analysis, as well as higher-level thinking based on causal analysis, like prediction, hypothetical thinking, planning, design, and related kinds of systematic problem solving (Stewart, 1984).

In a causal map, the causal agents or forces usually make up the nodes. The direction of causation is usually indicated by arrows, with positive causation running left to right and resistance running in the opposite direction. Each arrow on a causal map gives a student a chance to experiment with causal verbs of various strengths. Fat arrows can indicate strong forces. Dotted lines can show weaker ones. Each node can represent a force to consider in constructing a small model of some aspect of experience. Causal mapping is one way to involve students in searching experience for potential relationships of cause and effect. In developing a causal map, students may be creating hypotheses, explanatory models, planning frames, decisions, or predictions, depending on the teacher's purpose and direction. Creating a causal map is always a hypothetical exercise. Experience should be the test of whatever models students develop. Changing the model or map to fit new information or research should be considered part of the exercise of causal mapping.

ANALYTIC BACKMAPS: MAKING CAUSAL CHAINS THAT EXPLAIN EVENTS

A causal map can be very simple, as reflected in the test Nilah Cote gave to her second-grade students to measure comprehension after a social studies unit on colonial transportation (see Figure 9.8). All of the proposi-

FIGURE 9.8 Matching Quiz for Cause/Effect Relationships: Grade 2

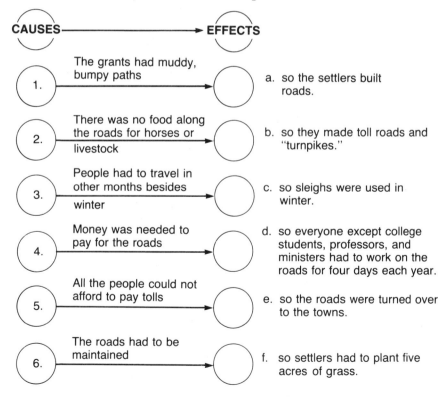

A Cause/Effect Test on Early Roads
Connect each of the causes in the left-hand column to one main effect listed in the right-hand column.

CAUSES   ⟶   EFFECTS

1. The grants had muddy, bumpy paths

2. There was no food along the roads for horses or livestock

3. People had to travel in other months besides winter

4. Money was needed to pay for the roads

5. All the people could not afford to pay tolls

6. The roads had to be maintained

a. so the settlers built roads.

b. so they made toll roads and "turnpikes."

c. so sleighs were used in winter.

d. so everyone except college students, professors, and ministers had to work on the roads for four days each year.

e. so the roads were turned over to the towns.

f. so settlers had to plant five acres of grass.

tions in the test are factual, as taken from the social studies text. Cote arranged them so that each proposition in the left column would have a consequence in the right column. Each of the propositions in the right column begins with the causal conjunction, *so.* The test takes the form of matching exercise, but the stems and responses all reflect cause and effect relationships. To succeed on the test, the students have to recognize the facts and deduce some "effects" for causes they understood from the transportation unit.

A backmap may separate several parallel chains that all contribute to one effect. By using parallel chains to show how something happened, students can gain a better sense of multiple, simultaneous "causes." In light of the tangle among causes, they may also become more circumspect about looking for quick solutions. Donna Wells taught her third-grade students to backmap as part of her science unit on endangered species. She planned to have students backmap the process of extinction for several species. Then, when her students had assembled a model of things causing extinction, she could shift focus to the present day and involve her students in planning ways to save endangered species. If her students could map causes of extinction from the past, they could map causes of endangerment today, and then discuss how to reduce or eliminate some of the threats to animal species.

Donna Wells taught her third-grade students to backmap from the written accounts of extinction in *As Dead as a Dodo* written by Paul Rice and Peter Mayle. First, her students read the stories included in the book and listed all the causes they could see. Then, working in collaborative groups, they created as many parallel chains as they could extract from their lists. Working together, the students looked for separate causal paths, simultaneous sequences of events leading toward extinction. In backmapping the extinction of the great auk, for example, her students discovered they could distinguish between two causal lines, one for natural causes and the other for human error, as represented in Figure 9.9.

The combintion of human error and natural disaster brought an end to the auk. The third-grade backmaps provided students with experience in summarizing events and making causal links from a chronological story.

As Donna Wells's third grade gained experience with backmapping, they also discovered that they could distinguish direct from indirect causes for extinction. Figure 9.10 represents the extinction process of the dodo, in which one original cause triggered two different chains, one directly causal and one indirectly causal. Both chains contributed to the dodo's demise. The arrival of the Portuguese sailors triggered two kinds of problem, one for the dodo and the other for dodo eggs. Which cause of extinction is more important: having a reason to kill an animal (for food) or a simple mistake that has permanent effects, like letting some pigs escape? In considering solutions to the problem of endangered species,

FIGURE 9.9 Backmap with Two Parallel Chains: Grade 3

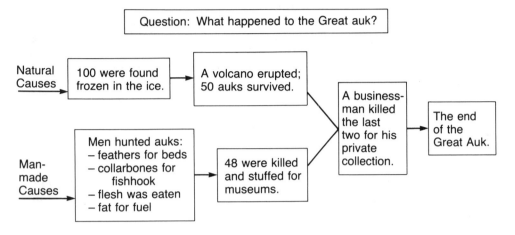

the third-grade class had to consider intentional attacks on some species and unintentional mistakes. Could the dodo have escaped its fate? What might have been changed to save the bird? Wells's third-graders could not save the dodo, but they could learn to think about today's endangered species with an eye toward options.

An analytic causal map can be expanded to include different levels of abstraction, like a concept map. A theoretical construct, for example, could be explained by a process model and then illustrated with evidence showing real effects that the senses can verify.

Greg Wright wanted his ninth-grade earth science class to link two related theories, one explaining the origin of the galaxies and the other explaining the origins of the solar system. He also wanted the class to consider both theories as aspects of one integrating process. With the

FIGURE 9.10 Backmap with One Cause and Two Effect Chains: Grade 3

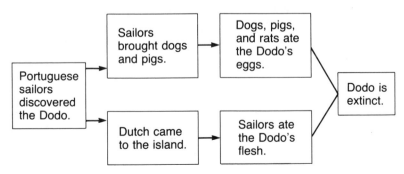

theoretical flow of events from the beginning of the universe as an organizer, Wright wanted to introduce the factual evidence for the theories that we have accumulated from scanning the heavens. On the blackboard, he set up a note-taking schema for his students with three levels: a level of theory, a level of process, and a level of supporting evidence. As he explained the theories, the process, and the evidence, each student developed notes in the form of a causal chain map (see Figure 9.11).

At the level of abstract theory, Wright's students mapped the overlap between the Big Bang Theory, which tries to explain how the core of the universe may have blown apart at birth, and the Dust Cloud Theory, which tries to explain how particles are gathering again to form the solar system as we now know it. At the process level, the students mapped stages in the theoretical sequence from the beginning of time to the present moment. The causal map describing the process included the collapse of original matter, the resulting explosion, and then the processes of condensation and gravitational attraction which may be bringing it all back together. Finally, throughout the unit, Wright's students made a record of the evidence supporting both theories: including physical evidence of red dwarfs, black holes, quasars, pulsars, and gaps in the record where the

FIGURE 9.11   Causal Chain for Theories, Processes, and Evidence: Grade 9

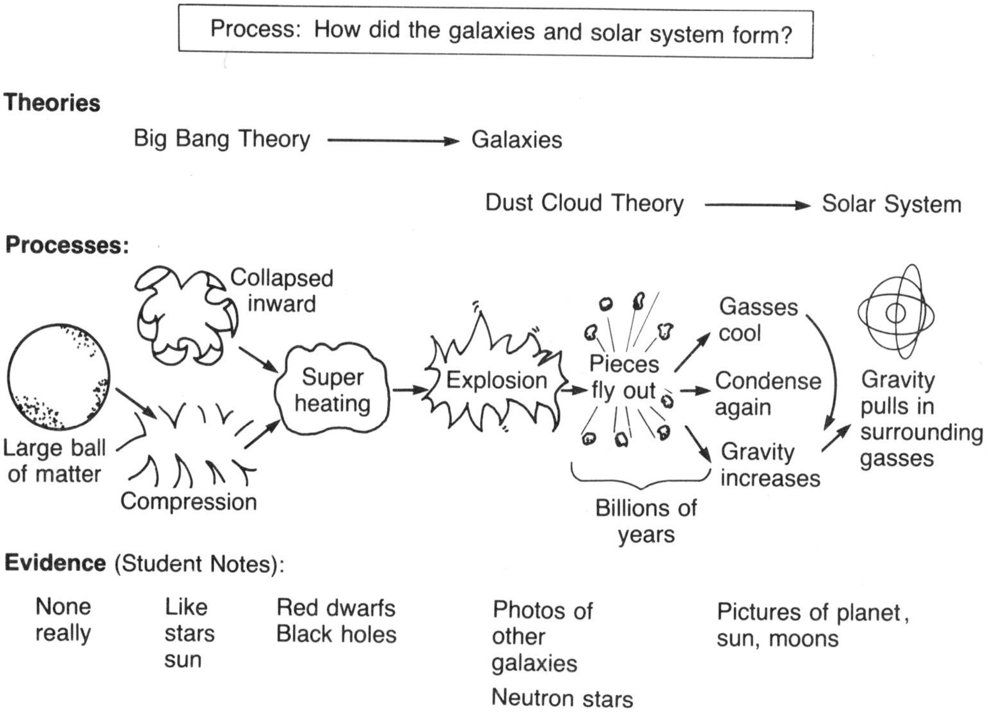

evidence has to be interpolated. The causal map showing stages in this long process thus serves as a medium linking highly abstract theory to a record of scientific evidence.

Backmapping can create an organizing process for large units in which individual projects constitute most of the learning activity. Hanging on the classroom wall, a backmap serves as a reminder or the overriding purpose of study within the unit. A causal map on the wall can continually say, "Our purpose is to find out why the civil war occurred" or "We are looking at microscopic life in pond water to discover what happens when you interrupt the food chain." To organize her sixth-grade class to investigate the effects of the geological periods on Vermont culture, Lisa Bovatt developed a large causal map that explained the relationship between geological history and daily affairs in Vermont. Hanging on the wall, this causal map remained there to help her students generate research questions and organize research papers (see Figure 9.12). Each student could use the general map to tailor a different inquiry project.

A causal map with this number of nodes and links can generate a very large number of research questions, only some of which have accessible answers:

QUESTION: How did mountain building from the Appalachian period contribute to recreation in Vermont?

ANSWER: We ski on them.

FIGURE 9.12 Chain Map Organizing Sixth-Grade Research Questions

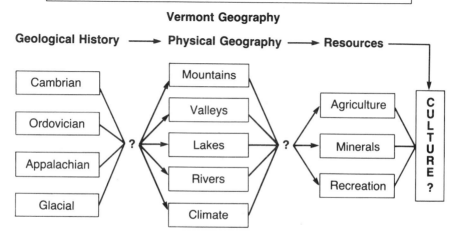

Other questions are much more difficult.

> **QUESTION:** How did the glacial period make mineral extraction more difficult?
>
> **PARTIAL ANSWER:** The ice dumped gravel all over the place.

With this map hanging on the wall, students could see both the purpose of their individual work and the structure of their investigation. Each student would have to identify some aspect of Vermont culture; for example, the centrality of skiing, the logging industry, fishing in Lake Champlain, or poverty in the Northeast Kingdom. Working backwards, they would use the library to identify the state's resources in supporting that cultural attribute. Working backwards again, they could research the geographic basis for the resource. Finally, they could examine the geological events that produced the resource. The causal map was built to provoke questions. Each individual would then produce a report tracing a current cultural attribute to its geological roots. As a whole class, the students would be able to describe Vermont culture, in part, as a result of geological events happening millions of years ago.

FORWARD CHAINING: CAUSAL MAPPING TO PREDICT OR CONTROL

Causal mapping offers the biggest payoff as a prediction device. By looking at a causal sequence in the past and present, students can practice projecting aspects of the future. Whether they are predicting the winner of a horse race or population figures for the next century, prediction can be exhilarating. As students look at information, devise causal models, and make predictions about what will happen next, they also earn the chance to check their predictions against what actually happens. A new information comes in, students may want to refine their models for greater accuracy. Prediction is the game played by research scientists, political consultants, and stockbrokers for big money. Anyone can learn to play. In learning to use causal models to predict, students can develop a healthy skepticism for sure winners and for loose promises.

In the sciences and social sciences, computer-based simulations are being developed to model cause/effect relationships in different physical or social systems. Used with simulations, causal mapping can help students recognize and control the forces represented by the computer program. John Cote wanted his fourth-grade students to understand the network of relationships implied by the word *ecology*. He introduced them to a computer-based simulation, a commercially available program representing a lake ecology. He also devised exercises using causal mapping that would let them understand the interdependence of species in the lake.

In a lake environment, the most important causal verb is the word *eats*, a word that implies the idea of dependency between species. John Cote began by asking each student to take the place of an animal in the ecosystem. Each student then mapped the species on a complex "eats" chain, a causal chain showing only one kind of causal relationship. Figure 9.13 shows how the whitefish could be mapped between eating and being eaten by other species in the computer simulation of a lake.

Each student specialized in one species, drawing a causal analytic map for "eats" and using the computer simulation to figure out what would eat or be eaten by the animal they represented. When each student had created an "eats" chain for one kind of animal, the teacher put each student in a group with other students representing other animals. Within the larger group, the students' task was to map the ecosystem as a network. A network map of causes uses an arrow to specify a causal relationship between any two elements. As each student explained what eats his or her animal, and then what his or her animal eats, the group could map the interrelations among all species in the lake, using arrows to link the "eating" animals to the eaten (see Figure 9.14).

As general maps of the ecosystem, these maps were not particularly comprehensible to any of us who were not in the classroom. The students who developed the network maps, however, were able to predict far-ranging consequences of even minor tinkering with life forms in the lake.

"Let's use some poison to get rid of those mosquito larvae!" Cote would suggest. The class could show him that four species would suffer directly and several others would suffer indirectly.

"Let's trap the otter so we'll have more sport fishing in the lake." In the short term, all of the larger fish would benefit from an otter-free

FIGURE 9.13   Analytic Map for One Fourth-Grade Whitefish Specialist

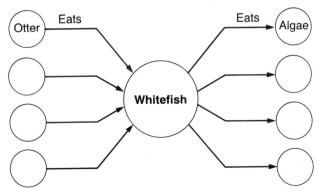

Causal Chain for One Species

FIGURE 9.14   Map of Interactions Developed by Fourth-Grade Specialists

Causal Network Map: "Odell Lake Ecosystem"

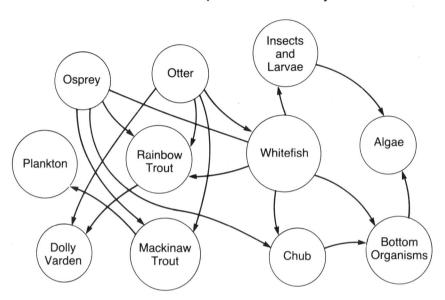

lake. As the population of all fish expanded, however, what would happen to the food chain? What would happen to oxygen in the water? Which fish that had been "otter food" would be more successful when the population of large fish had increased? Which species would benefit in the longer term, if any? John Cote's fourth-graders were not prepared to tangle with "chaotics," the study of unpredictability in complex systems, but they surely gained greater respect for the degree of uncertainty that can follow a small change in a large and complex system. At the end, with the otters gone, the students were aware that they did not know what would happen to other species. Their causal maps predicted everything from fishing paradise to a dead lake. Causal analysis could not get them firm answers. It could only raise the right questions.

HYPOTHETICAL CAUSE/EFFECT THINKING: PLANNING AND DECISION MAKING

"What if?" we ask. "What if?" The question opens the door to the future. Prediction and planning give us a way to control the future. Prediction and planning are often the purpose for causal analysis. If the future proves partially unmanageable, planners gain an increased respect for the extent to which unpredictable events intervene in even the most systematic planning sequence. Still, a map of the future gives us a standard, a sense of necessary process and, most important, a vision of ourselves trying to take hold of future events. Causal mapping gives us a lens through which we can see our hopes take form.

Causal mapping can also provide a vehicle for the if/then conditional logic that supports the skill of decision making. To decide well, we have to be able to imagine the chain of effects that will follow our decision to do one thing, as opposed to another. In deciding, we are causing something to happen. In deciding, however, we are responsible not only for the final effect we generate but for all the effects along the causal chain. Decision making involves complex hypotheses; we have to imagine more than one effect resulting from one decision. If we can predict all the effects along the chain, we can estimate the cost of our decision. In deciding, we start a process with four phases:

1. *Defining choices:* In relation to a present condition, we separate a number of choices.
2. *Chaining the effects:* For each choice, we map out all the effects, good and bad, that will follow that choice.
3. *Assessing the costs:* For each choice and all the steps resulting from each choice, we calculate both the costs and the benefits.
4. *Choosing:* We choose to maximize benefits at the least cost.

A decision is the right one if we arrive at an end we desire—and if all the steps along the way are not too costly. Examining decisions is more challenging than planning. Potentially, any choice may unleash a pack of stray "effects," some of which may have nothing to do with our getting the effect we desire.

DECIDING: THE SUFFERING BUTTON

A decision map (or tree) can look like any causal map, except that the choices make up the first steps in parallel chains. In asking students to choose and helping them map out the path from their choices, we are showing them how to avoid impulsive leaps. Many students have learned to love their impulsivity, despite its costs. In mapping out choices, perhaps at the least they will recognize the importance of choosing to choose.

Choosing requires extensive hypothetical reasoning. "What if?" becomes the question. For each answer to the first "what if?", more "what ifs" await. In tracing answers to "what if" questions toward the future, students are *forward chaining* causally linked events.

The "suffering button" exercise, which is familiar to many teachers, requires extended hypothetical thinking. The suffering button is an imaginary device that a teacher can bring to any classroom. It guarantees to eliminate all suffering on the globe, instantly and for all time, once a bright group of young people decides to push the button. To begin the exercise, the teacher brings the suffering button (or something that looks a bit like such a device) to class and offers to push it at the expressed wish of the class. If a class decides to "hit the switch" on suffering, the teacher agrees to push the button to see what happens. At first, most students respond impulsively to the choice. They want to eliminate suffering. "Hit it!" some say. After some thought, some may begin to question. Then, with support, they may begin to chain forward the effects that might result from eliminating suffering from human experience. Their hypothetical chains form the base of decision making.

Mary Heins and I introduced the suffering button during a sixth-grade social studies unit in which her class had been investigating natural disasters and their effects around the globe. "Who thinks we should push the suffering button?" she asked. Virtually every hand was in the air, at least temporarily. "OK," we said, "Let's give it a push. Get ready for the end of suffering!" We paused. Some hands began to fall and some faces were suddenly clouded with doubt. "We have to agree on this one," Heins said. "Come on, let's get the hands up again." This time, only half the hands went up. "OK," she continued. "I guess we will have to think this through." We broke the class into cooperative groups of three students, all of whom either wanted to push the button or did not want to push it. She showed each group how to map out a chain of effects they believed would follow the end of suffering. "Create a map of the effects you would expect after suffering ends," she said. "You will use your map to convince the rest of the groups that your decision is right."

Creating a hypothetical argument in the abstract was not the first step for most groups. Some groups, like Frank's in Figure 9.15, anchored their causal maps in specific events among the people they knew. To think hypothetically, they had to take it down to specifics. Working with specific cases gave them confidence. Frank's group created a chain in which the end of suffering leads Frank to relax all summer. In Figure 9.15, Frank smiles all summer, but does not cut or stack firewood. In the winter, Frank freezes to death. Would the end of suffering lead us all to our deaths? Frank's group decided to argue against pushing the suffering button. Other groups decided the opposite. To focus the debate, Mary Heins and I created a larger decision map on the blackboard, explaining the place of suffering in human experience and the results of a decision to eliminate suffering.

In the end, the sixth grade decided not to push the suffering button. Together, they designed a chain map showing the reasoning that led to that decision. The decision map in Figure 9.16 shows that suffering can

FIGURE 9.15   Decision Chain at the Concrete Level

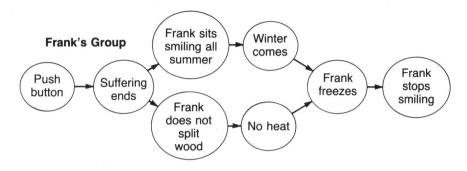

A Prediction Chain from a Specific Example

Question: What will happen when we push the button to eliminate all suffering?

FIGURE 9.16   Abstract Model as a Basis for Decision Making

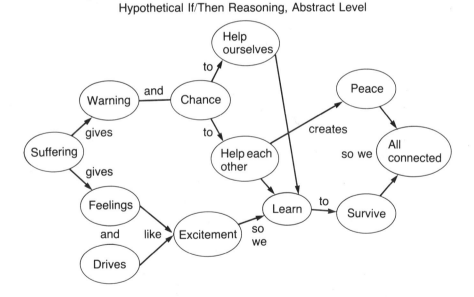

Why the Sixth Grade Chose Not to Push the Suffering Button
Hypothetical If/Then Reasoning, Abstract Level

be both a warning and a source of good feelings, like excitement. As a warning, suffering is a signal that we should help ourselves or help others, which creates peace. As a source of positive feelings, suffering helps us learn to survive and shows us that we are all connected. It is not likely that any single member of the class could have expressed the complexity of thought leading to this final assessment. The causal map allowed the whole class to map all the reasons why suffering might have some value. There is, in fact, no suffering switch. Do people try to remove their suffering without a switch? Yes. Drugs, sex, fast cars, clothes, food—all aim to eliminate suffering. There are many ways to escape. Shall we map out a chain of effects for any of those decisions?

A CASE STUDY: FORWARD CHAINING
FROM AN INDUCTIVE TOWER

In teaching eighth-grade language arts, Jori Dean had one primary goal: to make her students active readers who are aggressive about finding meaning in the literature they read. Dean developed an approach to her literature unit that used both filmed and written versions of old tales to teach close analytic observation. Being aggressive involves seeking answers before they appear in the text or on the screen. Finding meaning may involve thinking ahead to foresee where the stories might lead. To do both, her students had to locate facts in the stories that would give them the power to foresee how the stories might end. Jori Dean teaches her literature unit with a focus on prediction.

To learn how to predict, Dean's eighth-grade students had to combine inductive and deductive forms of thinking. First, they had to think inductively. They had to use a narrow base of facts to discover causal trends or themes in the literature. Second, they had to think deductively, using their hypotheses to predict the future. To support inductive thinking, Dean taught her students how to build inductive towers (see Chapter 6). As a medium for predicting, she taught her students how to make causal chain maps. If they could identify the main problem and the causal forces from a few pieces of text, they could map out the rest of the story. Throughout the literature unit, reading or watching a film would involve using a story to check and modify predictions, a facility developed by good readers (Paris, Lipson, & Wixson, 1983). In becoming strategic readers, Dean's students would actively generate hypotheses about the text they were reading, and then use their reading to modify their views.

At the beginning of one class, Jori Dean told the group that they would see a filmed version of an old story. "It's called *Bearskin*," she told them. They were delighted. A movie! Then she mentioned with a smile that they would see only three minutes of the tale. The class groaned. "You mean we have to predict again?" a student inquired. Their teacher nodded. They had done this before. "Don't worry," Dean assured them. "You will get a chance to check what you have predicted against the conclusion of the film." "Today?" a concerned student asked. "Yes, today," she answered, laughing. Silently, the eighth grade reached for paper and pens. They would need to watch closely to capture the necessary facts. The first three minutes would require intense concentration.

The three minutes passed all too quickly. The "factual" elements of the story were simple: an open field and a stranger in black who offered wealth to a soldier returning from the war poor and alone. Actually, the stranger's offer was a dare: If the soldier will go unbathed and sleep without a bed for seven years, wearing nothing but an old skin, he will have vast wealth and power. As if by magic, a bear suddenly reared up from behind a hill. The soldier shot the bear. Jori Dean turned on the lights and shut off the VCR.

She moved her students into collaborative groups to select facts that might help them make a reliable prediction. Working quickly, they built an inductive tower supporting the two choices the soldier faced (see Figure 9.17). Her students picked out three facts about the soldier from

FIGURE 9.17   An Inductive Tower as a Basis for Hypothetical Thinking

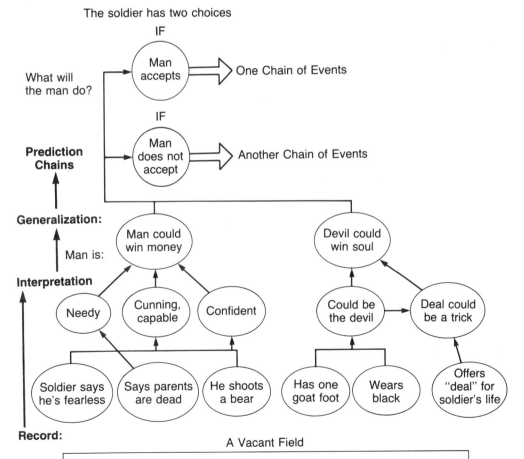

which they infer that he was both capable and he needed the money. Could he trust the man in black? The stranger had one goat foot, which led them to suspect a trick. The stranger in black could be the devil. The soldier was brave and strong enough to win the money but the devil could win his soul. In view of these facts, the soldier had but two possible choices: he could accept the dark stranger's deal or he could avoid the deal and the chance of a trick.

With the soldier's choices clear, Jori Dean asked the class to work in small groups to map out a causal sequence for both choices and then to predict the choice the soldier would make. When they had developed their thoughts, she brought the whole class back together and created a complex decision chain for the soldier's choice. As shown in Figure 9.18, there are two possibilities for the end of *Bearskin*. The soldier could win money or lose everything. There are also two main chains that result from the soldier's decision. Both chains could result in a victory for either the soldier or the devil.

The groups produced long causal chains, some with several levels for both the choices. After ten minutes, the class was confident that they had mapped the options and could predict the most probable path toward the most likely outcome. Dean compiled from the separate maps a single

FIGURE 9.18   A Complex Causal Map as a Basis for Predictions

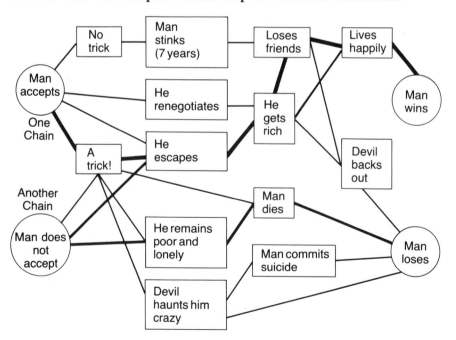

causal map, fusing both options the soldier faced. Among all the possible paths from the first three minutes of film, the class found two that looked probable.

First, it was possible that the devil was making a good offer: The soldier would wear the same clothes and "stink" for seven years, losing all his friends, but then he would receive the money and win. On the other hand, the man could refuse the offer of money and live in poverty for the rest of his life. What was the film about? Greed? Risk? Youth? Temptation? The class decided that the story was about greed: The soldier would make the deal with the devil and then suffer for it, but win in the end. He might lose the money but gain something better. When the class had made its predictions and reasoned them through, Dean turned the film back on without comment. As they had predicted, the soldier agreed to the devil's wager. At critical points along the path, the students cheered or sighed as they had to revise their prediction. Having made some claims about the meaning of the story and used reasoning to predict the end, the students had a stake in what would happen next.

After several opportunities to map stories, the eighth grade had also gained a sense of what skills it takes to make accurate predictions. In small groups they analyzed the process they had used to predict the path of a film or story and also to predict the future of their own efforts. "What does it take to make good predictions?" their teacher asked. They responded with guidance for those who would want to divine the future from the present:

How to Predict: Some Eighth-Grade Guidelines

1. Be realistic.
   a. Use your knowledge
   b. Try to comprehend

2. Think how others normally react.
   a. Think of obstacles
   b. Use the facts
   c. Then think ahead

3. Think everything through, analyze.
   a. Evaluate
   b. Synthesize

4. Use some imagination to simplify and cut details down.

Their formulation is a simple one, but it includes much of what we know about causal thinking and the process of making informed decisions.

SUGGESTIONS FOR TEACHERS

1. For a unit you are planning to teach, list the causal relationships that exist or may be implied by the content. Devise a simple pretest that will show you how aware your students are of these relationships.

2. For a unit you plan to teach, make a list of the events or ideas you want your students to be able to explain. Design a small group assignment that requires students to backmap those events or ideas.

3. Are there any events coming up in the school year for which student planning is required? (The prom is one possibility. Term papers, large tests, field trips and projects are more common.) To create a planning chart:
   a. Note the main goal or outcome at the right side of a page.
   b. By asking the question, What is it going to take to accomplish this goal? develop subgoals in a column to the left of the main goal.
   c. For each subgoal, map out the events in the order that will lead to the accomplishment of the subgoals, working backwards from the subgoal toward the present moment.
   d. Create a time line along the bottom of the page and note critical dates within the map itself.
   e. Assign small groups to take responsibility for each subgoal and all the steps along the causal path for that goal.

4. All of us try to predict the future. Not many use an approach to prediction that makes our thinking visible to others. For any important event coming up in the near future, ask your students to work together to develop prediction chains. As events occur related to the event being predicted, allow your students to use new information to change their predictions. When the event has occurred, ask them to explain any differences between what they predicted and what transpired.

5. What decisions are included in content you plan to teach, or are implied by the content? Do these decisions offer your students a chance to think hypothetically? Teach your students to forward map the causal chains that would follow different choices they might make.

6. Are there opportunities in your subject area for the question "What if?" Think of ways to get your students to develop hypotheses for what might happen under changed conditions. When they have declared an hypothesis, show them how to chain map their reasoning so they can explain it to other students.

Helping Students Reflect on Their Thinking

Even when your students experience success in using a graphic organizer for understanding the subject area, they will not automatically see wider usage for the technique they employed. They will need your help in finding other situations where the same technique would work as well. When your students are using a graphic to think about some part of content, make some effort to let them: (1) review the process they used to think and (2) look for other situations in or out of school where the same process might work. We can call the transfer of a thinking process a "Bridge."

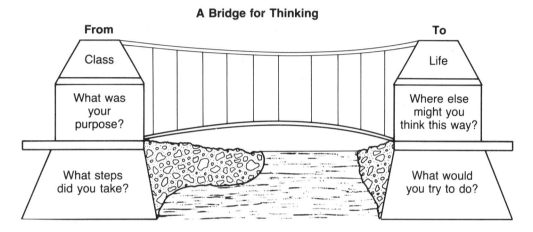

A Bridge for Thinking

- What jobs or careers depend on being able to analyze a series of events?
- What jobs or careers depend on prediction?
- Can you map out the chain of effects for a decision you face today?
- Try to identify three achievements in history that resulted from the question, "What if?"

REFERENCES

Anderson, R. C. (1977). The notion of schemata and the educational enterprise: General discussion of the conference. In R. C. Anderson, R. J. Spiro, & W. E. Montague (Eds.), *Schooling and the Acquisition of Knowledge.* Hillsdale, NJ: Lawrence Erlbaum.

Ault, C. R. (1985). Concept mapping as a study strategy in earth science. *Journal of College Science Teaching,* September/October, 38–44.

Brewer, W. F., & Nakamura, G. V. (1984). The nature and functions of schemas. In R. S. Weir & T. K. Krull (Eds.), *Handbook of Social Cognition.* Hillsdale, NJ: Lawrence Earlbaum.

Brooks, M. (1987). Curriculum design from a constructivist perspective. *Educational Leadership,* January, 63–67.

Camstra, B., & van Bruggen, J. (1984). Schematizing: The empirical evidence. In D. F. Dansereau & C. D. Holley (Eds.), *Spacial Learning Strat-*

egies: Techniques, Applications and Related Issues. New York: Academic Press.

Clarke, J. (1979). Homer and Aristotle in the classroom. *Liberal Education,* Fall, 395–399.

Clarke, J.; MacPherson, B.; & Holmes, D. (1982). Cigarette smoking and locus of control among young adolescents. *Journal of Health and Social Behavior,* 23(2), 203–211.

Clement, J. (1979). Mapping a student's causal conceptions from a problem solving protocol. In J. Lochhead & J. Clemmons (Eds.), *Cognitive Process Instruction.* Philadelphia: Franklin Institute Press.

French, L. A. (1985). Real world knowledge as the basis for social and cognitive development. In J. Pryor & J. Day (Eds.), *Development of Social Cognition.* New York: Springer-Verlag.

Glasser, W. (1984). *Control Theory.* New York: Harper and Row.

Glasser, W. (1985). *Control Theory in the Classroom.* New York: Harper and Row.

Holley, C. F., & Dansereau, D. F. (1984). *Spacial Learning Strategies: Techniques, Applications and Related Issues.* Orlando, FL: Academic Press.

Holloway, S. D. (1988). Concepts of ability and effort in Japan and the U.S. *Journal of Educational Research,* 58(3), 327–346.

Kassin, P., & Pryor, J. P. (1985). The development of attribution processes. In J. B. Prior & J. D. Day (Eds.), *The Development of Social Cognition.* New York: Springer-Verlag.

Kelley, H. H. (1972). Causal schemata and the attribution process. In E. E. Jones et al. (Eds.), *Attribution: Perceiving the Causes of Behavior.* Morristown, NJ: General Learning Press, Chapter 9, pp. 151–174.

Milligan, J. R. (1979). Schema learning theory: An approach to perceptual learning. *Review of Educational Research,* 49(2), 197–207.

Mirande, M. J. A. (1984). Schematizing: Technique and application. In D. F. Dansereau & C. D. Holley (Eds.), *Spacial Learning Strategies: Techniques, Applications and Related Issues.* New York: Academic Press.

Paris, S. G.; Lipson, M. Y.; & Wixson, K. K. (1983). Becoming a strategic reader. *Contemporary Educational Psychology,* 8, 293–316.

Piaget, J. (1964). *Judgment and Reasoning in the Child.* Patterson, NJ: Littlefield Adams and Company.

Rumelhart, D. E. (1984). Schemata and the cognitive system. In R. S. Weir & T. K. Krull (Eds.), *Handbook of Social Cognition.* Hillsdale, NJ: Lawrence Earlbaum.

Sherman, S. J., & Corty, E. (1984). Cognitive heuristics. In R. S. Weir & T. K. Krull (Eds.), *Handbook of Social Cognition.* Hillsdale, NJ: Lawrence Erlbaum.

Stewart, J. H. (1984). The representation of knowledge: Curricular and instructional implications for science teaching. In D. F. Dansereau & C. F. Holley (Eds.), *Spacial Learning Strategies: Techniques, Applications and Related Issues.* New York: Academic Press.

Surber, C. F. (1985). Application of information integration to children's social cognitions. In R. S. Weir & T. K. Krull (Eds.), *Handbook of Social Cognition.* Hillsdale, NJ: Lawrence Erlbaum, Chapter 3, pp. 59–93.

Vaughan, J. L. (1984). Concept structuring, the technique and empirical evidence. In D. F. Dansereau & C. F. Holley (Eds.), *Spacial Learning Strategies: Techniques, Applications and Related Issues.* New York: Academic Press.

Vygotsky, L. (1986). *Thought and Language.* Trans. by A. Kozulin. Cambridge, MA: MIT University Press.

Weiner, B. (1974). *Achievement Motivation and Attribution Theory.* Morristown, NJ: General Learning Press.

10

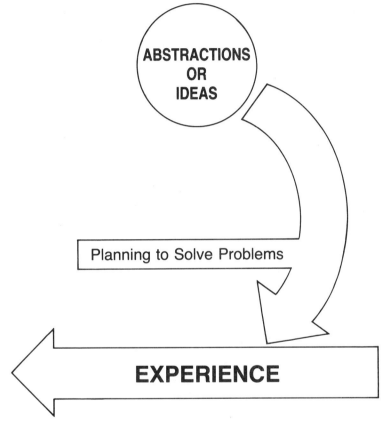

Can I solve the problem I have set? Do I like what I get when I solve this problem? Have I made the situation coherent? Have I made it congruent with my fundamental values and theories? Have I kept inquiry moving?
—DONALD A. SCHÖN, *The Reflective Practitioner*

Planning to Solve Problems

ANYONE WHO HAS EVER STRUGGLED UNSUCCESSFULLY with a problem may feel some sympathy for students who respond to all word problems in mathematics the same way—by impulsively adding up every number they see. Dates, distances, times, dollars—all may go into one pot. Impulsivity is one notable characteristic of poor learners and poor problem solvers (Letteri, 1982). Problems cause frustration. It doesn't feel good to face a problem. To feel better, we may throw everything we happen to have available at the problems that block our path. If we happen to have addition, we fire away with addition. If we have subtraction, we may throw in some of that, too. This chapter aims to encourage teachers to show students how to represent problems graphically so that they have a chance to:

1. *Induce:* Locate new information or activate their knowledge about the problem
2. *Deduce:* Plan out a reasonable sequence of steps toward solution

As students succeed in solving problems by using a planned approach, they may slowly put aside the delights of impulsive flailing and adopt a more reflective approach.

A PROBLEM SOLVING EPISODE: DO IT! DO IT AGAIN! DO IT HARDER!

The sixth-grade class had been waiting expectantly for last period. During last period, again they would have a chance to do puzzles. The classroom was set up in problem stations—areas where students could work together on problems of different types. Some stations were set up with puzzles based in arithmetic: a set of 16 numbers on a 4 × 4 matrix, for example, that must add up to 15—horizontally, vertically, and diagonally. Other stations required arranging geometric shapes, called *tangrams*, to make predefined figures. Other stations just had puzzles—an oval train track with two engines and two cars that must be "parked" on opposite sides of the "train yard." A bridge restricted free travel in the trainyard, stopping the engines from moving the caboose in a full circle. One station featured a box filled with cubes and rectangles that didn't quite fit their container. Making them all fit was the goal.

Throughout the fall, the students had been working on puzzles of different kinds. When at last it was time, several students rushed to stations to pick up a puzzle they had had to leave last time. Other students moved toward puzzles that did not include arithmetic, hoping to avoid struggling through calculations. Several others straggled toward stations where their friends had already arrived. A few complained listlessly about puzzles and how hard it is to do them.

I joined the kids at the oval train yard. I was just a visitor and, frankly, I had less confidence than they did about those calculation problems. The train crew looked as if they knew how to deal with problems.

"Well, how does it work?" I asked, hoping for an easy answer or perhaps some quick glory.

"Billy did it last time," one student said. I looked at Billy, who remained silent and kept his eyes down.

"Yeah," another said, "I saw him do it. And Carol did it last week."

"She did not."

"That's what I heard."

I watched Carol cringe slightly at another station—one of the stations requiring work with numbers. The group turned back to Billy. Billy reluctantly took one blue train engine and moved it half way around the track, pushing the red car ahead.

"The caboose won't fit through that bridge, there," Carol told me, pointing. Billy had the red car and caboose wedged up against the bridge. He set off in the other direction. But then the red car was on the wrong side of the blue engine. Nope, it wouldn't park.

"Yes, that's it," his friend applauded, as Billy brought the car around the track and into the right "yard." But in pulling out into the oval track again, he had his blue engine stuck between the bridge and the wedged caboose. So he was trapped. My heart sank. I was beginning to see the problem.

"How did you do it yesterday?" Carol asked Billy. I thought I heard some gloat in her voice.

"I can't remember," Billy said, quietly.

"Looks like a tough one," I said, to ease the pressure on Billy. "How did you solve it before?"

"Well," Billy said, "I just kept the red engine moving. Then I moved the blue engine. Then I might have played some more with the other engine. We were talking, and all. Then when I looked up suddenly I could see that the blue car was set up to go to its siding and the red car was already in here, where it belongs, and the caboose was—who knows where? So, I just stuck the red car back in the yard. Done."

"Do it!" Carol urged. Billy fiddled aimlessly with the blue car, running it toward the edge of the desk. "Do it."

He was saved temporarily by some commotion at the next station, where a group of kids had just figured out how to get those cubes and rectangles to fit in that little box.

"I did it," a female voice proclaimed in triumph, holding the box in the air.

"I saw her," says another.

"Do it," the gathering crowd exhorted. They didn't believe she could do it. One small boy poured the blocks out on a desk again. The slight young woman put all the wooden blocks loosely in the box and put the box top loosely over the unruly pile. Then she shook her hands vigorously. The box rattled. She stopped and looked. The blocks still didn't fit.

"Do it again," her friend suggested, looking around the room defiantly. The slight young woman covered all the blocks with the box top again. She shook it for a longer period of time.

"It worked before," her friend assured the crowd. "Do it harder, Marybeth."

Marybeth continued shaking the box and peaking under the lid, but the outer edge of the crowd was already drifting back to their own problem stations.

NOVICES IN PROBLEM SOLVING

To the extent that all learning involves asking questions and then finding answers to those questions, all learning is problem solving. To the extent that preceding chapters have described methods for helping students gather information and develop general models, each of the chapters also deals with the kinds of thinking that helps solve problems. The crucial difference between problem solving and other forms of thinking is that problem solving, even in the smallest way, aims to change the structure of the universe as we know it. We set out to solve problems because we are not quite satisfied with the experience we are having, for example:

- The second-grade student working out a sheet of math problems is changing the structure of the contents of her mind and then adding something new to the universe of information defined by the problem sheet.
- The engineer completing drawings for a new bridge is helping put a new face on a much larger part of physical reality.

Both are using their minds to create something that did not exist before they set out to create a new answer and "fill in the blank."

I asked members of this sixth-grade class what it took to be good at solving math problems. "Luck," was the prevalent answer. If they shook the box long enough and had some luck, all the cubes would fall into place. If you ran your trains around the track and turned your mind to other things, your cars would eventually end up on the right siding. "That's all it takes?" I asked, "Just luck?"

"Brains," was another common response. When I asked the students what it meant to have "brains," they assured me it was something you had to be born with.

"You mean you have to be lucky?" I asked again.

"Yep," they agreed.

Over the fall semester, the sixth grade had learned to stick with problems for a while. Time and obdurate persistence can grind away problems. To the sixth grade, and to others of us, I suspect, if you can stand the pain and keep moving, the problems will fall away. Persistence is basic to problem solving.

What more does it take to solve problems effectively? According to most research in problem solving, luck and ability are not the right answers to this question. Yet "luck and ability" may characterize our beliefs about what it takes to solve problems. If we believe in luck, we may rely on luck, even in problem situations that call for skill. If we have learned that luck and native ability are the basis of successful problem solving, we have also learned to see ourselves as somewhat helpless.

A vast and useful body of research has developed in psychology around the phenomenon of "learned helplessness" (Weiner, Neirenberg, & Goldstein, 1976; Lefcourt, 1974). At the heart of it, repeated instances of failure to manage problems may teach us that we are powerless before the problems we face (Wheaton, 1980; Clarke, MacPherson, & Holmes, 1982). Our minds are wonderful model makers, but some of us fashion a model of the world in which we see ourselves exerting little influence and solving few problems. Our mental models can empower us to solve problems aggressively or to withdraw passively from the problems we face. Every instance of successful problem solving contributes to the development of a self-concept that includes personal power. In teaching problem solving in the content areas, we are trying to expand the size of the universe in which our students see themselves exerting some control.

MAKING EXPERTS FROM NOVICES

Problem solving is an attempt to change the nature of the reality we experience. The simplest definition of a problem involves a situation in which what we need is not the same as what we have or where we are is not where we want to be. Problem solving then becomes a matter of changing what exists to better fit what we desire. Newell and Simon (1972) saw problem solving as resolving the difference between the current state and a goal state by defining steps through a "problem space." Figure 10.1 represents the "state-space" conception of problem solving, with steps through that space as by Nickerson, Perkins, and Smith (1985).

To move through the problem space and achieve a goal, a problem solver needs to represent the problem and determine a goal, plan out an approach, carry out the planned approach, and use feedback along the way to self-correct (Bransford, Sherwood, & Sturdevant, 1987). Although this model has been useful, particularly in describing the trial and error

FIGURE 10.1   A State-Space Representation of Problem Solving

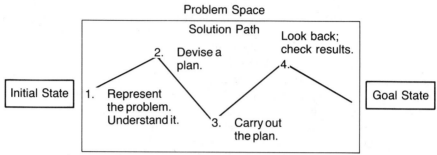

Any step that moves us closer to the goal state is a solution.

Adapted from R. S. Nickerson, D. N. Perkins, and E. E. Smith, *The Teaching of Thinking* (Hillsdale, NJ: Lawrence Erlbaum, 1985).

problem solving of novices like the sixth-graders above, it does not account for the role of knowledge in problem solving or well describe the work of expert problem solvers.

Research has shown that what we already know about a problem has a profound influence on the way we move through a "problem space" (Larkin et al., 1980). When a problem has no single solution, as in the social sciences, expert problem solving may amount to the ability to organize a large amount of information in support of a relatively large number of solutions or parts of solutions (Voss et al., 1985). People who know a lot about a subject are generally better problem solvers. Novices, who have little knowledge on which to rely, must resort to inductive thinking to understand the problem. They have to gather lots of information first—perhaps by trial and error tinkering—to understand the problem. Novices tend to work backward from the goal, as in backmapping (Chapter 9), because the only real measure of progress they have is whether they are perceptibly closer to reaching a solution. They lack a general model on which they can rely to support deductive thinking and to guide them through planned steps.

Experts, perhaps guided by deeply embedded mental models of the problems they face, can work deductively, using a few rules, principles, and established concepts to understand the whole framework (Gentner & Stevens, 1983). Experts work forward from the information they have toward the goal they desire, confident that their general knowledge will allow them to recognize progress and errors along the way (Larkin et al., 1980, p. 1338). Experts rely on deduction; once they recognize the general pattern or type of the problem, they use their stored networks, models, and scripts to work through solution steps quickly and efficiently. Experts know a lot. Experts also use what they do know to figure out what they do not know. Experts work efficiently. They can postulate and then look for the shortest route between the current state and their goal. They avoid random trials and exert considerable effort simply in designing an approach to the problem they face.

Novices may not systematically review what they know or design a methodical approach. They may act impulsively, hoping that good luck will churn up enough information and ideas to get them from current state to goal state. Novices flail. Lacking information organized in comprehensive models, novices try to create experience that will bring them some kind of information, perhaps even "the right answer" if they flail hard and long enough. Novices have to work inductively first. They have to develop a model at the same time they are trying to solve the problem. In a sense, the flailing of novices is an attempt to quickly make up for their lack of knowledge. The student in the sixth-grade class who shook the box to make the cubes fit felt she had no recourse except to create information about boxes with her own hands. Shake the box. Look at it. Shake it again, harder. Look again. Chance gave her "the right answer" once. Chance could repeat the gift. Experience in problem solving is essential to learning. Still, if we want our students to solve problems in the content areas, we must make sure that they can access all the information they need, organize that information into telling patterns, and then design an approach that will let them change the situation.

ACTIVATING INDUCTION AND DEDUCTION: IF/THEN RULES

By watching experts solve problems, researchers have been able to refine a view of successful problem solving. Larkin (1979) has identified three general attributes of expert problem solvers:

1. They see tasks in terms of condition-action units or if/then relationships. "*If* the caboose blocks the track, *then* move the caboose to a siding," they say. That is, they see a problem in terms of conditions that imply a related set of responses or actions. In this sense, their problem-solving skills are embedded in a much larger network of understandings particular to a problem domain.
2. The larger network or schema includes assumptions about the way things behave under different conditions. Before they start to calculate, experts run through a general model of the way things work to see whether the model applies to the specific case.
3. They begin planning for problem solving with a "low detail" model of the problem situation—a mental sketch. If they can make the low detail model work, they can then add details that will let them run through any necessary calculations. They are

looking first for the larger patterns that define basic relationships, and then for the smaller patterns that imply particular steps or calculations.

Larkin's research supports a view of expert problem solving as a deductive process, supported by inductive information gathering.

Among both experts and novices, the basic pattern of problem solving may be similar. Both depend on if/then patterns of thinking. Both have to rely on a process of inductive data collection and analysis followed by a deductive process of model making and solution steps or trials. Experts have reduced laborious induction/deduction sequences to scriptlike "rules" in which a specific observed problem condition (an "if") is linked to a specific kind of response (a "then") (Holland et al., 1986, p. 14). One kind of if/then rule generates simple categorical definitions: "*If* it has hair and a long nose, *then* it could be a collie." For problem solving, the more powerful if/then rules use a present condition to predict the future or to prescribe future actions.

Predictions:

If the dog growls, then he might also bite.
If the dog sees your cat, he will take off after it.

Prescriptions:

If the dog goes after your cat, call the fire department.
If he doesn't, why don't we sit and have a soda?

If/then rules have the same basic structure as the cycle tying inductive to deductive thinking.

Problem solving can involve a specific application of the Thinking Wheel introduced in Chapter 1 and clarified through examples thereafter. Under most conditions, problem solving occurs in two phases, an inductive phase of information gathering and analysis followed by a deductive phase of planning and applying procedures (see Figure 10.2). In this sense, the Thinking Wheel simply reformulates the steps of the scientific method:

Inductive Phase:

1. A problem is observed in nature.
2. The problem is clarified and hypotheses are developed.

Deducticve Phase:

3. An experiment is designed.
4. The experiment is carried out and data are gathered.
5. The data are analyzed and conclusions are drawn.

FIGURE 10.2   Problem Solving as Representation

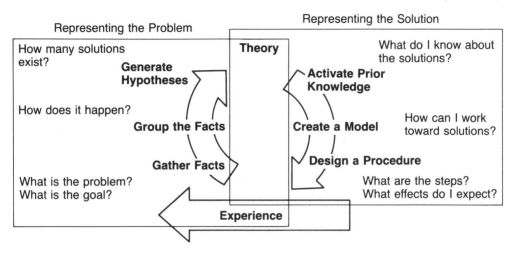

The inductive phase includes looking carefully at the problem, getting the facts straight, organizing those facts so their meaning is clear, recalling additional information as necessary, and setting a clear goal. The deductive phase includes proposing a general model for how the problem works, designing a set of procedures for solving the problem, and working the steps toward solution, gaining corrective feedback with each step. Any specific problem might require one inductive/deductive cycle— or many, each refining the information and approach of that which preceded it. If students know a great deal about the subject, the teacher may focus attention on the deductive application of rules and procedures. If the students are still developing knowledge, the teacher should consider working on the inductive and the deductive sides with equal emphasis. As in the state-space approach, students can continue acting and checking for reduction between current state and goal state until all the differences have disappeared—and the goal state has been achieved (Newell & Simon, 1972).

THE ROLE OF REPRESENTATION
IN PROBLEM SOLVING

Representation is essential to problem solving. It takes the problem from the world of events and creates from it an abstract model. By converting problems from the world of experience into abstract versions or models, we are reducing our reliance on our hands and increasing the extent to which we can use our mental powers. For our minds to work at all, they need an abstracted representation to work on. Our hands may be essential in gathering information and trying out solutions, but hands cannot solve problems alone. Graphic organizers can give us a concrete representation for our minds to work over.

A problem representation is a cognitive structure corresponding to a problem that is constructed by a solver on the basis of domain-specific knowledge (Glaser, 1984). An expert, in any field, usually tries to represent a problem simply, on paper, before trying for solutions. "Paper and pencil provide an unlimited extension of the problem solver's working memory" (Larkin, et al., 1980). Novices may have to wade in and get involved in order to draw a representation. Sternberg (1987) has concluded from his own studies of problem solving that either verbal representation or graphic representation may play a role in problem management. The quality of solutions we develop for a problem depends on the detail and accuracy of a problem we represent. More simply, we cannot solve what we cannot see. As an inductive step, drawing can identify the problem space or the conditions—the "ifs." As a deductive step, a drawing can outline the general model or plan for solution making—or the "thens." By putting the conditions and actions in one representation, the student can better control the whole problem-solving process.

Drawing makes us focus on the problem and scan for all relevant information. A drawing suggests clusters or groups that can form steps or simplify. A drawing can force inference by raising questions of relationship or pointing to gaps in the given information. It can cue the problem solver to draw upon prior knowledge (concepts). A drawing can also amount to a plan of attack, imposing order on the general approach, setting a schedule of steps, and preventing diffusion of effort. Finally, drawing a representation can provide the student with an outline of indicators for success. Like any graphic, a problem representation opens the door to dialogue among teachers and students, creating a space where each might share some expertise.

Graphic representation can serve several purposes in teaching problem solving:

1. *By helping students organize the "problem space,"* a graphic can support planned movement from current state to goal state. A graphic can frame the whole problem, allowing students to work through specific steps without losing the path.

2. *By representing the problem conditions (the "ifs"),* students can organize a record of what they know about the problem. Potentially, they can see parts of the problem arranged to reveal relationships.Visible relationships may help them recall additional facts or rules that they can use to solve the problem.

3. *By representing the actions (the "thens"),* students can control the sequence of steps they use to solve the problem. As they complete steps, they can use their results to monitor progress toward the goal they have set.

Sketching, drawing, or diagramming a problem can give students a way to control problem solving. It may free up space in short-term memory for higher-level functions needed in thinking through a problem. No matter what symbols are used in calculating, representation gives the student a way to look at the whole frame before wading in with calculation or "right answer" generation.

USING GRAPHIC ORGANIZERS TO TEACH PROBLEM SOLVING

If students can get a clear enough view of a problem, they are often surprised to discover that they have also obtained a fairly clear view of implied solutions. Descriptions of simple problems often carry their solutions on their backs. When we see the marshmallow fall in the fire, we pull it out. If we lose a pencil, we try to find it. If we see there are not enough chairs, we go get some more. These simple problems have an inductive and deductive side, a period of information gathering and goal setting followed by a period of application or "solving."

Drawing a picture of a problem brings the details, and their relationship, into view, creating a vision of the whole problem space. To the extent that they bring the facts into view, graphics may support inductive thinking. If the drawing suggests a model of how things happen, we can use it to derive specific solutions, a deductive step. The following two examples emphasize the importance of representation to the inductive stages of problem solving, during which the conditions are outlined and analyzed.

Diane Quebec noticed that all the stories her second-grade students were reading involved some kind of problem. Her students, however, often failed to see the problems embedded in the fairy tales. They were not seeing the stories in a problem/solution format. Instead, they were seeing the stories as linked episodes or strings. Two of her students created Figure 10.3 as a way to represent fairy tales. Rather than seeing the stories of how characters solve problems, the students saw fairy tales as an aggregate of some themes, like "power" and "beauty," with accretions of undifferentiated examples, like "Snow White" and other character types. As they began to read fairy tales, the stories were simply events lined up in chronological order. To help them see a problem/solution structure in short stories, Diane Quebec created a simple story frame that guided them in identifying problems and then looking for solutions.

In Figure 10.4, the preliminary questions, Where? Who? When? helped students scan the story for details they could use to identify the problem. Those are inductive steps. Then, the question, "How is it solved?" asked the student to relate problem definitions to solutions, the deductive steps, which should be proven out in the story ending. Quebec

FIGURE 10.3   Second-Grade Conception of Fairy Tales as an Accretion of Partially Linked Ideas

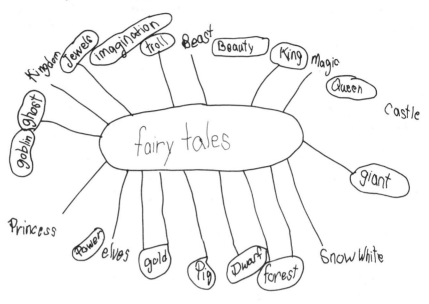

FIGURE 10.4   A Problem-Solving Frame for Second-Grade Readers

What Is the Problem?	How Is It Solved?
Where?	
Who?	
When?	Ending of the Story

was using a graphic organizer to focus student reading on problems and solutions.

Simply asking students to draw a picture may have a similar effect. In teaching natural science to fourth-graders, John Cote wanted to increase their skills in observation and inductive thinking. By setting out problems for fourth-grade students to solve, he found he could accomplish both purposes. For the problems he defined, Cote asked his students to draw a picture that would help them understand the situation thoroughly. Different drawings of the same situation might suggest different kinds of solutions.

THE FENCE LINE: A FOURTH-GRADE PROBLEM

As you are walking along an old barbwire fence, you notice that it passes almost through the middle of a large tree that is perhaps two feet thick. The wire is about two and a half feet off the ground. What does this tell you about how trees grow?

Without a fairly close look at the tree and the wire, an impulsive student might leap to the conclusion that a particularly strong farmer had hammered the wire through the middle of the tree. Working in groups of two, Cote's students drew the tree and the fence line, represented in Figure 10.5. The group that drew Figure 10.5 drew a top view and a side view of the tree. Most students could see from a side view drawing and from prior knowledge that the tree was growing taller. Since the fence was still at about the right level to stop cows, they could infer that not the whole tree was growing taller, only the tips of the branches (labeled 1 in Figure 10.5). Since the tree was large but still stood against the wind, they also inferred that the roots must also be growing fast enough to stabilize the growing branches (labeled 2). Both of these conclusions could be drawn from the side view of the tree. A cross-section of the tree gave some students a third conclusion about tree growth; it must be growing sideways (labeled 3). Since the wire ran through the center of the tree, the students inferred that the fence had been strung when the tree was only a sapling. The tree bark had grown away from the center, stabilizing the tree but burying the wire fence. For this fourth-grade class, two drawings of the situation produced better solutions than may have been possible from a single representation.

FIGURE 10.5   Fourth-Grade Representation of Tree Problem

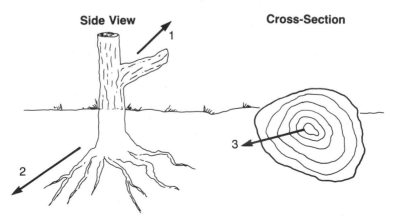

PROCEDURAL MAPPING: WRITING SCRIPTS

Showing the students a problem solving organizer (Figure 10.4) or having them organize facts by drawing a picture (Figure 10.5) can help students manage the inductive or deductive aspects of problem solving. One way to help them plan an approach for themselves involves showing them how to represent a procedure graphically. Using a graphic map to set up a procedure can help an impulsive student organize an approach to a word problem, for example.

Arnell Sherwin teaches a multiage class, grades 4–6. "Math is hard for some students," she explained. "Particularly word problems. They used to look at any problem and just add up the numbers they saw— including dates and addresses. We began to map word problems so we would only use what we needed for a purpose." Sherwin developed a process for mapping word problems that also gives her students a medium for talking through the procedures with each other. Sherwin's process for word problems has four steps:

1. *Set the purpose:* Look for the question mark. What is being asked?
2. *Choose an operation:* Look for cue words in the question.
3. *Map the steps:* Link numbers and operations in a map.
4. *Do calculations and check answers.*

Sherwin and her students have developed a list of cue words on a wall chart that let them figure out which operation is required by a word problem. Figure 10.6 is a word problem mapped out by one student as an addition problem and by another as multiplication. Both maps start with the same purpose—to figure out how much Andrew paid. The first student chose to see the operation as addition, mapping it out as a linear sequence. The second student saw the operation as multiplication, mapping it out in two layers, pencils × pennies.

When a word problem contains irrelevant information, the map helps the students put it to one side. In Sherwin's approach, subtraction maps have the same linear form as addition; division maps have the same form as multiplication. In combination, these simple graphics can produce quite complex problem-solving plans.

As her students gain skill in mapping word problems, Sherwin. asks them to write word problems for each other. Figure 10.7 (page 246) contains problems designed by some of the students and mapped for solution by others. Both problems require at least two distinct phases with different operations. "It's really the same thing as regular math," one student explained, "but the map makes it easier. It shows you whether to 'minus' or 'plus' or 'times' or whatever. The maps help you read the problem and get it straight."

FIGURE 10.6   Two Maps of a Word Problem

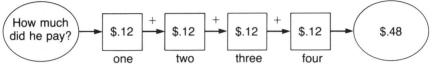

Problem: Andrew bought 4 pencils at the drug store for $.12 each. How much did they cost altogether?

A Map for Addition:

Purpose

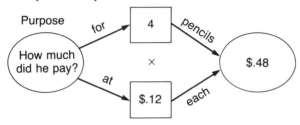

A Map for Multiplication:

"After a while," another student added, "You don't even need the map."

In other words, the purpose of writing out scripts for problem solving is to eliminate the need for writing out scripts.

FROM SCRIPTS TO FLOWCHARTS: MAKING THEM EXPERTS

Problem solving requires a certain bravado. Bravado gives experts another advantage over novices in approaching a new problem. Experts generally know a great deal about a very narrow array of events. They have organized what they know in highly efficient networks and schemata. They have experience in solving problems of different types. Additionally, experts usually know that they know a great deal. All of that gives them courage. Young people in school usually do not feel that they know a lot, either about subject areas or the process of solving problems. They are apt to be more timid than experts in asserting what they know or in aggressively attacking problems. By asking students to create a graphic showing how they solve a particular kind of problem, we can give them some of the psychological advantage enjoyed by experts.

An easy way to put students into the position of expert is to ask them to draw a schematic frame for a problem-solving approach they

FIGURE 10.7   Word Problems Designed and Mapped by Multiaged Students

Jamie's Problem: Jamie went to the store with $10.00. She bought milk for $2.65 and cookies for $1.59. How much did she get back?

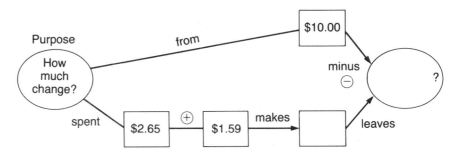

Kevin's Problem: Kevin sells miniature football helmets after school for $.25 each. Yesterday, he sold 10, but bought two candy bars for $.60 each. How much did he take home?

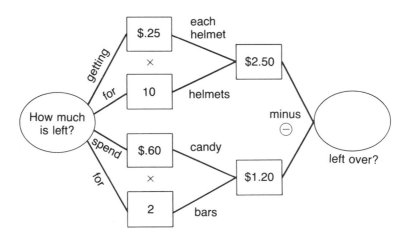

have learned to use. Flowcharts give teachers a relatively simple medium for representing student expertise. A flowchart uses four symbols to represent procedural steps in a problem-solving operation (see Figure 10.8).

Flowcharting is most often taught in computer science, where step-by-step analysis and design are necessities. Increasingly, flowcharts are being used to describe procedures in mathematics. In virtually any area of content, teachers can show students how to flowchart basic procedures, from conducting an interview, to using library resources, to design-

FIGURE 10.8 Symbols Used in Designing Flowcharts

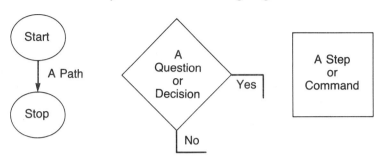

ing a film. From my perspective, the products of this activity have more value in confirming the expertise of the designer than in conveying expertise to others. A student designing a flowchart must cycle through his or her knowledge repeatedly, breaking out steps, decisions, and paths. With a flowchart on paper, students usually find ways to economize, collapsing steps and shortening the path (activities that closely mimic expertise in larger realms). Designing a flowchart forces us to look at a procedure with a critical eye.

Lisa Bovatt teaches her sixth grade to design flowcharts for mathematics, as well as for everyday activities. Before they try to map technical or complex procedures, her students practice with "scripted" events in their daily lives, activities in which they are experts indeed. Figure 10.9 represents a practice flowchart devised by one of Lisa's sixth-graders for the process of cleaning a bedroom. Clearly, this student has discovered the basics of flowcharting, as well as some advanced techniques, such as using feedback loops to represent repeating procedures. Lisa Bovatt's students refine their flowcharts by asking their classmates to walk through the steps and troubleshoot the process. When they have become proficient in flowcharting, and they have also had some fun, they begin work on mathematical procedures, some of which are quite difficult to design.

Figure 10.10 is a flowchart for adding and subtracting fractions, designed by a sixth-grade student in Lisa Bovatt's class. To develop the flowchart, the student needed some practice with flowchart symbols. More important, however, she needed to walk herself through a simple problem requiring the addition of fractions with a common denominator. When she had designed a flowchart for one simple example of addition, she had to try the flowchart with larger numbers—with fractions carrying a denominator smaller than its numerator. Would the flowchart provide a general model for solving this kind of problem? Many trials with increasingly complex problems were necessary to test the increasingly comprehensive "model." When she could make her flowchart work for simple

FIGURE 10.9 Flowchart: How to Clean My Room (If You Really Want to)

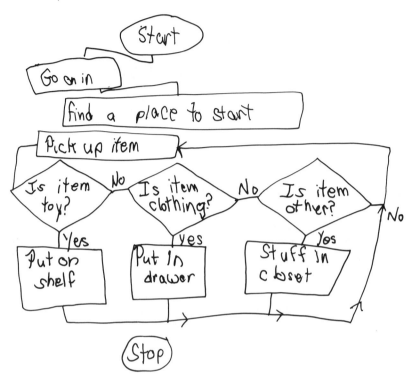

addition problems, she could begin to adjust it to accommodate both addition and subtraction. The adjustment was relatively easy. One loop did the trick. The most formidable step involved adjusting the flowchart to deal with different denominators. Equalizing denominators turned out to be a separate set of procedures; it fit only one place in the flowchart, the beginning. The final product hung on the wall outside of class for several weeks.

Designing and then troubleshooting a flowchart for a computer program proved most challenging to the sixth grade, probably because the computer would accept fewer errors or omissions than Lisa Bovatt herself. Bovatt's students take considerable pride in their ability to map out complex processes. One student wrote:

> *I think flowcharts are very helpful to me and they can help me some day if I become a teacher, which I hope to be. Flowcharts got very frustrating when we had a unit on Computer and Addition. When I got through that— everything else was a piece of cake. . . . I like flowcharts and would do them every day—over class work.*

FIGURE 10.10 A Sixth-Grader's Flowchart for Adding and Subtracting Fractions

How to Add and Subtract Fractions

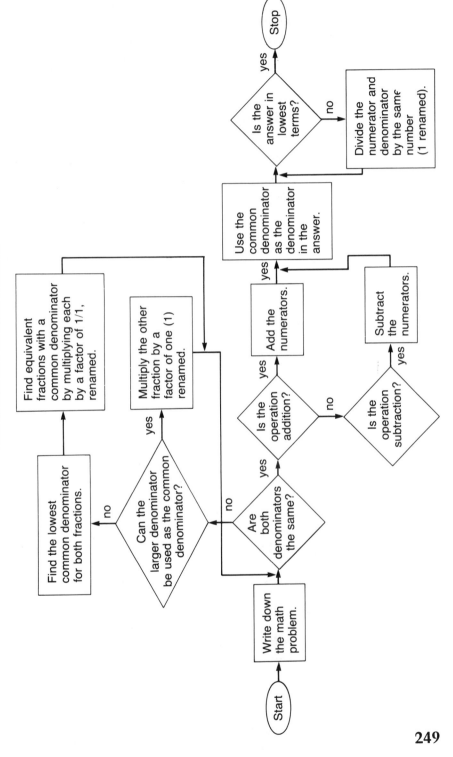

From this student's perspective, designing flowcharts makes other school work look easy. Another student wrote about his flowchart for addition with a different slant, "I'm surprised how hard it is to add if you don't know how."

A flowchart represents in physical form the kind of thinking our minds usually reduce to automatic "scripts." Scripted knowledge is fine, as long as it adequately solves a problem. Counseling psychologists tell us that some of our scripts for everyday behavior actually cause more problems than they solve (Wheaton, 1980; Glasser, 1986). In showing students how to flowchart common activities, we are asking them to take a script off automatic pilot, look at it in an objective form, and consider rearranging or developing some of its parts. If we ask students to flowchart the steps of academic tasks, we may give them a chance to look for gaps in the flow and consider more promising approaches to their own learning.

Lynn Currier teaches her sixth-grade class to design flowcharts for the process of doing their homework. Figure 10.11 is a representation of doing routine homework. The flowchart consists of four or five subroutines. Getting home is the first and most straightforward subroutine, walking from the school bus to a work space. Setting up the work space is a second subroutine, nicely defined. The third subroutine looks more sketchy. "Start work," the chart commands. "Do you understand?" "No?" "Ask for help!" Compared to "getting home," the homework itself is an ill-defined routine.

Could this student be led to revise his routine? Could he include an investigation of the purpose and scope of the homework assignment? Could he include reviewing necessary background material? He knows how to "loop back" to find additional assignments. Could he write in a feedback loop on the homework itself—before seeking help from others? This student seems to manage well the physical steps of homework. Could he gain equivalent control over the intellectual steps? By creating a representation of the process, this student also created a way to look at what he does and consider revision. Surely, a helpful teacher would not suggest all these revisions, but the flowchart creates a medium in which many kinds of questions about homework can be asked and many options can be discussed.

A flowchart need not be cold and linear. Lynn Currier encourages her students to include both feelings and higher-level "judgments" in the flowcharts they create, in addition to "metacognitive" instructions to themselves as they go about an academic task. As part of her vocabulary program, for example, she has included a dictionary word-search game called "Quest." During a Quest, her students work in groups of four to solve different kinds of dictionary problems. On one day, for example, the Quest teams had to work through a list of words with double meanings to identify all the words, which were kinds of tools, in addition to other

FIGURE 10.11   Sixth-Grader's Flowchart of a Routine Academic Task

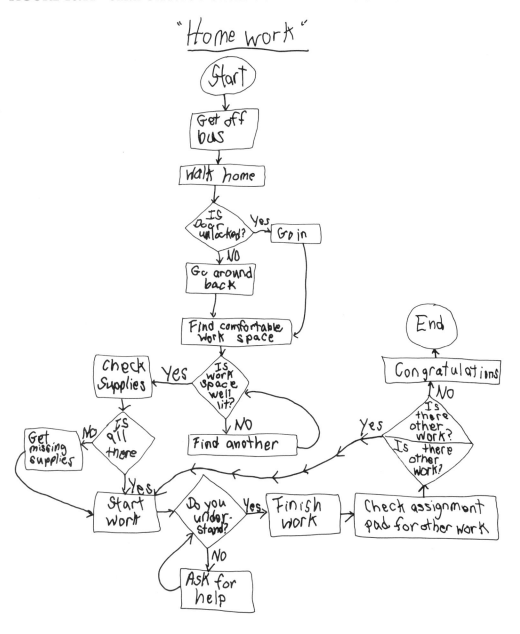

meanings. Words such as *plane, saw, maul,* and *level* made the list difficult. To win the game, a team has to define all the words quickly, using all the prior knowledge of all its members, designing a system of dictionary search, dividing the words within the team to increase efficiency, and creating a recording system. Lynn Currier asked her students to design the approach they would use for this task, in the form of a flowchart (see Figure 10.12).

Figure 10.12 includes most of the guidance sixth-grade students need to complete a dictionary search. It also includes some metacognitive

FIGURE 10.12   Sixth-Grade Flowchart of Dictionary Skills with a Personal Flair

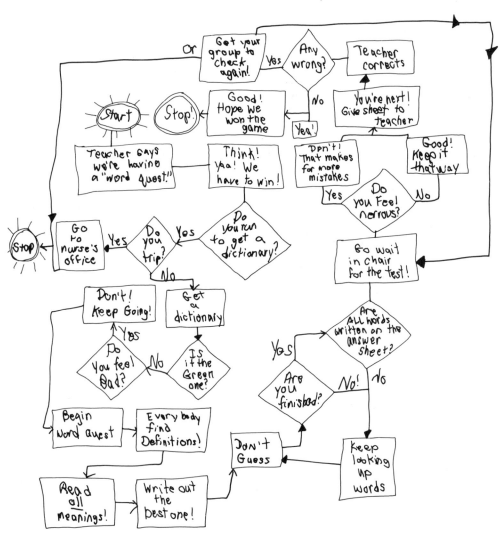

advice, like "Don't guess!" and "Read all meanings," with some purely inspirational boxes, such as "Think! Yaa, we have to win" or "Feel Glad!" Several charts included advice on teamwork, such as "Let the others know what you are doing" and "Arguing slows you down." A careful view of the flowchart in Figure 10.12 may even reveal the presence of some flowchart jokes. As a graphic organizer helping students see how they think, flowcharts should not aim for perfection. If flowcharts have the purpose of representing how an individual thinks, they too can have personality, even charm.

USING FLOWCHARTS TO GUIDE LEARNING

Student-made flowcharts are probably preferable to teacher-made flowcharts in learning to plan an approach to problems. Like concept maps or causal chains, a flowchart can give both the teacher and the student a vision of what the student's mind is doing with information. Student-made flowcharts let the teacher work forward from the base of prior knowledge in the students. Still, teacher-made or commercial charts may contribute something to cognitive skills development by giving students a guiding framework for their work with complex problems. After all, if every student had to "discover" routines that work for content area problems, school study would stand no chance of keeping pace with a changing society.

Schoenfeld (1979) has described a general approach to mathematical problem solving that he teaches to his students. Each student has one copy of his problem-solving flowchart; a large version of the same flowchart hangs on the wall. Early in the course, his students may be able to make little sense of the chart. As they engage new material, however, and work through one problem after another, they begin to find meaning in the flow diagram. Through practice with many kinds of problems over a whole semester, they slowly adopt Schoenfeld's general "script" for problem solving in mathematics.

Most disciplines include similar sequences of activity that are the central processes or methods of discovery. Teachers can create flowcharts to guide students through complex procedures in the disciplines. With repetition, those procedures may become part of "scripted" student knowledge.

Writing is a recursive process that requires simultaneous attention to many kinds of questions at many different levels. Writing teachers often notice that students neglect the procedures they already have learned to use whenever they try to move on to a new area. It would be useful to have available a representation of the whole writing process to remind students of what they know as they labor with any new part.

FIGURE 10.13   Teacher-Designed Flowchart of the Writing Process as a Course Overview

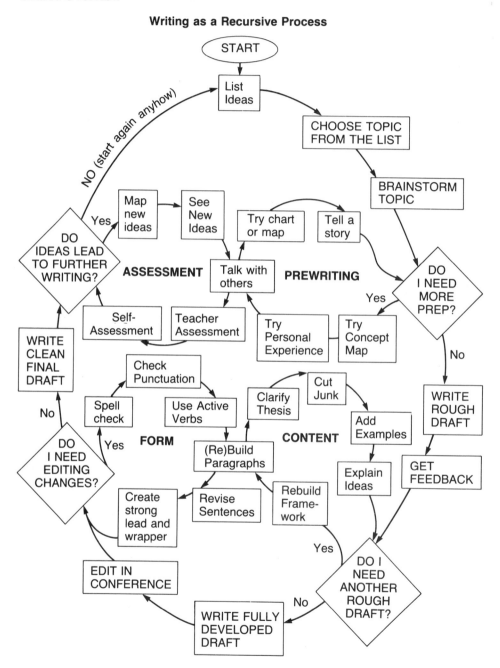

Judy Boucher was teaching English composition in a community college when she developed the flowchart for the writing process in Figure 10.13. The outer ring of the flowchart is a linear representation of the writing process. Four subroutines inside the main ring list options for students who are stuck with defining a topic, focusing on content, creating a structure, or editing. Boucher's flowchart consists of all the aspects of writing included in her composition course. By making the whole process visible throughout the course, she always had a way to show her students where they were individually with a composition, or where the whole group was stuck on a particular day.

FROM INDUCTION TO DEDUCTION IN SCIENCE: A CASE STUDY

In working with complex subject matter and more difficult problems, a stepwise approach to problem representation may be required. Like John Cote and Arnell Sherwin, Ellen Fogarty wanted her eleventh-grade biology students to observe carefully. In addition, she wanted her students to use models of the processes that drive biological growth to think their way through problems.

Ellen Fogarty designed a careful stepwise process of representation to let her students understand concepts related to metamorphosis and then use those concepts to solve problems in biology as a scientist might solve those problems:

Induction: Fogarty would give them information on the stages of metamorphosis that would allow them to develop a "model" of the forces behind insect growth and development.

Deduction: The students would then use their "models" to solve several kinds of problems confronted by biologists when they try to understand growth and development. If her students could begin to develop models of biological processes, they could also begin to think like research scientists, using the models they devised to solve problems.

Figure 10.14 represents Fogarty's plan for teaching scientific problem solving to her eleventh-grade biology class. By putting her students in the position of research scientists, she forced them to solve problems, using what they learned to deduce facts they would not actually "see" within the biology class. Figure 10.14 represents the steps she took to support problem solving in her students, and the steps they took to work through to solutions. In this graphic organizer and those that follow, Fogarty's input is represented with a circle, whereas the response of her students is enclosed in a square. With Fogarty's guidance, the students

FIGURE 10.14 Four Stages in a Problem-Solving Process in Eleventh-Grade Biology

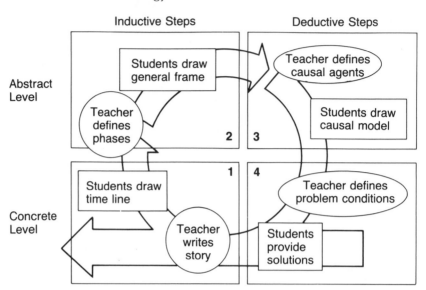

incrementally drew a graphic organizer for metamorphosis that would allow them to predict the effects of different experimental conditions.

Ellen Fogarty's approach required four steps, arranged to represent scientific thinking—beginning with pure description and ending with solutions to experimental problems. In each of the four steps, she provided her students with a different kind of information, and asked them to work in groups to include that information in a "drawing" or representation. At first, she gave them a physical description of an event in nature. They drew a time line from her description. Then Fogarty gave them facts that would let them recognize relationships in the description. They created categorical frames, phases, or "chunks" for their time lines. She provided some definitions of chemical hormones causing different transformations in insects. They drew a causal model that included those agents. With the general model drawn, her students were ready for problem solving. As Fogarty changed parts of the "story," her students used their models to predict the experimental results. Her plan corresponds to one full cycle of the Thinking Wheel (Chapter 1), within which there were many smaller cycles of induction and deduction.

Each stage required a different kind of representation, including information necessary to understanding the circumstance or working out specific answers.

Figure 10.15 is a "story" Ellen Fogarty wrote for her class, with the
instruction to create a *time line* of what they had read.
Figure 10.16 includes relational facts she gave her students and an
abstract model that they developed to make the process visible.
Figure 10.17 adds causal agents to the abstract model of metamorphosis from which *if/then condition* statements may be derived.
Figure 10.18 illuminates the *problems* by changing the basic story
in different ways and asking students to predict the results of experiments.

By creating a planned sequence of steps in problem solving, Fogarty
was reducing the chance that prior knowledge or differences in ability

FIGURE 10.15   From Story to Representation

The (round white) object begins to vibrate. Finally, it emerges, (its large jaws)
having eaten through its tomb. Once fully free, it rests, biding its time while its skin
hardens and darkens. Suddenly, it begins to move, pushing and pulling its body
forward, (devouring) everything in its path. As it eats, it (grows,) growing so large that
its hardened skin can no longer contain it. The skin cracks. A softer, larger animal
crawls out and continues on with shedding its skin. Then as suddenly as it started to
eat, it (stops, and ties) itself securely to a leaf surface. Ceasing to grow, its skin turns
very (dark and hard.)
    The dormant creature appears dead, but a trained eye can see subtle changes in
the brown structure. Finally, a different looking creature emerges, flexes its (wings)
and (flies off,) leaving the empty brown structure flapping in the wind.

BASIC TIME LINE

Draw a representation of this story: a time line

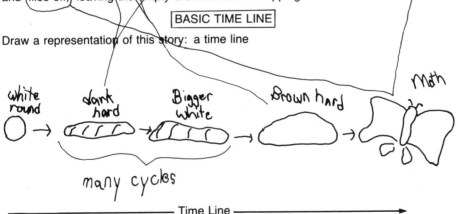

FIGURE 10.16 From Teacher-Defined Phases to Student-Designed Frame

**Teacher-Defined
Phases**

FACT: The caterpillar is the larval stage of moths and butterflies.
FACT: An instar is the period of time between molts.
FACT: After the last instar the caterpillar turns into a pupa or cocoon.
FACT: A larva in its last instar is about to become a pupa.
FACT: On the 8th day of the last instar, something happens that allows
   this change.
FACT: After the 8th day, it takes two weeks for the larva to become a full pupa.
FACT: Caterpillars are very hardy animals. It is possible to remove their
   brains, their thoracic glands, and their corpora allata without killing them.
   Because they are so hardy, it is also possible to hook several of them
   together.

**Student-Defined
General Frame**

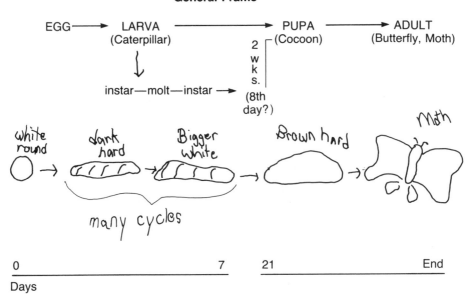

would prevent some students from working with their peers to solve very challenging problems. From carefully devised representations of the problem, indeed, any of us might be able to work through to solutions.

  Figure 10.15 is the "story" Ellen Fogarty wrote about metamorphosis, with a web diagram devised by a student to identify important elements of the story. From the webbed story, the students abstracted a time line with at least four phases (see Chapter 3). At this point, none of the points on the time line had a label other than the descriptive adjectives from Fogarty's story. The students enjoyed the story, because Fogarty's

FIGURE 10.17   From General Frame to Causal Model

Causal Agents

Brain Hormone: This hormone is secreted by the brain throughout the caterpillar's larval development. The brain hormone travels to the the thoracic center where it stimulates the thoracic center to produce molting hormone.

Molting Hormone   This hormone is produced by the thoracic center. It travels through the body and causes the larva to molt. When the amount of juvenile hormone is low, it causes the larva to pupate—to become a pupa.

Juvenile Hormone   This hormone is produced by the corpora allata. It is made in large quantities when the caterpillar is young. As the caterpillar molts and goes through its instars, the amount of juvenile hormone produced decreases. In the last instar the amount of juvenile hormone is so low that the caterpillar does not molt, but instead becomes a pupa.

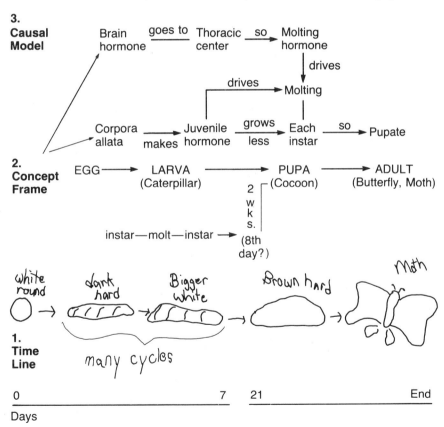

FIGURE 10.18 Introducing Specific Problems for Processing through Model

Problems for Research Team

Teacher introduces problems:

Problem A: You and your research team are given two caterpillars, both in first instar. From one you remove the corpora allata. The other one you leave alone. What happens to each caterpillar? Why has this happened?

Problem B: You and your research team are given two more caterpillars in their first instar. From one you remove the thoracic gland. The other you leave alone. What happens to each caterpillar? Why has this happened?

Problem C: You and your research team are given two caterpillars in their last instar. One is 7 days old; the other is 10 days old. You tie a knot around the center of both. You wait 14 days. What has happened to each half of both caterpillars? Why has this happened?

Problem D: You and your research team are given lots of caterpillars, each in its first instar. After cutting off their heads and tails, you connect the the abdomens together with glass tubing. You take another caterpillar in its last instar—7 days old—and you cut off its head. You take the head and attach it to the abdomens of the other caterpillars. You wait two weeks. What has happened to the abdomens? Why has this happened?

Students use models to solve problems:

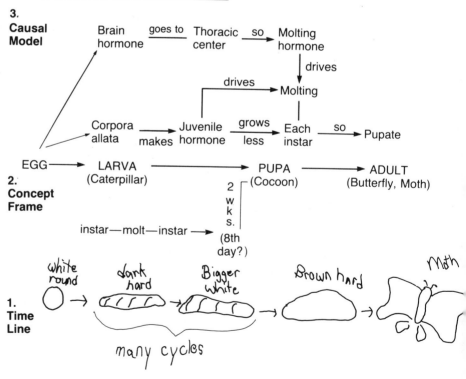

260

version captured some of the magic that makes science so interesting. The student time lines became the basis for three additional student representations, all of which would finally constitute one fully developed "model" of metamorphosis.

To make the time line more useful, Fogarty gave her students seven facts about caterpillars and moths which would give the students labels they could use to break the time line into distinct stages. Fogarty helped them revise their original time lines to include the new information, as shown in Figure 10.16. Having labeled the four phases of metamorphosis and inserted additional facts in their schematic, the students were almost ready to predict effects of changes in "the story."

Fogarty preceded problem descriptions with the three definitions, included in Figure 10.17, which would allow her students to carry out steps of problem solving. Each of the definitions identified a hormone (causal force) and its physical origin. The hormones, however, are not in simple serial order. They each represent simultaneous, interacting causes in the process of changing larvae to pupae. Her students used the three definitions of causal hormones and the organs that produce them to create a more abstract model of the phases of metamorphosis. Their drawing of the causal process gave them a way to solve the "What if?" problems she had developed.

"What if?" she began to ask. Figure 10.18 shows the problems Ellen Fogarty introduced to her class, now divided into groups of four "research scientists." "What if a caterpillar loses its corpora allata?" To answer the question, her students had to resort to their "models." The could see that the caterpillar without the corpora allata would not produce any juvenile hormone. Without juvenile hormone, the caterpillar might start to pupate. What would happen to a caterpillar driven to pupation during its first instar? It might make a very small cocoon, if it lived. Would it live? The students could see nothing in their models that would kill the pupating larva, which was still dark and hard, but potentially viable. Would the cocoon also be dark and hard? The students were left with questions, even to the simplest problem. As the problems grew more difficult, their questions grew more penetrating.

Fogarty arranged the problems from relatively simple to more complex. Still, with the introduction of the first problem, her students found that they had to refine their representation of the process in question in order to begin working toward solutions. Because Fogarty designed this unit to develop both the inductive information gathering of problem solving and the deductive applications, virtually all her students had everything they would need to solve the problems she presented. None were excluded from participation by gaps in prior knowledge or inadequately developed skill.

The more information we supply our students and the more carefully we design problem-solving situations, the greater our confidence can be that we have removed most barriers to this "higher-level" thinking skill. If we show our students how to develop graphic organizers for problem situations, we may increase the extent to which they control the problem-solving process.

SUGGESTIONS FOR TEACHERS

1. As an exercise in problem analysis, ask your students to identify a task they have mastered and then to write out a set of instructions showing an inexperienced person how to complete that task. When the instructions are written, you may ask the students to identify points in the procedure where problems can easily arise. For each problem, you can show them how to write out if/then conditional rules for solving those problems.

2. If you have a flair for the dramatic, consider posing as an intergalactic space traveler who recently arrived on this planet with little more than English instruction via the AM/FM radio. Request written help with common tasks, such as:
   a. Opening a can of tuna
   b. Making a peanut butter and jelly sandwich
   c. Buying a can of Drano
   d. Contacting NASA
   e. Catching a bus to Denver
   f. Dressing appropriately for a visit with the president
   g. Moving undetected through a school day

3. Consider introducing the symbols and techniques of flowcharts or scripts as a way to develop graphic organizers for procedures. Working on common daily tasks is both easy and enjoyable. Have other students troubleshoot the completed charts by reviewing them and then suggesting alternatives.

4. Identifying events or issues as problems is the first step in problem solving. To give your students practice in isolating problems from the surrounding landscape, consider using a history, literature, or science text as a source of pure description and ask them to identify problems within the text. Newspapers supply an endless flow of description rich in problems. Sometimes, the systems chart in Figure 10.19 may help them convert a problem definition to a general problem-solving approach.

5. Are there procedures your students carry out impulsively, ritualistically, or without understanding? Word problems are only one example of such procedures. Show your students how to flow-

FIGURE 10.19   Helping Students Distinguish between Problems, Goals, Solutions, and Effects

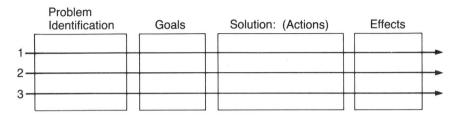

chart and assign them to design a flowchart for an activity they complete impulsively. Working in a group of two or three others may improve the quality of final charts. When they have finished, the whole class can discuss what they have learned by breaking the procedure down. What have they learned about procedures? What have they learned about their minds?

Helping Students Reflect on Their Thinking

Even when your students experience success in using a graphic organizer for understanding the subject area, they will not automatically see wider usage for the technique they employed. They will need your help in finding other situations where the same technique would work as well. When your students are using a graphic to think about some part of content, make some effort to let them: (1) review the process they used to think and (2) look for other situations in or out of school where the same process might work. We can call the transfer of a thinking process a "Bridge."

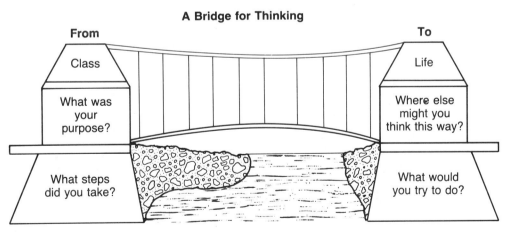

A Bridge for Thinking

- Make a list of careers that require a great deal of problem solving and another list of careers requiring little problem solving. What does each list have in common?
- What is an expert? How does a person become an expert?
- Make up a letter of application for a job which describes your skills as a problem solver.

REFERENCES

Bransford, J. D.; Sherwood, R. D.; & Sturdevant, T. (1987) Teaching thinking and problem solving. In J. B. Baron & R. Sternberg (Eds.), *Teaching Thinking Skills: Theory and Practice.* New York: W. H. Freeman, pp. 163–181.

Chase, W. G., & Simon, H. (1973). The mind's eye in chess. In W. G. Chase (Ed.), *Visual Information Processing.* New York: Academic Press, pp. 215–278.

Clarke, J. H.; MacPherson, B. V.; & Holmes, D. R. (1982). Cigarette smoking and locus of control among young adolescents. *Journal of Health and Social Behavior,* 23(3), 253–259.

Gagne, R. M. (1980). Learnable aspects of problem solving. *American Psychologist,* 15(2), 84–92.

Gentner, D., & Stevens, A. L. (1983). *Mental Models.* Hillsdale, NJ: Lawrence Erlbaum.

Glaser, R. (1984). Education and thinking: The role of knowledge. *American Psychologist,* 39(2), 93–104.

Glasser, W. (1986). *Control Theory in the Classroom.* New York: Harper & Row.

Holland, J; Holyoak, K. J.; Nisbett, R. E.; & Thagard, P. R. (1986). *Induction: Processes of Inference, Learning and Discovery.* Cambridge, MA: MIT Press.

Larkin, J. (1979). Information processing models and science instruction. In J. Lochhead & J. Clemmons (Eds.), *Cognitive Process Instruction.* Philadelphia: Franklin Institute Press.

Larkin, J; McDermott, J.; Simon, D. P.; & Simon, H. A. (1980). Expert and novice performance in solving physics problems. *Science,* 208, 20 June, 1335–1342.

Lefcourt, H. (1974). *Locus of Control: Current Trends in Theory and Research.* New York: Wiley.

Letteri, C. (1982). Teaching students how to learn. *Theory into Practice,* 24(2), 112–121.

Letteri, C. (1983). An introduction to information processing, cognitive controls and cognitive profiles. Manuscript from author.

Marzano, R. J.; Brandt, R.; Hughes, C.; Jones, B.; Presseissen, B.; Rankin, S.; & Suhor, C. (1988). *Dimensions of Thinking.* Alexandria, VA: ASCD Publications.

Newell, A., & Simon, H. A. (1972). *Human Problem Solving.* Englewood Cliffs, NJ: Prentice-Hall.

Nickerson, R. S.; Perkins, D. N.; & Smith, E. E. (1985). *The Teaching of Thinking.* Hillsdale, NJ: Lawrence Erlbaum.

Schoenfeld, A. H. (1979). Can heuristics be taught? In J. Lochhead & J. Clemmons (Eds.), *Cognitive Process Instruction.* Philadelphia: Franklin Institute Press, pp. 315–338.

Sternberg, R. M. (1987). Teaching intelligence: The application of cognitive psychology to the improvement of intellectual skills. In J. B. Baron & R. Sternberg (Eds.), *Teaching Thinking Skills: Theory and Practice.* New York: W. H. Freeman.

Voss, J. F.; Greene, T. R.; Post, T. A.; & Penner, B. (1983). Problem solving skill in the social sciences. In *The Psychology of Learning* (Vol. 17). New York: Academic Press.

Weiner, B. R.; Neirenberg, B. R.; & Goldstein, M. (1976). Social learning (locus of control) versus attribution (causal stability) interpretations of expectancy of success. *Journal of Personality,* 44, 1–20.

Wheaton, B. (1980). The sociogenesis of psychological disorder. *Journal of Health and Social Behavior,* 21, 100–124.

SECTION IV

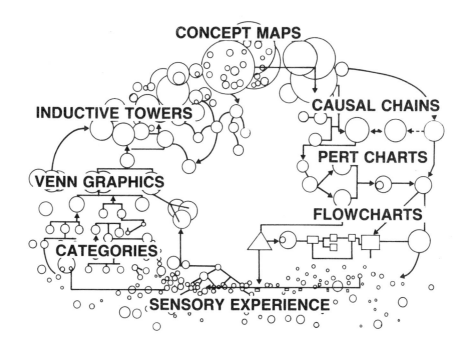

CONCEPT MAPS

INDUCTIVE TOWERS

CAUSAL CHAINS

PERT CHARTS

VENN GRAPHICS

FLOWCHARTS

CATEGORIES

SENSORY EXPERIENCE

Beyond Graphic Organizers

11

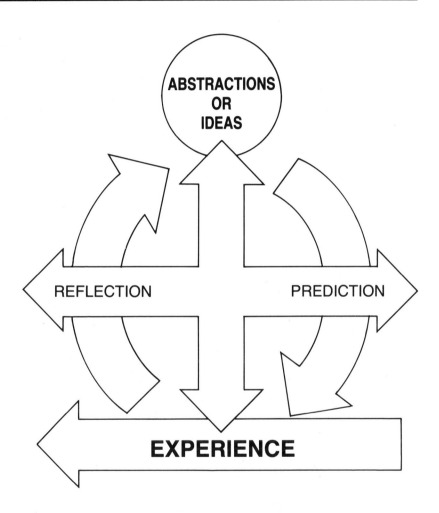

Complex Graphic Organizers

THE POWERS   Among the People, a child's first Teaching is of the Four Great Powers of the Medicine Wheel. To the North on the Medicine Wheel is found Wisdom. The color of the Wisdom of the North is White, and its medicine animal is the Buffalo. The South is represented by the Sign of the Mouse, and its Medicine Color is Green. The South is the place of Innocence and Trust, and for perceiving closely our nature of heart. In the West is the sign of the Bear. The West is the Looks-Within Place, which speaks of the introspective nature of man. The color of this place is Black. The East is marked by the Sign of the Eagle. It is the place of Illumination, where we can see things clearly, far and wide. Its color is the Gold of the Morning Star.

At birth, each of us is given a particular Beginning Place within these Four Great Directions on the Medicine Wheel. This Starting Place gives us our first way of perceiving things, which will be then our easiest and most natural way throughout our lives.

But any person who perceives from only one of these Four Great Directions will remain just a partial man.
—HYEMEYOHSTS STORM,
Seven Arrows

THE GRAPHIC APPROACH TO THINKING SKILLS INSTRUCTION described in the previous sections relies on very simple forms of graphic organizers. Their purpose is to help students increase their control over basic patterns of thinking so that they can move on to develop and manage more complex forms. The purpose of this chapter is to point outward from these simple beginnings toward more complex patterns of thinking. Although related to one or several basic patterns, complex patterns are usually much more specialized to a subject area. They may be more difficult to use across the subject areas and throughout the K–12 continuum. This chapter will not include all of the complex forms that may be related to simple forms; instead, the chapter presents just a few that suggest directions a teacher might choose for particular kinds of teaching projects.

Teachers who want to develop a teaching approach based on a complex pattern of thinking might seek out alternative models within the academic disciplines closely tied to their subject area. Teachers who want to develop a general thinking or study skills program might begin their quest by looking at thinking skills programs that already exist. Nickerson, Perkins, and Smith (1985) provide descriptions of comprehensive thinking skills programs and some evaluation in a manner that should prove helpful to readers of this book, as does Chance (1986). Baron and Sternberg (1987) and Costa (1985) include program descriptions written by their developers that can lead the reader toward more complete descriptions.

COMPLEX APPLICATIONS OF THE WHEEL

The Thinking Wheel, which provides the organizing metaphor for this book, is itself a basic pattern related to some complex patterns of thinking. Cut into pieces of different sizes, the inductive and deductive aspects of thinking form the basis for many methods of inquiry, including the scientific method. Many patterns of prose writing and even poetic forms follow the natural logic of the wheel, moving from data to theory and back, or moving from analysis to synthesis, and back, as represented in Figure 11.1.

A sonnet moves from verification to idea generation in 14 lines. Jefferson wrote the Declaration of Independence beginning with a synthesis, "When in the course of human events . . . ," moving to verification of the King's transgressions, "He has harbored troops . . ." and so on, and then moving through analysis to a new idea—that the colonies should be free. Different disciplines or professions have chosen to start "thinking" from different points on the wheel.

As a four-part rather than six-part cycle, the wheel has helped guide thinking in a number of specific areas. As represented in Figure 11.2, the scientific method is often represented as one full cycle on the wheel, beginning and ending with a theory, idea, or problem statement. For the

FIGURE 11.1   The Thinking Wheel as Two Interacting Fields or Axes

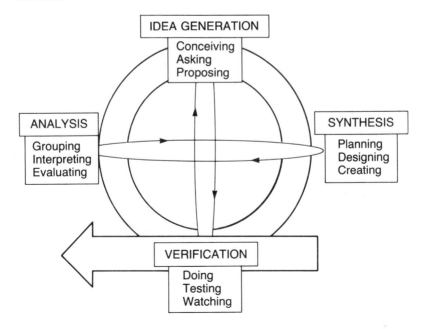

FIGURE 11.2   The Scientific Method as a Complex "Wheel"

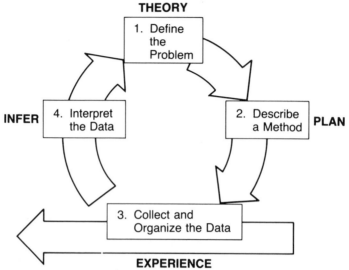

problem statement, a method or procedure is designed, and data are collected and organized for analysis and evaluation, modifying the original
idea. As Kuhn (1970) and Costa (1985) point out, Figure 11.2 may not
describe how scientists actually think through experiments as much as it
describes how they represent their work to others. Within a conventional
structure, their thinking becomes more comprehensible to others. This
may be true of other complex graphics as well—that they have become
ways of communicating among specialists rather than ways of thinking.

   Physicians may use the structure of the wheel for a similar purpose,
but they usually start at a different point. Figure 11.3 represents the same
wheel as a process of clinical diagnosis and treatment, which can begin
literally with "the record" of a patient's medical history. Anyone who
has watched a physician work can attest to the flexibility of assessment
and planning in the hands of an expert. Great elaboration of the pattern
is possible. Skillful physicians may work up to five separate concerns
through several simultaneous cycles of investigation and confirmation
before they recommend a treatment.

   What happens to the wheel in the hand of students? The reading
pattern SQ3R is one application of the wheel: *Survey*—for general ideas;
Question—as in planning; *Read*—to answer questions; *Recite*—do some
interpretive cycling; *Remember*—restructure in long-term memory. Writing essays may often follow the same pattern, beginning anywhere on the
wheel and cycling once or several times. The wheel has become thoroughly conventional in Western thought. It is commonplace. The possi-

FIGURE 11.3   Medical Diagnosis and Planning as a Cycle

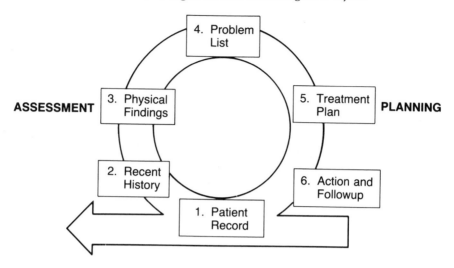

ble adaptations to teaching and learning are numerous. Adaptation of the pattern of the wheel to complex learning tasks in the classroom should depend on the purpose of the teacher. What do we want our students to do with their minds?

COMPLEX SCANNING AND FOCUSING

Mathematicians, scientists, and other observers of the human scene noticed not long ago that their observations of most phenomena fell into a few different patterns. When variability was possible and when extraneous factors did not interfere, their count of observed phenomena tended to fall into one main pattern, the distribution pattern described as falling the "normal curve" (see Figure 11.4). The normal curve describes a pattern of distribution for both human and material phenomena. When we watch things happen long enough and carefully count repetitions, we often find that the pattern falls within the normal curve.

The pattern of the normal curve lets us answer difficult questions about the events we are observing. Is what I am seeing normal? Are some of the things I see quite probably unusual? Have I counted enough to represent a normal population? When some event occurs at the edge of expected normal range, what are the chances that it is still "normal"? Is one class of objects or people different from another in some respect? Developed inductively, the pattern of the normal curve came around the circle and became, for better or worse, a model forming the basis of judg-

FIGURE 11.4   The Normal Curve: One Pattern for Advanced Focusing and Scanning

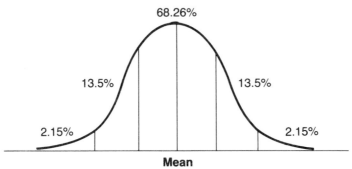

ment. Teachers used the normal curve to guide the distribution of their grades, for example, whether or not student achievement could be described by the curve. The normal curve creates an expectation for what we will see when we are focusing and scanning.

The normal curve has become the basis for a way of thinking about events, creating one basis for the subdiscipline of mathematics called statistics. There are other patterns of data search as well, many of which are applications of probability theory. Halpern (1984, Chapter 5) offers an excellent introduction to probability and probabilistic reasoning. Neimark (1987, Chapter 9) explains hypothesis testing and statistical reasoning. Books on the topic and on different approaches to research would fill a great deal of shelf space. Can students use the pattern of the normal curve as a basis for judging their own observations and measurements? Would other patterns describing probability help? Again, our use of patterns to shape thinking should depend on our purpose.

COMPLEX CATEGORIZATION

Grouping physical objects into categories can be a useful activity. Grouping abstract ideas into categories can also be useful, though more difficult. When one is grouping arguments on either side of an issue, the result amounts to an advanced form of the two-celled, lapped Euler Diagram. For any issue, some arguments favor a point of view; other arguments lean the other way. By analyzing conflicting ideas, we can usually find a synthesis, a creative summing of parts. Dialectical argument—thesis, antithesis, and synthesis—is ancient in our culture. Opposition of arguments or forces can be represented graphically for students, as shown in Figure 11.5.

FIGURE 11.5 Advanced Categorization: Grouping Arguments by Thesis, Antithesis, and Synthesis

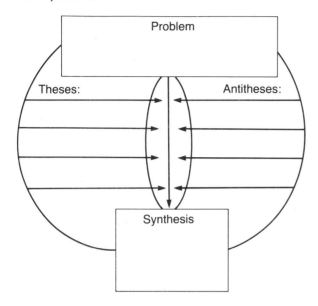

Almost any complex issue can be managed through this pattern for dialectical argument, from "raising the drinking age to 32" to "opening more trade in Cuba." With room for illustrations for each opposed argument, the pattern in Figure 11.5 can be used to prepare an outline for writing a position paper that accommodates both sides of an issue. It can also be used to prepare students for a debate, with one side taking the "pro" and the other the "con." The pattern can be useful in current events and language arts classes.

PROPOSING COMPLEX RELATIONSHIPS

Perhaps the best way to represent advanced inductive or abductive thinking is to show how the process of designing a survey or questionnaire reflects the exercise of inductive thinking. Unlike inductive towers, which presume the existence of a factual record, the process of designing a survey is at first entirely hypothetical.

Figure 11.6 represents a process of survey design that would have the students define their thinking before they actually write questions.

FIGURE 11.6   Advanced Inductive Logic through Survey Design

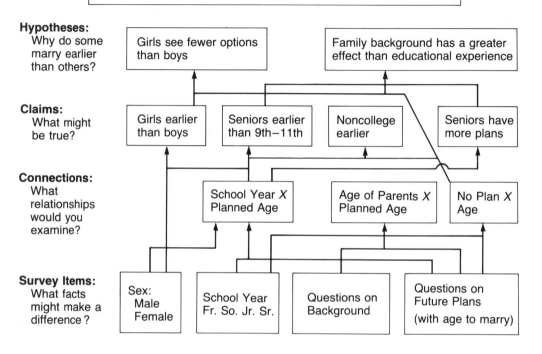

Question: What influences the age at which high-school students see themselves getting married?

Hypotheses:
Why do some marry earlier than others?

- Girls see fewer options than boys
- Family background has a greater effect than educational experience

Claims:
What might be true?

- Girls earlier than boys
- Seniors earlier than 9th–11th
- Noncollege earlier
- Seniors have more plans

Connections:
What relationships would you examine?

- School Year X Planned Age
- Age of Parents X Planned Age
- No Plan X Age

Survey Items:
What facts might make a difference?

- Sex: Male Female
- School Year Fr. So. Jr. Sr.
- Questions on Background
- Questions on Future Plans (with age to marry)

Student designers would use Figure 11.6 to develop a clear purpose, and then to imagine a process of investigation that would bring them the facts they need. By prethinking a survey though this kind of structure, a student could avoid a lengthy survey which loses responses and brings in excess information.

In this illustration, a student would first define a purpose: to find out what makes students want to marry early. Then the student would sketch out a list of factors that might make a difference, and put them down as the base. With an overwhelming mass of potential relationships to consider, the student designer would then have to isolate a few relationships with the greatest potential importance. Based on prior knowledge (or a guess), the student would then have to write out some claims necessary to the support of the hypotheses. How could the claims be substantiated? Is the structure in place that would allow the student to answer the question? In carrying out the study, and having unforeseen findings bring surprises, students working with this kind of model might gain increased respect for the risks of inductive thinking.

COMPLEX CONCEPT MAPPING

With the further addition of structure, concept mapping can be used as a vehicle for creative thinking or for evaluation arguments. A map with either purpose would no longer consist of concepts linked by relational lines and verbs (as in Chapter 8); instead, it would consist of sentences. Neimark (1987, pp. 168–185) has described a process for mapping the structure of arguments either to improve them (if they are yours) or to dismiss them (if they belong to someone else.)

In a related manner, Perkins (1986) has described four design questions he uses to evaluate any kind of knowledge:

Perkins's Design Questions
1. What is its purpose?
2. What is its structure?
3. What are model cases of it?
4. What are arguments that explain or evaluate it?

These questions also follow the pattern of the Thinking Wheel. If we combine Perkins's questions with a mapping technique for arguments, we get an advanced form of concept mapping that students could use to create or evaluate ideas. Figure 11.7 is an example of an advanced map evaluating the design of a paragraph. Students could be shown how to map the relationship of propositions in their own writing, the writing of their friends, or selections from the texts they are using.

COMPLEX CAUSAL MAPPING

Causal argument has been built into the process of developing proposals for government or foundation contracts as a pattern of argumentation. Designing a response to a problem in a simulation of a proposal/contract situation can be fun. Students of almost all ages may enjoy simulations of contract competitions. Teachers may present students with serious problems to solve, such as the lack of available, low-cost housing for the poor, or less serious problems, such as that described in Figure 11.8. Some students might treat the Mississippi Bridge problem with levity, proposing floating ice bridges, made in Minnesota, for seasonal travelers along the entire length of the river. Students who live by the Mississippi River might take the problem more seriously and actually examine alternate sites.

Taken lightly or seriously, proposal writing is an exercise in extended causal thinking. Every problem has causes; when we eliminate the causes, we believe we will eliminate the problem. The proposal for-

FIGURE 11.7 Advanced Concept Map—Evaluation of a Paragraph, Guided by Perkins's Design Questions

Editorial

She is doing it again. The governor's office announced today that the state will hold town's responsible for an appropriate arts program in the schools, at whatever level of funding the state provides. Some towns receive 65% of their budget from the state; other towns receive less than 10%. In 1986, one small school raised an outcry because its funding was withheld pending replacement of substandard doorknobs. Many schools have protested the use of funding to enforce the new school approval standards. Other schools have protested the applications of general standards without regard for the unique relationship between schools and their communities. Until state legislators are put on notice by the voters, the governor will have her way.

Perkins's Design Questions (1986)

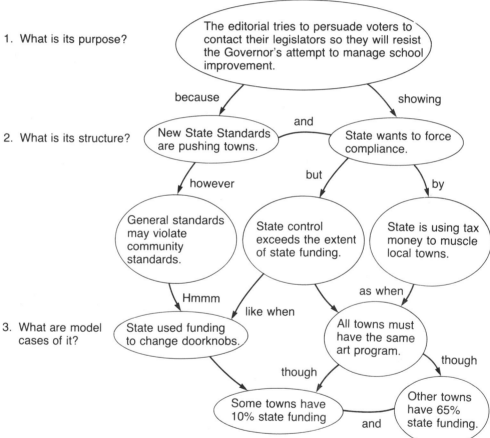

1. What is its purpose?

The editorial tries to persuade voters to contact their legislators so they will resist the Governor's attempt to manage school improvement.

because   showing

2. What is its structure?

New State Standards are pushing towns.   and   State wants to force compliance.

however   but   by

General standards may violate community standards.   State control exceeds the extent of state funding.   State is using tax money to muscle local towns.

Hmmm   as when

3. What are model cases of it?

State used funding to change doorknobs.   like when   All towns must have the same art program.   though

though   and

Some towns have 10% state funding   Other towns have 65% state funding.

4. What are arguments that explain or evaluate it?

The editorial writer has one main purpose and two supporting ideas. The writer wants to pump up the readers so they will call their representative against her. The writer believes that state influence should be proportionate to state funds. Ridiculous. Since when did money buy rights? Rich towns have no right to buy their way free of standards. What we need is a vote. The people should deliberate the standards at town meeting, then stick with their vote.

FIGURE 11.8   Advanced Causal Analysis

CALL FOR PROPOSALS:
Mississippi Bridge Project

A recent transportation department study has revealed a flaw in this country's road system: There are simply not enough bridges across the Mississippi River to carry eastern travelers West or western travelers East. "The problem is the same all the way from New Orleans to St. Paul," a department spokesman has said. "Though the southern end has fewer bridges and greater need because the cost of long bridges is higher." Congress has allocated up to $1 billion for projects which will solve the problem. Contractors should be prepared to make an oral presentation within three weeks. The proposal review board will use four criteria to judge all proposals:

1. *The need for the project:* Contractors should be able to show that a number of problems will be solved by locating the bridge on the river.
2. *Innovative design:* Contractors should recognize that the successful proposal will represent a model for all bridges to be rebuilt on the river.
3. *Feasibility:* Contractors should be able to show how they will carry out each aspect of the project.
4. *Cost:* Contractors should show the best bridge for the fewest dollars.

No written proposals will be accepted. Use graphics to clarify each part of your oral proposal.

Recommended Outline for Design Teams

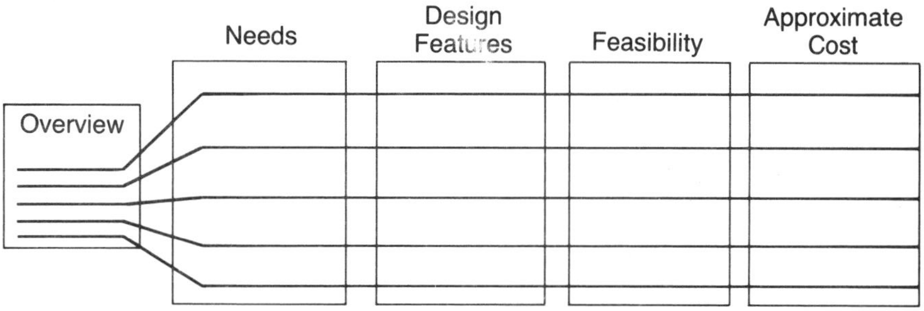

mat in Figure 11.8 intertwines the problems, forcing students to do some kind of cost/benefit analysis. Long bridges solve more problems, but they are also more expensive. Ice bridges are cheap, but are they durable? Whether presenting proposals to their own class, a panel of teachers, parents, or even a part of the school community, students have to make a persuasive argument. Commonly, the graphic representation of both problems and their solution carries persuasive weight.

A panel of judges may use another complex graphic to render its verdict on student proposals. Decision making is often represented in a

FIGURE 11.9   Decision Matrix for Mississippi Bridge Problem

DESIGN GROUP

CRITERIA	River Rat Construction	American Bridge, Inc.	Brooklyn Bridge Bldrs.	Sky Hook Designers
Demonstration of need	6	7	9	9
Design innovation	9	6	4	10
Feasibility	5	9	9	2
Cost	3	4	7	6
	23	26	29	27

complex graphic, either as a "tree," a flow diagram, or a matrix. Figure 11.9 is a decision matrix for the evaluation of Mississippi Bridge that can be used to evaluate any item against a set of established criteria.

Do the numbers favoring Brooklyn Bridge Builders represent sufficient cause for the award of a contract? What is the proper weight for different criteria? Students face the same issue if they are evaluating breakfast cereal, political candidates, or aspects of the defense budget. Is a cause the same as the sum of its parts? In thinking about causes as reasons for a decision, what is the place of judgment?

COMPLEX PROBLEM SOLVING

A large number of protocols or systems have been developed to guide people throughout the process of solving problems. Koberg and Bagnall (1974) described an elaborated version of a problem-solving routine. Bransford, Sherwood, and Sturdevant (1987) offered a simpler version, one that may be represented graphically to students. Their IDEAL problem solver is an open-ended approach to which many kinds of problems may respond. It aims to keep the student's mind working while several different solutions are explored.

Figure 11.10 is a graphic representation of the IDEAL problem

FIGURE 11.10   Graphic Representation of IDEAL Problem Solver

Student Dies at Horseshoe Curve

An eighteen-year-old high-school student lost his life early Saturday morning when the car he was driving went out of control at Horseshoe Curve in Huntington and plunged into the icy river. Snowy road conditions prevented police from obtaining skid estimates but the distance the car traveled into the river points toward high speed. Police had been called earlier to break up a party the youth had been attending. Community leaders have called for an investigation.

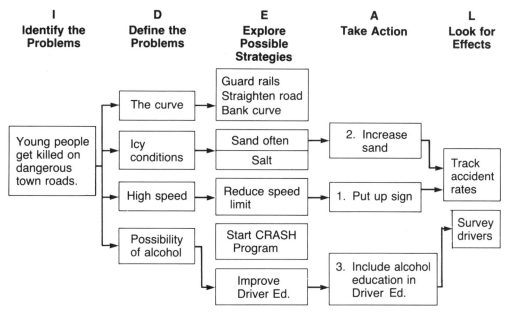

Adapted from J. D. Bransford, R. D. Sherwood, and T. Sturdevant, "Teaching thinking and problem solving," in J. B. Baron and R. J. Sternberg (Eds.), *Teaching Thinking Skills: Theory and Practice* (New York: Freeman, 1987).

solver, applied to the problem of accidents on a bad curve, as described in a short newspaper report. There are many ways of looking at the accident. The curve, ice, speed, and alcohol may all have had influence. What are the solution options for each cause? We could change the road, eliminate ice, slow the car, or sober the driver. What solutions appear most feasible? The figure indicates three—all relatively cheap. Would they work? Possibly, but if they didn't, survey results and accident rates would provide a signal. More accidents would occur. The process would begin again. The authors have applied the IDEAL system to everyday problems, such as the car accident, and to academic problems as well, such as how to factor a quadratic equation.

ARTIFICIAL VERSUS ORGANIC INTELLIGENCE

Why not include the advanced forms with the simpler forms in teaching thinking across the content areas? Some teachers may see a place for them and choose to do so. Many of these approaches have found a place in study skills courses or programs. I have not included them with their simpler forebearers because they seem, to me, specific to certain kinds of course content. They also seem more like conventions of communications than natural expressions of human intelligence which spring from our yearning to find order in experience. The advanced forms are more artificial and more prescriptive than their primitive cousins, and less adaptable across contexts than the simpler forms.

The use of graphics in teaching, however, is closely tied to a parallel movement in cognitive science—the development of artificial intelligence, which also is using graphics to develop and express network or schematic structures for machine thinking (Sharkey, 1986).

Part of developing artificial intelligence in "Expert Systems" has included techniques similar to those described here. The history of development of artificial intelligence and thinking skills instruction is partially intertwined (Simon, 1979; Bobrow & Collins, 1975; Galambos, Abelson, & Black, 1986). No matter how closely these efforts parallel each other, they will remain dedicated to goals that are mutually exclusive. Both movements use graphics to make thinking visible; visible forms of thinking become manageable. Once learned, however, patterns of thinking become visible again, either in the mind of the individual or in the relational calculations of the computer. As the processes become invisible again, management again becomes an issue. Human judgment cannot be applied after the thinking is done. Judgment must be part of the whole thinking process.

Designers of artificial intelligence software may design systems that can diagnose illness and prescribe treatment better than most doctors can. They may create artificial intelligence that assembles all relevant legal cases and creates more powerful summative arguments than any lawyer. But machines will never wonder about purposes and dream of different ways to think about what is good and how to make good things better. That will remain for us and our students, with the few pounds of organic intelligence we carry into our classrooms.

REFERENCES

Baron, J. B., & Sternberg, R. J. (Eds.) (1987). *Teaching Thinking Skills: Theory and Practice.* New York: Freeman.

Bransford, J. D.; Sherwood, R. D.; & Sturdevant, T. (1987). Teaching thinking and problem solving. In J. B. Baron & R. J. Sternberg (Eds.), *Teaching Thinking Skills: Theory and Practice*. New York: Freeman.

Bobrow, D. G., & Collins, A. (Eds.) (1975). *Representation and Understanding: Studies in Cognitive Science*. New York: Academic Press.

Chance, P. (1986). *Thinking in the Classroom*. New York: Teachers College Press.

Costa, A. (1985). How scientists think when they are doing science. In A. Costa (Ed.), *Developing Minds: A Resource Book For Teaching Thinking*. Alexandria, VA: ASCD Publications.

Galambos, J. A.; Abelson, R. P.; & Black, J. B. (1986). *Knowledge Structures*. Hillsdale, NJ: Lawrence Erlbaum.

Halpern, D. (1984). *Thought and Knowledge: An Introduction to Critical Thinking*. Hillsdale, NJ: Lawrence Erlbaum.

Heiman, M. (1985). Learning to learn. In A. Costa (Ed.), *Developing Minds: A Resource Book for Teaching Thinking*. Alexandria, VA: ASCD Publications.

Koberg, D., & Bagnall, J. (1974). *The All New Universal Traveler*. Los Altos, CA: Kaufmann.

Kuhn, T. S. (1970). *The Structure of Scientific Revolutions*. Chicago: University of Chicago Press.

Neimark, E. (1987). *Adventures in Thinking*. New York: Harcourt Brace.

Nickerson, R. S.; Perkins, D. N.; & Smith, E. E. (1985). *The Teaching of Thinking*. Hillsdale, NJ: Lawrence Erlbaum.

Perkins, D. N. (1986). *Knowledge as Design*. Hillsdale, NJ: Lawrence Erlbaum.

Sharkey, N. E. (1986). A model of knowledge based expectations in text comprehension. In J. A. Galambos, R. P. Abelson, & J. B. Black (Eds.), *Knowledge Structures*. Hillsdale, NJ: Lawrence Erlbaum.

Simon, H. A. (1979). *Models of Thought*. New Haven, CT: Yale University Press.

12

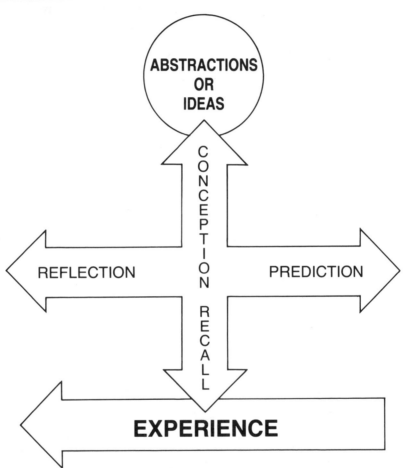

Thinking will make you smart. Pay attention.
—THIRD-GRADE STUDENT, Swanton, Vermont

Assessing Organizers for Thinking

T HE MOST IMPORTANT QUESTION IN EVALUATION IS THE question of purpose: "Why do I want to evaluate?" The second most important question is the question of audience: "Who wants to know?" It is hard to put these questions in order because, in practice, the two are hopelessly entangled: "What will we do with the information we gather from this evaluation?" That question tangles purpose and audience; it is also a question that generates heat in debates on education. Many, like myself, believe that effective thinking is the purpose of education. In behalf of that belief, we will have to produce a great deal more evidence than we have today that education can indeed improve thinking, preferably not at the expense of content knowledge.

THE QUESTION OF AUDIENCE

I believe that the purpose of thinking skills instruction is to increase students control over the workings of their own minds; consequently, I believe that the first audience for evaluation results is the individual student. The many audiences for evaluation results may be assembled in widening circles around that student. In widening circles, each audience brings a different purpose to the question of evaluation (see Figure 12.1).

FIGURE 12.1 Audiences for Thinking Skills Evaluation, with Some of their Purposes

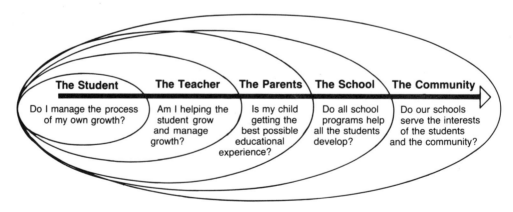

The several audiences for evaluative information clearly do not have the same need. The students need to see a product of their work and to judge that product in light of clear standards. The school board may want only to see evidence that students in each grade are making steady progress as they go through school. Different audiences imply different purposes for evaluation.

THE QUESTION OF PURPOSE

In evaluating graphic organizers, we have to remember we are evaluating a "tool." We will have to apply the same logic to evaluating them that we apply to the use of any tool. Does it work in behalf of the purposes we assign to it?

The purpose of evaluation for the benefit of the student should be to increase the sense of control the student feels over the content and the process of thinking by creating clear evidence of competence. For the individual student, each use of a graphic organizer can be used as a basis for evaluation. Does the graphic really represent what the student thinks? Does it represent how the student thinks? Are there skills reflected in the graphic that the student may use again? Are there other ways to look at thinking? How much has student thinking changed? What other steps are possible, based on what the student has already done? Hung on classroom walls, graphic organizers can begin to represent student achievement to other students—and to the larger public.

To help students think about their thinking, and potentially gain further control over thinking processes, some further evaluation steps may help. Having students write journals or essays on different approaches to thinking may help them objectify subjective experience and support transfer to other subject areas.

Sally Kaufman asked her third-grade students to write something about the graphic organizers they had been using in their reading and writing. "Which kind of map is easiest for you?" she asked. "What tricks have you developed to make mapping work?" Figure 12.2 includes some of one student's responses to that question, arranged to reflect the Thinking Wheel. Written comments can help the student and the teacher assess progress and set new goals.

Students such as Lauren focused much of their commentary on techniques, particularly whether those techniques are easy or hard. In her comments, one can see a preference for inductive towers and concept maps. Why does Lauren prefer these graphic organizers? She says that they do not require any particular initial order. The order flows out of the process. Story frames (time lines) and causal maps both require some attention to initial order, either chronological sequence or causal se-

FIGURE 12.2   Selections from one Third-Grade Journal on Graphic
Organizers

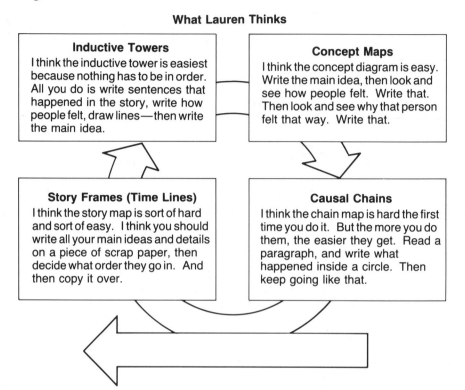

What Lauren Thinks

Inductive Towers

I think the inductive tower is easiest because nothing has to be in order. All you do is write sentences that happened in the story, write how people felt, draw lines—then write the main idea.

Concept Maps

I think the concept diagram is easy. Write the main idea, then look and see how people felt. Write that. Then look and see why that person felt that way. Write that.

Story Frames (Time Lines)

I think the story map is sort of hard and sort of easy. I think you should write all your main ideas and details on a piece of scrap paper, then decide what order they go in. And then copy it over.

Causal Chains

I think the chain map is hard the first time you do it. But the more you do them, the easier they get. Read a paragraph, and write what happened inside a circle. Then keep going like that.

quence. Lauren's learning style, or a pattern of earlier success, has led her to prefer working up order from chaos. Should she know that about herself? Should the teacher adapt to that preference or help strengthen areas of weakness?

Teachers bring a different set of purposes to evaluation. Formatively, they want information that will help them adjust their approach. Summatively, they need some solid measures of attainment. For teachers, evaluation is an ongoing process. Formative evaluation can be conducted informally, simply by glancing around a room full of students or by talking with someone on the playground. It can be conducted formally, as well, by watching for shifts in standardized test scores or by applying a structured research technique. One advantage of graphic organizers is that they provide the student and the teacher with immediate *prima facie* evaluation material. Graphic organizers sit out in the open. They can be discussed, analyzed, and understood. Most of the time, however, their format is unacceptable to others to whom the teacher must report results. A teacher is the gateway to the adult community. To a large extent, the teacher must act as evaluator and translator for the whole school community.

In communicating student need and student achievement to the adult community, a teacher needs to look for measures that are comprehensible and acceptable to that community. Figure 12.3 list several kinds

FIGURE 12.3   Evaluation Questions Responding to Purposes for Graphic Organizers

Purposes	Questions

Increase student control
—over content
	Do students who use graphics score as well on tests as students who do not?
	  1. on questions requiring factual recall?
	  2. on questions requiring application of procedures?
	  3. on questions requiring analytic skill, creativity, or problem solving?

—over process of thinking	Do students who have used graphic organizers manage the process of their thinking?
	  1. describing their thinking process, with a rationale?
	  2. selecting an approach after examining several options?
	  3. designing an approach to assignments that "fit" purpose of the assignment?
	  4. showing evidence of self-correction and revision?

Increase student involvement in learning	Do students using an organizer to learn or think actively engage the content?
	  1. persisting in the task longer than they would without a graphic organizer?
	  2. pursuing alternate interpretations, theories, or methods of solving problems?
	  3. doing more than they are required to do in particular assignments?
	  4. expressing preference for a specific kind of learning?

Increase student interaction around the content	Do students engage each other over subject area content?
	  1. helping each other work on assignments?
	  2. challenging each other's view of the content?
	  3. challenging each other's process of thinking?
	  4. working cooperatively to solve problems?

Increase student intellectual confidence	Do students see themselves as competent thinkers?
	  1. recognizing their own style or preference?
	  2. allowing differences in approach and outcome?
	  3. reflecting upon the limitations and advantages of the approach they have taken?
	  4. treating their approach to learning as a process they can shape and direct?

of purpose for a thinking skills curriculum embedded in subject area content, with questions that point toward different kinds of evaluation. Costa (1985) has composed a similar list of questions. There may be many kinds of indicators for each question. Focusing on a particular kind of question and using a particular set of indicators should depend on purpose, as seen by the audience that will make use of the results.

For an audience of school officials and other professionals, a formal evaluation of any thinking skills curriculum may be required. Baron has outlined a general approach to formal evaluation and provided a list of research instruments that have been used to measure the development of intellectual skill (Baron & Sternberg, 1987, Chapter 11; Baron & Kallick, 1985). To the extent that these instruments will produce results for a larger audience, members of that audience should be included in their selection. Selection of a research instrument should also depend on consistency between the language of the instrument and the language employed during instruction to describe thinking.

In the area of research, a persistent question remains: If we focus instructional time and effort on thinking, will we sacrifice content acquisition or basic skills? Does knowing *how* always cost something of knowing *what?* The future of current work in thinking skills may well rest on the answer to this question (Alexander & Judy, 1988). We can teach thinking skills through a general approach apart from content, through infusion with existing content courses or by total immersion in some specific context (Ennis, 1989). Do each of these approaches have the same effect on content acquisition? Do some approaches actually increase content acquisition, particularly with respect to long-term memory and problem-solving ability? Perkins and Salomon (1989, p. 23) believe that evaluators should distinguish between "educating memories versus educating minds." If we educate minds but measure memories, we are bound to be disappointed at the fruits of our work. If we aim at improving our students' ability to locate and use information, we should measure thinking skills, transferred across the content areas. We do not presently have research findings that answer these questions.

No doubt, research will begin to take on the question of how thinking relates to learning. For faster results, fitting a particular group of kids in a particular school located in a real community, I would look to practicing teachers for useful evaluation results. Practicing teachers may be the first to find answers to the following questions:

> What is the optimal age for introducing graphic frames of different kinds?
>
> Once a frame is introduced, how much practice is required to support transfer and elaboration?
>
> What specific lesson plans are effective in teaching frames to students of different ages?

What motivational props assist learning? What motivational effects accompany the use of graphic frames?

In watching teachers work, I have been amazed at the extent to which they help students use organizers for aspects of thinking that are not supposed to be possible at certain ages and levels of ability. Terri Sturgeon (in Chapter 6) and kindergarten students making inductive inferences. I watched Sara McKenny (Chapter 8) teach deductive thinking to noncollege-prep students with little academic confidence. We do not yet know the limits of the technique—or the real limits of the human mind.

The issue of motivation is also unresolved. How do students feel about their school study? Can they describe the way they think? Can they invent different ways to locate information or list alternatives in solving problems? Do they attack problems rather than retreat? Can they work with others to understand information and create new ideas? Answers to these questions will take us toward the future.

THE QUESTION OF TRANSFER

The real signature of success for thinking skills instruction is the reapplication of skills to a new context, preferably an unstructured one that does not resemble the context in which the skill was learned. Each chapter in the central portion of this book contains some guidance for supporting transfer. Perkins (1986, Chapter 8) has written an entire chapter on different approaches to bridging thinking skills from one context to another. Teachers who see a graphic organizer emerge for use in a new context should not be appalled if the organizer has been revised almost beyond recognition. Restructuring is a necessary aspect of long-term learning. Students cannot create if they cannot modify what they encounter in the classroom. By far, I have felt the greatest delight when some 8-year-old invents an organizer for a particular subject for which there is no known precedent but that is perfectly matched to the task.

THE QUESTION OF FEELINGS

As a culture, we have come to think of thought and feeling as if they were of different worlds. For better or for worse, however, thought and feeling live in the same house and eat off the same plate. In the house of the mind, thinking and feeling stalk the floor as one. In watching students work through some cold-looking subject matter in graphic form I am always impressed with the intensity of the exchange. Our view of the world is infused with feelings.

When Mary Heins began her year with problem solving for her sixth grade, she asked the students to brainstorm all the feelings they had about the process. "What do you feel when you try to solve problems at a math station?" she asked. Figure 12.4 lists their responses.

What struck Heins was the distinctly negative leaning in the student responses. In fact, it took some probing and cuing to get them to list any positive feeling about solving problems. How different might the list be for any of us? Control is the central issue. None of us wants to seem less than the tasks we face. None of us likes being "managed" by a problem we have not chosen to solve. If we face a page of text, a science experiment, or rows of problems on a page, we need to feel able to manage the situation. In considering evaluation, we need also to consider feedback to students that will help them recognize and feel pride in their capabilities. Graphic organizers, as elaborate and even gaudy artifacts of thinking, do allow teachers a vehicle for recognizing and celebrating the thinking process.

A graphic organizer has the advantage of remaining visible, even after learning and thinking have occurred. Maps, chains, towers, and circles may be treated as emblems of thinking in different patterns. Unlike written text, however, graphics are very difficult to compare, either against each other or against external standards. To assess the value of a graphic organizer, we may have to ask the students to walk us through, perhaps in the talk-aloud method developed by Whimbey and Lochhead (1982). If students can describe their strategy, perhaps they will prove able to transfer it to new settings. If they can criticize their strategy, perhaps they can adapt it to novel problems.

FIGURE 12.4   Feelings Expressed
by Sixth-Grade Students about
Problem Solving (arranged from
negative to positive)

Negative	Positive
hate	curious
surprise	proud
frustrated	gleeful
silly	contented
stupid	finally great
bad	exhausted
disgusted	variably confident
all impossible	(up and down)
embarrassed	
doubtful	
mad	

THE QUESTION OF STYLE

In watching students think their way through graphic organizers, we can easily see the differences that mark what students know about a subject —and how they know it. Students can know a subject equally well, at least as represented by multiple-choice or matching-type questions, and still conceive of the subject in entirely different ways. Students may have equivalent scores on aptitude tests, but show marked dissimilarities in the way they learn (Kolb, 1976). Style differences affect the way we organize the mental landscape, the way we perceive new information, the way we organize learning tasks, and our preference for the physical context in which our learning takes place. Learning style inventories have been developed to measure facets of all these areas of difference (Keefe, 1979; Hyman & Rosoff, 1984; Whimbey, 1984; Letteri, 1983). Evaluation and research should aim to determine the extent to which cognitive style affects a preference for graphic organizers in thinking, or preference for other techniques.

The development of this book was based, in part, on the Learning Style Inventory designed by David Kolb. In Kolb's (1976) inventory, some students show a preference for inductive thinking, from the concrete to the abstract. Others feel more comfortable working deductively, using abstractions to pick their way through details. Some are more reflective than others, looking at the facts from sufficient distance to perceive the organizing patterns. Others prefer active experimentation, wading in to have an experience at closer range.

Watching students develop graphic organizers reveals a related set of differences. Degree of preference for order, need for an overview, field dependence, and independence all are issues that affect the way students work with information. Apart from the informal tests and inventories available, graphic organizers give teachers and students a way to talk about different styles of thinking. Cooperative learning creates a situation in which stylistic differences become apparent. With help, students can use their interactions as a source of evaluative feedback, seeing their strengths from a new perspective and seeing other styles work to visible effect.

THE QUESTION OF EFFECTS

Though hardly a major innovation in itself, the use of graphic organizers in teaching may have a fairly profound effect on the way teaching and learning take place in the classroom. The use of graphic organizers may demystify a process that many students see as obscure. It may put students at the center of the learning process, a position they otherwise may easily lose to teaching, to technology, or to administrative control. To some extent, the use of graphic organizers may catalyze a larger change—the return of learning to the center of school activity. Given what we know about how the mind works, the structure of the school day is not always fully aligned with learning:

- Learning is an active process requiring engagement, yet we may keep our students in their seats for much of the day.
- Learning is idiosyncratic to the individual, yet we dispense content as if all students were the same receptacle.
- Learning is recursive, requiring continual revision of knowledge, yet we teach-test-teach-test-teach new material in an endless line of hours.
- Learning inspires a passion of the mind, yet we freeze-dry learning into granules and deal it out by the spoonful.
- Learning asks the mind to speak to the senses, yet we use the classroom walls to hold off sensation, for terms up to 16 years.
- Learning endows the individual with personal power, yet we design the day to ensure a large measure of helplessness.

If graphics may support thinking within the curriculum, it remains to be measured what thinking may do to the conventions of education in our schools.

REFERENCES

Alexander, P. A., & Judy, J. E. (1988). The interaction of domain specific and strategic knowledge in academic performance. *Review of Educational Research*, 58:4, 375–405.

Baron, J., & Kallick, B. (1985). Assessing thinking: What are we looking for? And how can we find it? In A. Costa (Ed.), *Developing Minds: A Resource Book for Teaching Thinking*. Alexandria, VA: ASCD Publications.

Baron, J., & Sternberg, R. (Eds.) (1987). *Teaching Thinking Skills: Theory and Practice*. New York: Freeman.

Costa, A. (1985). How can we recognize improved student thinking? In A. Costa (Ed.), *Developing Minds: A Resource Book for Teaching Thinking*. Alexandria, VA: ASCD Publications.

Ennis, R. H. (1989). Critical thinking and subject specificity: Clarification and needed research. *Educational Researcher*, 18:3, 4–6.

Hyman, R., & Rosoff, B. (1984). Matching learning and teaching styles: The jug and what's in it. *Theory into Practice*, 23(1), 36–43.

Keefe, J. W. (1979). *Student Learning Styles: Diagnosing and Prescribing Programs.* Reston, VA: NASSP.

Kolb, D. (1976). *Learning Style Inventory (Manual).* Cambridge, MA: McBer and Associates.

Letteri, C. (1983). An introduction to information processing, cognitive controls and cognitive profiles. Manuscript from author.

Morante, E. A., & Ulesky, A. (1984). The assessment of reasoning abilities. *Educational Leadership,* September, 71–74.

Perkins, D. N. (1986). *Knowledge as Design.* Hillsdale, NJ: Lawrence Erlbaum.

Perkins, D., & Salomon, G. (1989). Are cognitive skills content bound? *Educational Researcher,* 18:1, 16–25.

Sternberg, R. J. (1984). How can we teach intelligence? *Educational Leadership,* September, 38–44.

Whimbey, A. (1984). The key to higher order thinking is precise processing. *Educational Leadership,* September.

Whimbey, A., & Lochhead J. (1982). *Problem Solving and Comprehension* (3rd edition). Philadelphia: Franklin Institute Press.

Bibliography

Alexander, P. A., & Judy, J. E. (1988). The interaction of domain specific and strategic knowledge in academic performance. *Review of Educational Research*, 58(4), 375–404.

Alverman, D. (1987). Strategic teaching in social studies. In B. F. Jones, A. S. Palincsar, D. S. Ogle, & E. G. Carr (Eds.). *Strategic Teaching and Learning: Cognitive Instruction in the Content Areas*. Alexandria, VA: ASCD Publications.

Anderson, R. C. (1977). The notion of schemata and the educational enterprise: General discussion of the conference. In R. C. Anderson, R. J. Spiro, & W. E. Montague (Eds.), *Schooling and the Acquisition of Knowledge*. Hillsdale, NJ: Lawrence Erlbaum.

Armbruster, B. B., & Anderson, T. H. (1984). Mapping: Representing informative text diagrammatically. In C. T. Holley & D. F. Dansereau (Eds.), *Spacial Learning Strategies: Techniques, Applications and Related Issues*. Orlando, FL: Academic Press.

Arnaudin, M. W.; Mintzes, J. J.; Dunn, C. S.; & Shafer, T. S. (1984). Concept mapping in college science teaching. *Journal of College Science Teaching*, November.

Ault, C. R. (1985). Concept mapping as a study strategy in earth science. *Journal of College Science Teaching*, September/October, 38–44.

Ausubel, D. (1968). *Educational Psychology: A Cognitive View*. New York: Holt, Rinehart and Winston.

Ausubel, D. (1978). A defense of advance organizers. *Review of Educational Research*, 48(2), 259-272.

Baron, J. (1987). Evaluating thinking skills in the classroom. In J. Baron & R. Sternberg (Eds.), *Teaching Thinking Skills: Theory and Practice*. New York: Freeman.

Baron, J., & Kallick, B. (1985). Assessing thinking: What are we looking for? And how can we find it? In A. Costa (Ed.), *Developing Minds: A Resource Book for Teaching Thinking*. Alexandria, VA: ASCD Publications.

Baron, J., & Sternberg, R. (1987). *Teaching Thinking Skills: Theory and Practice*. New York: Freeman.

Baron, R. F., & Schwartz, R. M. (1984). Graphic postorganizers: A spacial learning strategy. In D. F. Dansereau & C. Holley (Eds.), *Spacial Learning Strategies: Techniques, Applications and Related Issues*. Orlando, FL: Academic Press.

Beratta-Norton, M. (1976). *Mathematics Their Way.* Menlo Park, CA: Addison-Wesley.

Beyer, B. (1987). *Practical Strategies for the Teaching of Thinking.* Boston: Allyn and Bacon.

Bloom, B. S. (Ed.) (1956). *Taxonomy of Educational Objectives. Handbook I: Cognitive Domain.* New York: McKay.

Bobrow, D. G., & Collins, A. (Eds.) (1975). *Representation and Understanding: Studies in Cognitive Science.* New York: Academic Press.

Bransford, J. D.; Sherwood, R. D.; & Sturdevant, T. (1987). Teaching thinking and problem solving. In J. B. Baron & R. J. Sternberg (Eds.), *Teaching Thinking Skills: Theory and Practice.* New York: Freeman.

Breuker, J. A. (1984). A theoretical framework for spacial learning strategies. In *Spacial Learning Strategies: Techniques, Applications and Related Issues.* (pp. 21–46). Orlando, FL: Academic Press.

Brewer, W. F., & Nakamura, G. V. (1984). The nature and functions of schemas. In R. S. Weir & T. K. Krull (Eds.), *Handbook of Social Cognition.* Hillsdale, NJ: Lawrence Erlbaum.

Brooks, M. (1987). Curriculum design from a constructivist perspective. *Educational Leadership*, January, 63–67.

Bruffee, K. (1986). Social construction, language, and the authority of knowledge: A bibliographical essay. *College English*, 48(8), 773–790.

Bruner, J. (1975). *Toward a Theory of Instruction.* Cambridge, MA: Harvard University Press.

Bruner, J. (1986). *Actual Minds, Possible Worlds.* Cambridge, MA: Harvard University Press.

Camstra, B., & van Bruggen, J. (1984). Schematizing: The empirical evidence. In D. F. Dansereau & C. D. Holley (Eds.), *Spacial Learning Strategies: Techniques, Applications and Related Issues.* New York: Academic Press.

Chambers, J. H. (1988). Teaching thinking throughout the curriculum: Where else? *Educational Leadership*, 45(7), 3–4.

Chance, P. (1986). *Thinking in the Classroom.* New York Teachers College Press.

Chase, W. G. (Ed.) (1973). *Visual Information Processing.* New York: Academic Press.

Chase, W. G., & Simon, H. (1973). The mind's eye in chess. In W. G. Chase (Ed.), *Visual Information Processing* (pp. 215-278). New York: Academic Press.

Chomsky, N. (1973). *Language and Mind.* New York: Harcourt Brace Jovanovich.

Clarke, J. (1979). Homer and Aristotle in the classroom. *Liberal Education*, Fall, 395–399.

Clarke, J. (1980). The learning cycle: Frame of discourse for paragraph development. *New England Association of Teachers of English Leaflet*, 79(3).

Clarke, J. (1983). The effectiveness of remediation among high risk students of different ages. ERIC HE 015-832, ED227-723

Clarke, J. H. (1987). Building a lecture that works. *College Teaching*, 35(2), 56–58.

Clarke, J. H. (1989). Designing discussion on the inquiry cycle. *College Teaching*, October.

Clarke, J. H.; Gilbert, G.; & Raths, J. (1989). Inductive towers: Helping students see how they think. *Journal of Reading*, 33(2), 86–95.

Clarke, J. H., & Hood, K. (1986). School improvement in a rural state. *Educational Leadership*.

Clarke, J. H.; MacPherson, B. V.; & Holmes, D. R. (1982). Cigarette smoking and locus of control among young adolescents. *Journal of Health and Social Behavior*, 23(3), 253-259.

Clarke, J. H., & Wittes, S. (1977). *The Clarke Reading Self Assessment Survey*. San Rafael, CA: Academic Therapy Publications.

Clement, J. (1979). Mapping a student's causal conceptions from a problem solving protocol. In J. Lochhead & J. Clemmons (Eds.), *Cognitive Process Instruction*. Philadelphia: Franklin Institute Press.

Costa, A. (1985). *Developing Minds: A Resource Book for Teaching Thinking*. Alexandria, VA: ASCD Publications.

Costa, A. (1985). How can we recognize improved student thinking? In A. Costa (Ed.), *Developing Minds: A Resource Book for Teaching Thinking*. Alexandria, VA: ASCD Publications.

Costa, A. (1985). How scientists think when they are doing science. In A. Costa (Ed.), *Developing Minds: A Resource Book for Teaching Thinking*. Alexandria, VA: ASCD

Costa, A. (1985). Toward a model of human intellectual functioning. In A. Costa (Ed.), *Developing Minds: A Resource Book for Teaching Thinking*. Alexandria, VA: ASCD Publications.

Costa, A. (1988, November). *What human beings do when they behave intelligently and how they can become more so*. Paper presented at "Creative Thinking," Vermont ASCD Conference, Burlington, VT.

Costa, A.; Hanson, R.; Silver, H. F.; and Strong, R. W. (1985). Other mediative strategies. In A. Costa (Ed.), *Developing Minds: A Resource Book for Teaching Thinking*. Alexandria, VA: ASCD Publications.

Dansereau, D. F., & Holley, C. (1984). *Spacial Learning Strategies: Techniques Applications and Related Issues*. Orlando, Fl: Academic Press.

Derry, S. J., & Murphy, D. A. (1986). Designing systems that train learning ability. *Review of Educational Research*, 56(1), 1–39.

diSessa, A. (1979). On "learnable" representations of knowledge: A meaning for the computational metaphor. In J. Lockhead & J. Clement (Eds.), *Cognitive Process Instruction* (pp. 239–266). Philadelphia: Franklin Institute Press.

Donald, J. G. (1983). Knowledge structures: Methods for exploring course content. *Journal of Higher Education*, 54(1), 31–41.

Ducharme, E. (1970). Close reading through gradual disclosure. *English Journal*, Fall.

Ennis, R. H. (1985). Goals for a critical thinking curriculum. In A. Costa (Ed.), *Developing Minds: A Resource Book for Teaching Thinking*. Alexandria, VA: ASCD Publications.

Ennis, R. H. (1987). A taxonomy of critical thinking dispositions and abilities. In J. B. Baron & R. M. Sternberg (Eds.), *Teaching Thinking Skills* (pp. 1–26). New York: W. H. Freeman.

Ennis, R. H. (1989). Critical thinking and subject specificity: Clarification and needed research. *Educational Researcher*, 18:3, 4–6.

Feuerstein, R.; Rand, R.; Hoffman, M.; & Miller, R. (1980). *Instrumental Enrichment; An Intervention Program for Cognitive Modifiability*. Baltimore: University Park Press.

Flavell, J. H. (1985). *Cognitive Development*. Englewood Cliffs, NJ: Prentice Hall.

Flower, L., & Hayes, J. R. (1984). Images, plans and prose. *Written Communication*, 1(1), 120–160.

French, L. A. (1985). Real world knowledge as the basis for social and cognitive development. In J. Pryor & J. Day (Eds.), *Development of Social Cognition*. New York: Springer-Verlag.

Fulwiler, T. (1987). *Teaching with Writing*. Upper Montclair, NJ: Boynton/Cook.

Fulwiler, T. (1987). *Writing to Learn*. Upper Montclair, NJ: Boynton/Cook.

Fulwiler, T. (1989). *The Journal Book*. Upper Montclair, NJ: Boynton/Cook.

Gagne, R. M. (1980). Learnable aspects of problem solving. *American Psychologist*, 15(2), 84–92.

Gagne, R. M., & White, R. T. (1978). Memory strategy and learning. *Review of Educational Research*, 48(2), 187–222.

Galambos, J. A. (1986). Knowledge structures for common activities. In J. A. Galambos, R. P. Abelson, & J. B. Black (Eds.), *Knowledge Structures*. Hillsdale, NJ: Lawrence Erlbaum.

Galambos, J. A., Abelson, R. P.; & Black, J. B. (1986). *Knowledge Structures*. Hillsdale, NJ: Lawrence Erlbaum.

Gardner, H. (1983). *Frames of Mind: The Theory of Multiple Intelligences*. New York: Basic Books.

Gentner, D., & Stevens, A. L. (1983). *Mental Models*. Hillsdale, NJ: Lawrence Erlbaum.

Glaser, R. (1984). Education and thinking: The role of knowledge. *American Psychologist*, 39(2), 93–104.

Glasser, W. (1984). *Control Theory: A New Explanation of How We Control Our Lives*. New York: Harper and Row.

Glasser, W. (1986). *Control Theory in the Classroom*. New York: Harper and Row.

Gould, S. J. (1987). Animal, vegetable or mineral? *Harvard Magazine*, November/December, 74–77.

Gray, R. L. (1979). Toward observing that which is not directly observable. In J. Lockhead & J. Clements (Eds.), *Cognitive Process Instruction*. Philadelphia: Franklin Institute Press.

Gregorc, A. F. (1979). Learning/teaching styles: Their nature and effects. In *Student Learning Styles: Diagnosing and Prescribing Programs* (pp. 19–26).

Halpern, D. (1984). *Thought and Knowledge: An Introduction to Critical Thinking*. Hillsdale, NJ: Lawrence Erlbaum.

Hawking, S. W. (1988). *A Brief History of Time: From the Big Bang to Black Holes*. New York: Bantam.

Heiman, M. (1985). Learning to learn. In A. Costa (Ed.), *Developing Minds: A Resource Book for Teaching Thinking*. Alexandria, VA: ASCD.

Hill, J. M. (1986). Geometry for grades K-6. *Readings from the Arithmetic Teacher*. Reston, VA: National Council of Teachers of Mathematics. ED280699

Holland, J. H.; Holyoak, K. J.; Nisbett, R. E.; & Thagard, P. R. (1986). *Induction: Processes of Inference Learning and Discovery*. Cambridge, MA: MIT Press.

Holley, C. F., & Dansereau, D. F. (1984). Networking: The technique and the empirical evidence. In C. F. Holley & D. F. Dansereau (Eds.), *Spacial Learning Strategies: Techniques, Applications and Related Issues*. Orlando, FL: Academic Press.

Holloway, S. D. (1988). Concepts of ability and effort in Japan and the US. *Journal of Educational Research*, 58(3), 327–346.

Hunt, M. (1982). How the Mind Works. *The New York Times Magazine*, January 24, 1982.

Hunt, M. (1982). *The Universe Within*. New York: Simon and Schuster.

Hunter, M. (1982). *Mastery Teaching: Increasing Instructional Effectiveness in Secondary Schools, Colleges and Universities*. El Segundo, CA: TIP Publications.

Husaim, J. S., & Cohen, L. B. (1981). Infant learning of ill defined categories. *Merrill-Palmer Quarterly*, 27(4), 443–456.

Hyman, R., & Rosoff, B. (1984). Matching learning and teaching styles: The jug and what's in it. *Theory into Practice*, 23(1), 36–43.

Johnson, D. W., & Johnson, R. T. (1986). *Learning Together and Alone.* Englewood Cliffs, NJ: Prentice-Hall.

Jones, B. F., Palincsar, A. S.; Ogle, D. S.; & Carr, E. G. (1987). *Strategic Thinking and Learning: Cognitive Instruction in the Content Areas.* Alexandria, VA: ASCD Publications.

Jones, B. F.; Pierce, J.; & Hunter, B. (1989). Teaching students to construct graphic representations. *Educational Leadership,* 46(4), 21–25.

Joyce, B., & Weil, M. (1986). *Models of Teaching* (3rd ed.). Englewood Cliffs, NJ: Prentice-Hall.

Justice, E. M. (1985). Categorization as a preferred memory strategy: Developmental changes during elementary school. *Developmental Psychology,* 21(6), 1105-1110.

Kassin, P., & Pryor, J. P. (1985). The development of attribution processes. In J. B. Prior & J. D. Day (Eds.), *The Development of Social Cognition.* New York: Springer-Verlag.

Kay, D. S., & Black, J. B. (1986). Explanation driven processing in summarization: The interaction of content and process. In J. A. Galambos, R. P. Abelson, & J. B. Black (Eds.), *Knowledge Structures.* Hillsdale, NJ: Lawrence Erlbaum.

Keefe, J. W. (1979). *Student Learning Styles: Diagnosing and Prescribing Programs.* Reston, VA: NASSP.

Kelley, H. H. (1972). Causal schemata and the attribution process. In E. E. Jones et al. (Eds.), *Attribution: Perceiving the Causes of Behavior* (pp. 151-174). Morristown, NJ: General Learning Press.

Kinnison, L. R.; & Pickens (1984). Teaching vocabulary to the learning disabled student from an interactive view of reading comprehension. ED276222

Koberg, D., & Bagnall, J. (1974). *The All New Universal Traveler.* Los Altos, CA: Kaufmann.

Kolb, D. (1976). *Learning Style Inventory* (Manual). Cambridge, MA: McBer and Associates.

Kolb, D. (1977). *Learning Style Profile.* Cambridge, MA: McBer and Associates.

Kuhn, T. S. (1970). *The Structure of Scientific Revolutions* (2nd ed.). Chicago: University of Chicago Press.

Larkin, J. (1979). Information processing models and science instruction. In J.Lochhead & J. Clemmons (Eds.), *Cognitive Process Instruction.* Philadelphia: Franklin Institute Press.

Larkin, J.; McDermott, J.; Simon, D. P.; & Simon, H. A. (1980). Expert and novice performance in solving physics problems. *Science,* 208 (20 June), 1335–1342.

Lefcourt, H. (1974). *Locus of Control: Current Trends in Theory and Research.* New York: Wiley.

Letteri, C. (1982). Teaching students how to learn. *Theory in Practice*, 24(2), 112–121.

Letteri, C. (1983). An introduction to information processing, cognitive controls and cognitive profiles. Unpublished manuscript.

Letteri, C. (1988). The NASSP learning style profile and cognitive processing. In J. W. Keefe, (Ed.), *Profiling and Using Learning Style* (chapter 2). Reston, VA: NASSP Publications.

Lingle, J. H.; Altom, M. W.; & Medin, D. L. (1984). Of cabbages and kings: Assessing the extendability of natural object concept models to social things. In R. S. Wyer & T. K. Krull (Eds.), *Handbook of Social Cognition*, Vol. l. Hillsdale, NJ: Lawrence Erlbaum.

Lipson, M. Y. (1982). Learning new information from text: The role of prior knowledge and reading ability. *Journal of Reading Behavior*, 14(3), 243–261.

Lord, A. (1969). *A Singer of Tales*. Cambridge, MA: Harvard Univ. Press.

Marzano, R. J.; Brandt, R. S.; Hughes, C. S.; Jones, B. F.; Presseisen, B. Z.; Rankin, S. C.; & Suhor, C. (188). *Dimensions of Thinking: A Framework for Curriculum and Instruction*. Alexandria, VA: ASCD Publications.

Mayer, R. (1989). Models for understanding. *Review of Educational Research*, 59(1), 43–64.

McGuigan, S., & Black, J. B. (1986). Creation and comprehension of arguments. In J. A. Galambos, R. P. Abelson, & J. B. Black (Eds.), *Knowledge Structures*. Hillsdale, NJ: Lawrence Erlbaum.

McKeachie, W. (1984). Spacial strategies: Critique and educational implications. In C. F. Holley & D. F. Dansereau (Eds.), *Spacial Learning Strategies: Techniques, Applications and Related Issues*. Orlando, FL: Academic Press.

McTighe, J., & Lyman, Jr., F. T. (1988). Cueing thinking in the classroom: The promise of theory embedded tools. *Educational Leadership*, 45(7), 18–25.

Milligan, J. R. (1979). Schema learning theory: An approach to perceptual learning. *Review of Educational Research*, 49(2), 197–207.

Mirande, M. J. A. (1984). Schematizing: Technique and application. In D. F. Dansereau & C. D. Holley (Eds.), *Spacial Learning Strategies: Techniques Applications and Related Issues*. New York: Academic Press.

Morante, E. A., & Ulesky, A. (1984). The assessment of reasoning abilities. *Educational Leadership*, September, 71–74.

Neimark, E. (1987). *Adventures in Thinking*. New York: Harcourt Brace Jovanovich.

Newell, A., & Simon, H. A. (1972). *Human Problem Solving*. Englewood Cliffs, NJ: Prentice-Hall.

Nickerson, R. S.; Perkins, D. N.; & Smith, E. E. (1985). *The Teaching of Thinking* (chapter 5). Hillsdale, NJ: Lawrence Erlbaum.

Nisbett, R. E.; Fong, G. T.; Lehman, D. R.; & Cheng, P. W. (1987). Teaching reasoning. *Science, 238* (30 October), 625–631.

Norman, D. A. (1983). Some observations on mental models. In A. L. Stevens & D. Gentner (Eds.), *Mental Models.* Hillsdale, NJ: Lawrence Erlbaum.

Novak, J. D. (1977). *A Theory of Education.* Ithaca, NY: Cornell University Press.

Novak, J. D., & Gowin, D. B. (1984). *Learning How to Learn.* Cambridge: Cambridge University Press.

Paris, S. G.; Lipson, M. Y.; & Wixson, K. K. (1983). Becoming a strategic reader. *Contemporary Educational Psychology, 8,* 293–316.

Perkins, D. N. (1986). *Knowledge as Design.* Hillsdale, NJ: Lawrence Erlbaum.

Perkins, D. N. (1987). Thinking frames: An integrating perspective on teaching cognitive skills. In J. Baron & R. Sternberg (Eds.), *Teaching Thinking Skills: Theory and Research.* New York: W. H. Freeman.

Perkins, D. N. (1988). Thinking Frames. *Educational Leadership, 43*(8), 4–11.

Perkins, D. N., & Salomon, G. (1989). Are cognitive skills context bound? *Educational Researcher, 18*(1), 16–26.

Perkins, D. N., & Simmons, R. (1988). Patterns of misunderstanding: An integrative model for science, mathematics and programming. *Review of Educational Research, 58*(3), 303–326.

Piaget, J. (1964). *Judgment and Reasoning in the Child.* Patterson, NJ: Littlefield Adams.

Postman, N., & Weingartner, C. (1969). *Teaching as a Subversive Activity.* New York: Dell.

Presseisen, B. (1985). Thinking skills: Meanings, models, materials. In A. Costa (Ed.), *Developing Minds: A Resource Book for Teaching Thinking.* Alexandria, VA: ASCD Publications.

Presseisen, B. (1988). Avoiding battle at curriculum gulch: Teaching thinking and content. *Educational Leadership,* April, 7–10.

Reder, L. M. (1980). The role of elaboration in the comprehension and retention of prose: A critical review. *Review of Educational Research, 50*(1), 5–54.

Reed, S. K. (1973). *Psychological Processes in Pattern Recognition.* New York: Academic Press.

Reigeluth, C. M. (1987). *Instructional Theories in Action.* Hillsdale, NJ: Lawrence Erlbaum.

Resnick, L. (1987). *Education and Learning to Think.* Washington, DC: National Academy Press.

Resnick, L. B. (1987). Learning in school and out: The 1987 presidential address. *Educational Researcher, 19*(9), 13–19.

Rumelhart, D. E. (1975). Notes on a schema for stories. In D. G. Bobrow & A. D. Collins (Eds.), *Representation and Understanding: Studies in Cognitive Science.* New York: Academic Press.

Rumelhart, D. E. (1984). Schemata and the cognitive system. In R. S. Wier & T. K. Krull (Eds.), *Handbook of Social Cognition.* Hillsdale, NJ: Lawrence Erlbaum.

Rumelhart, D. E., & Ortony (1977). The representation of knowledge in memory. In R. C. Anderson, R. J. Spiro, & W. E. Montague (Eds.), *Schooling and the Acquisition of Knowledge.* Hillsdale, NJ: Lawrence Erlbaum.

Schoenfeld, A. H. (1979). Can heuristics be taught? In J. Lochhead & J. Clemmons (Eds.), *Cognitive Process Instruction* (pp. 315–338). Philadelphia: Franklin Institute Press.

Sharkey, N. E. (1986). A model of knowledge based expectations in text comprehension. In J. A. Galambos, R. P. Abelson, & J. B. Black (Eds.), *Knowledge Structures.* Hillsdale, NJ: Lawrence Erlbaum.

Sherman, S. J., & Corty, E. (1984). Cognitive heuristics. In R. S. Weir & T. K. Krull (Eds.), *Handbook of Social Cognition.* Hillsdale, NJ: Lawrence Erlbaum.

Shuell, T. J. (1986). Cognitive conceptions of learning. *Review of Educational Research,* 56(4), 411–436.

Simon, H. (1979). How big is a chunk? In H. A. Simon (Ed.), *Models of Thought.* New Haven, CT: Yale University Press.

Simon, H. A. (1979). *Models of Thought.* New Haven, CT: Yale University Press.

Simon, H. A. (1979). The information storage system called the "human memory." In H. Simon (Ed.), *Models of Thought.* New Haven, CT: Yale University Press.

Slavin, R. E. (1983). *Cooperative Learning.* White Plains, NY: Longman.

Slavin, R. E. (1987). Cooperative learning and the cooperative school. *Educational Leadership,* 45(3), 7–12.

Sternberg, R. J. (1984). How can we teach intelligence? *Educational Leadership,* September, 38–44.

Sternberg, R. J. (1985). *Beyond IQ. A Triarchal Theory of Intelligence.* Cambridge/New York: Cambridge University Press.

Sternberg, R. J. (1986). *Intelligence Applied: Understanding and Increasing Your Intellectual Skills.* San Diego: Harcourt Brace Jovanovich.

Sternberg, R. J. (1987). Questions and answers about the nature and teaching of thinking skills. In J. Baron & R. Sternberg (Eds.), *Teaching Thinking Skills: Theory and Research.* New York: W. H. Freeman.

Sternberg, R. J. (1987). Teaching intelligence: The application of cognitive psychology to the improvement of intellectual skills. In J. B. Baron & R. Sternberg (Eds.), *Teaching Thinking Skills: Theory and Practice.* New York: W. H. Freeman.

Stewart, J. H. (1984). The representation of knowledge: Curricular and instructional implications for science teaching. In D. F. Dansereau & C. D. Holley (Eds.), *Spacial Learning Strategies: Techniques, Applications and Related Issues.* New York: Academic Press.

Storm, H. (1972). *Seven Arrows,* New York: Harper & Row.

Surber, C. F. (1985). Application of information integration to children's social cognitions. In R. S. Weir & T. K. Krull (Eds.), *Handbook of Social Cognition* (pp. 59–93). Hillsdale, NJ: Lawrence Erlbaum.

Surber, J. R. (1984). Mapping as a testing and diagnostic device. In C. F. Holley & D. F. Dansereau (Eds.), *Spacial Learning Strategies: Techniques, Applications and Related Issues.* Orlando, FL: Academic Press.

Travers, R. M. W. (1982). *Essentials of Learning: The New Cognitive Learning for Students of Education* (5th ed.). New York: MacMillan.

Tulving, E. (1983). *Elements of Episodic Memory.* Oxford: Oxford University Press.

Van Patten, J.; Chao, C.; & Reigeluth, C. M. (1986). Strategies for sequencing and synthesizing information. *Review of Educational Research,* 56(4), 437–472.

Vaughan, J. L. (1984). Concept structuring, the technique and empirical evidence. In D. F. Dansereau & C. D. Holley (Eds.), *Spacial Learning Strategies: Techniques, Applications and Related Issues.* New York: Academic Press.

Vobeija, B. (1987). A mathematician's research on math instruction. *Educational Researcher,* 16(9), 9–11.

Vosniadou, S., & Brewer, W. S. (1987). Theories of knowledge restructuring in development. *Review of Educational Research* 57(1), 51–67.

Voss, J. F.; Greene, T. R.; Post, T. A.; & Penner, B. (1983). Problem solving skill in the social sciences. In *The Psychology of Learning* (Vol.17). New York: Academic Press.

Vygotsky, L. (1986). *Thought and Language* (A. Kozulin, trans.). Cambridge, MA: MIT University Press. (Original work published 1926)

Weiner, B. (1974). *Achievement Motivation and Attribution Theory.* Morristown, NJ: General Learning Press.

Weiner, B. R.; Neirenberg, B. R.; & Goldstein, M. (1976). Social learning (locus of control) versus attribution (causal stability) interpretations of expectancy of success. *Journal of Personality,* 44, 1–20.

Wheaton, B. (1980). The sociogenesis of psychological disorder. *Journal of Health and Social Behavior,* 21, 100–124.

Whimbey, A. (1984). The key to higher order thinking is precise processing. *Educational Leadership,* September.

Whimbey, A., & Lochhead, J. (1982). *Problem Solving and Comprehension* (3rd ed.). Philadelphia: Franklin Institute Press.

Wilson, J. (1963). *Thinking with Concepts.* Cambridge: Cambridge University Press.

Winocur, S. L. (1987). Developing lesson plans with cognitive objectives. In A. Costa (Ed.), *Developing Minds: A Resource Book for Teaching Thinking.* Alexandria, VA: ASCD Publications.

Witkin, H. A.; Moore, C. A.; Goodenough, D. R.; & Cox, P. W. (1977). Field dependent and field independent cognitive styles and their educational implications. *Review of Educational Research*, 47(1), 1–64.

Young, R. M. (1983). Surrogates and mappings: Two kinds of conceptual models for interactive devices. In D. Gentner & A. Stevens (Eds.), *Mental Models*. Hillsdale, NJ: Lawrence Erlbaum.

Index